THE ARCHEOLOGY
OF A GOOD RAGÙ:

Discovering Naples, My Father, & Myself

GUERNICA WORLD EDITIONS 36

THE ARCHEOLOGY
OF A GOOD RAGÙ:
DISCOVERING NAPLES, MY FATHER, & MYSELF

John Domini

GUERNICA
World
EDITIONS

TORONTO—CHICAGO—BUFFALO—LANCASTER (U.K.)

2021

Michael Mirolla, editor
Cover design: Rafael Chimicatti
Cover artwork: "Partenope," by Oni Wong,
Cortile Artestesa, Naples.
Interior layout: Jill Ronsley, suneditwrite.com
Guernica Editions Inc.
287 Templemead Drive, Hamilton (ON), Canada L8W 2W4
2250 Military Road, Tonawanda, N.Y. 14150-6000 U.S.A.
www.guernicaeditions.com

Distributors:
Independent Publishers Group (IPG)
600 North Pulaski Road, Chicago IL 60624
University of Toronto Press Distribution,
5201 Dufferin Street, Toronto (ON), Canada M3H 5T8
Gazelle Book Services, White Cross Mills
High Town, Lancaster LA1 4XS U.K.

First edition.
Printed in Canada.

Legal Deposit—First Quarter
Library of Congress Catalog Card Number: 2020945665
Library and Archives Canada Cataloguing in Publication
Title: The archeology of a good ragù : discovering Naples, my father, & myself / John Domini.
Names: Domini, John, 1951- author.
Series: Guernica world editions ; 36.
Description: Series statement: Guernica world editions ; 36
Identifiers: Canadiana (print) 20200329294 | Canadiana (ebook) 20200329340 | ISBN 9781771835534 (softcover) | ISBN 9781771835558 (Kindle) | ISBN 9781771835541 (EPUB)
Subjects: LCSH: Domini, John, 1951- | LCSH: Naples (Italy)—Biography. | LCGFT: Autobiographies.
Classification: LCC PS3554.O462 Z46 2021 | DDC 813/.54—dc23

For Jennifer, out of Ghana,
& to the memory of Flavio Gioia.

Some nights I dream the taste
of pitch and bus fumes and leaf meal
from my old exacting street.
This time home, I'm walking to find

I don't know what. Something always
offers itself while I'm not watching.

—*W.S. DiPiero,*
"Oregon Avenue on a Good Day"

PART ONE

Mo' lo facc'—I'm on it.

*M*O': THE NEAPOLITAN "NOW." *Mo'*, a grunt, a moo, brought up from the middle of the chest with a thrust of the bottom lip, making for a sudden mouthy shrug, an extreme contraction wrung out of *al momento*, "at this moment." *Mo'*, they say, whatever the moment. Could be morning, as you consider taking Mass; could be midday, the bikes at full roar in the streets, and here's one bearing down, close, with two cold-eyed young toughs on the banana seat; could be evening, echoing with the clack of a woman in heels, a miracle when you consider the cobblestone, and you look around, where is she? Where's that intoxicating sashay?

"Now" could be any of these. You hear a special emphasis in the expression *mo' lo facc'*, roughly "I'm on it:" MOH loh fahh-chh, the last syllable a diminishing drawl. And me too, *mo'*, now, Naples. This hub of a Janus-faced Siren (to dream up an incongruous creature, bicultural, both Roman god and Greek monster), this city that triggers baroque aspiration yet burns away, infernally, all hope—incongruous as the creature may be, to me it remains one thing always. To me it's the locus of renewal. A very old metropolis, nonetheless it left me rejuvenated, remade in midlife.

So, me too, I'm on it. I'll find the coherence in this crowded place.

After all, regardless of the good it did for me, doesn't the city deserve this on its own? An informed treatment, for an eternal downtown? If Americans think of Naples at all, they think of the murderous Camorra and the crap in the streets. Maybe a few still think of the incomparable Sophia Loren, born and raised. They think of renewal Hollywood-style, one of those stories in which Loren restores the soul of some uptight Anglo (say, Jack Lemmon, lucky guy). She awakens him to a primal joy, enriched with mozzarella. If Americans haven't seen that movie, they've seen the feminist version, *Eat, Pray, Love.* Isn't it pizza that awakens Elizabeth, our heroine? Pizza in Naples? These days any self-respecting foodie will seek out the same, a Margherita, the True Pie, with its blistered crust and cooked whole leaves of basil. Those burnt green wrinkles, amid the sauce and cheese, can suggest a wilting old man's face.

In my mind's eye, that face isn't my own, not yet. Rather it's my father's, withered by his first heart attack. The final crisis came young, for this day and age. Pop broke down despite reaching, in his adopted country, a level of comfort well above the one to which he'd been born. Away from home, he'd found the good life, and yet during his final years I reconnected with his native city. Naples drew me back again and again, more deeply each time. I'd made previous visits, first in middle school and then in college. But now I arrived *nel mezzo del cammin*: my father sick and dying, my marriage more of the same, and always the wrong fit for the job. "At loose ends," would you say? My ends were droopy as cooked basil.

I had some idea how the place helped, the perspective it afforded, trimillennial and transoceanic. I had a notion it might provide a glimpse of a better outcome. The ululations of the Siren didn't always lead to drowning. Also I could see a thing or two, or three, about Pop. As this city put me around corners, it illuminated his long-ago turning points. A few of those looked unflattering, sins of the father. At the least, Enzo Domini faced choices so messy they left stains. He grew up amid hair-raising agglomeration and din—for a while under Nazi guns. As for that, the war in the old city, his story took especially long coming to light. Still, bad trouble of one kind or another kept confronting

me, poking out of some nook or cranny. It made what I was trying
to accomplish look like a party game, *Adventures in Reinvention*.
Nevertheless as my project took shape I could feel its full, adult
weight. In order to get a handle on the rest of my life, I needed to
know my father and his city.

The problem, in any case, was where to begin. Amid the
agglomeration and din, there's no end of "now." It's been three
thousand years, or close enough, since Greek immigrants laid
down the urban blueprint. You can find some of that first pavement still, c. 700 BCE, and since then of course other landmarks
have jutted up. In Pompeii you've got the Fall of Rome, petrified;
around the San Carlo Opera House you've got the incandescent
Borbon moment, with visitors like Mozart and Shelley. Exploring
my father's past, meantime, I turned up other climaxes, domestic
shocks. I heard a deathbed confession, exposing long-ago lies. I
saw my closest relatives ruined by the Naples Mafia; the goons
actually threatened a child barely able to walk.

Still, Naples offers no simple structure, no neat increments
of rising action. Rather, it's a confounding total immersion: an
eternal *mo'*.

* * *

One good choice for a starting point would be Anno Domini
1948, the year my father headed to New York. As for the hometown, he wanted no more of what it'd put him through—including
the things it took me years to discover.

Granted, he wasn't just leaving the one behind, he was headed
towards the other. Pop followed the call of a contemporary siren,
Golden America. Indeed, he'd already enjoyed what Neapolitans
call a *colpo d'oro*, a "golden wallop." He'd married a woman from
New York. Nevertheless, Pop's origins render him *Napoli D.O.C.*
The designation's a joke, one contemporary Italians use to estab-
lish their bona fides (filching the "D.O.C." from winemakers). But

my father could back his up with a baptism record—Vincenzo Vicedomini, 1925—just a stone's throw from the old docks. The church is now deconsecrated, like a number of others across the 21st-century town, some still hiding a magnificent altarpiece or a shameful past. But there's no mystery about the old-city pungency of his childhood, where a *passegiata* would take in both the incense from Mass and the stink of the night's fishing. Before the last World War this was the country's center for merchant shipping (now it's Salerno, farther south), and that bustle defined the boy's home piazza, *Piazza della Borsa*, "of the bank." The bank's granite lions still brood over the square, but the place-name, like my father's, has changed. In an attempt at civic renewal, it became Piazza Giovanni Bovio, after, ah … "Some philosopher," the Neapolitans shrug. "Years back."

Like Bovio, "Vicedomini" carried a certain fading glory. A portmanteau construction, the word translates as "God's helper," and young 'Enzo had relatives prominent in the Church. In '36, in San Pietro ad Aram, a chapel was dedicated to his cleric uncle Giovanni. This remains in service, some twenty centuries after its founding; in an annex sits the broad stone on which Peter baptized his first converts in Italy (*aram* is Latin for "altar"). These days, African sidewalk salesmen crowd the front doors, and the neighborhood, the Forcella, chokes in the grip of the Camorra. Still, I've visited. New-World "John," I've stood under the old priest's plaque, struggling with its grimy inscription: *in memoria di Giovanni Vicedomini …*

By the time I read the thing I was 40 and, though failing at so much else, I'd learned something of the city. I'd learned that my family's place in town, by those same 1930s, was precarious. My father's father had lost his own parents in the flu of 1918-19, yet somehow, getting raised by nuns had left him a cantankerous left-winger. Years later, out on a *passegiata* with his teenage American grandson, the man still got off lots of wisecracks about workers' rights. The Communist Party of Italy, if you asked him, was a farce.

Back at the end of the '20s, however, the Fascists weren't laughing. They banished him and his family—wife, daughter, Enzo, and a younger brother—to an outlying hamlet. They must've felt as if sent into the howling wilderness. Transport moved on hooves and water arrived via rope and bucket. The outback often served as a dumping ground for troublemakers, and in the case of Carlo Levi, "internal exile" led to the compassionate meditations of *Christ Stopped at Eboli*. Yet decades later, for me Eboli proved quite the opposite sort of stay. In the country where my grandfather had suffered abasement, the oldest son of his oldest son enjoyed an eco-tourist's hospitality.

That visit was another of my midlife efforts, tracing family whorls from past to present. My *Nonno*, I'd learned, had returned to his own *centro* and century by way of his wife. On the rusty scales of Naples aristocracy, her kinfolk carried weight. Their parish was another San Pietro, *a Maiella*, on a prestigious intersection several blocks uphill from the Forcello markets. Next door, rather, stood the Conservatory of Music. Its alumni included three of my grandmother's brothers (three more of my great-uncles), carving out careers on piano or cello. The social dynamics meant nothing to an American teenager, but by the time I was old enough to sample the Eboli cheeses and wines, I could see, if I squinted, what distinguished my father's father's clan from my father's mother's. The Vicedominis were the Lord's helpers, not Lords themselves. To clear his name, my Nonno needed his wife's name. He needed to kiss the wrinkled hand of some relation who'd never worked a day in her life. Okay, I'm exaggerating, but by the War years, my grandfather was back at the central Post Office.

"Brutalist" architecture, this Fascist edifice still raises its barrel chest over Via Monteoliveto. It never did make a good fit for Nonno. Before too long he'd be on a train to Auschwitz. What matters for the moment, however, is how swiftly my '90s re-engagement with the city revealed the way it felt, in the '40s, to my father. The town must've seemed ever more inhospitable, with even his extended family raising a chill, and for me too things got shivery, the few times I visited his mother's people. Their show china includes a sizeable St. Francis, preaching to lamb and bird, but I felt nothing like grace and peace. I found the family bread-winner especially hard to take. A Mercedes dealer, he dressed in rhinestone flash and liked gutter talk, and later I besieged another relative for an explanation. The dealership, it turned out, was a Camorra favorite.

To Vincenzo, half a century earlier, this all must've felt like no way to live. He must've started to think about leaving even before the nightmares of '42 and '43—just as, soon afterwards, he was eager to put them out of his mind. By the time I'd reached adolescence, Pop was sharing next to nothing out of that time, the Jewish musician who hid in their apartment, the bombing and starving and combat hand-to-hand. Rather he'd tossed such stuff in a box and stuck it in the back of the closet. On the box, two simple words: "the War." Before it was opened again, his sons and daughter would have growing kids of their own. Till his final years, and my first revisits, we knew little beyond his flight to Manhattan in '48.

He made occasional returns to the old hometown, to be sure, and at the start of the 1960s he brought along his young family. Back then, I didn't even have body hair (really? ever?), and of course I needed chaperones. But at the end of the decade, during college days, I made it over by myself. I got out into the city on my own, and these walkabouts at about age 20 then went through fresh iterations starting at about 40. It's this later cycle that gives me the "plot" of this memoir, about the old guy born again, with the Siren acting as midwife. Exploring the Siren City, that never ends; my story, however, wraps up back when the Twenty-Aughts turned over to the Twenty-Teens. It's a time capsule, this text, and so keeping the contents safe requires sealing out everything that's happened since. The coronavirus, in particular, must be locked out, despite its surreal effect—for weeks, COVID-19 emptied out these same busy, bewildering streets.

And this also provides my best beginning: these twinned encounters with the *centro storico*, parallel strata of the same man. Back at the end of my teens, there was a lot I didn't know, including the historical anomalies of cheap tuition and jet fuel. Still, my greater misunderstanding was the same as at the end of my 30s. In 1990 as in '70, I arrived thinking, this *terra* isn't so *incognita*—but I never reckoned on the bewilderment, the fascination.

* * *

In my reading, I keep coming across others stirred up in the Neapolitan sauces. Here's a 2018 text: "The orgy of images, fragrances (the smells of decay, street food, trees, melons, the sea …), and sounds—steals my breath, dizzies me, and prevents me from anchoring." The author, in this case, comes from across the Adriatic; it's the Croatian Dubravka Ugrešić, her sinuous novel *The Fox*. For an American, "anchoring" can seem out of the question.

Myself, I was as badly adrift at 40 as at 20: first a kid who'd never had a steady girl, then a man who'd somehow left his wife unsatisfied. Struggling for orientation, I discerned that the cauldron for the city's many active agents was *Spaccanapoli*, "split Naples," a thoroughfare that cuts through the historic center. The street's official name changes five times along the route, but the byway remains best known by its ear-pleasing slang handle: SPAHH-kah-NAHH-poh-lee. Why not use the shorthand? What's the point naming the tunnels in an anthill? My shoes and pants-cuffs quickly acquired a speckle of sulfur dust, and no matter the direction I tilted my nose, like Ugrešić I was confounded by yet another reek. A whiff of shellfish or acetylene, of garlic in oil or mixed tobacco and hashish. If I paused and put my head back, I spied the sky's sea-freshened *azzura*, but this was never wider than a streak of bright fingerpaint. Rooftops bristled with ornamental cornices, if not with unruly hedgerows, the weeds sprouting from the stonework. Everywhere, too, the sky's serenity was slapped aside by dangling laundry. Time and again, the overhead crisscross of sheets and shirts, pants and underpants, surprised my neck with a cold sprinkle. And with these alleyways threading off left and right unpredictably, with every third or fourth palazzo bearing a coat of arms in grime-blackened bas-relief, with the storefronts erupting in party colors and stirring up eddies in the crush of pedestrians—with all that, I couldn't imagine how anyone found their way. You wouldn't call the edges of Spaccanapoli sidewalks. Side-niches perhaps, or cobble-steps, their wear and tear suggested something out of Pompeii. Yet somehow thousands of downtowners, tens of thousands, came and went.

How could I claim to know more than most Americans? Didn't feel like it—though back in my late teens, when it came to describing Ugrešić's "orgy," it was another American who delivered my favorite line.

This was a Franciscan novice. He and I met in one of Spaccanapoli's landmark churches, Santa Chiara: the sisters of Clarisse, allied with the Franciscans. The monk-in-training was about my age and ethnic blend, out of Brooklyn, name of Henry. *Fratello Enrico* favored a chin beard that, had he worn black leather rather than brown robes, would've rendered him hip. We overlapped in town for hardly a month and yet, half a century later, this book glistens with nuggets Henry first turned up. Inside Santa Chiara, it was he who pointed out a couple of tiny scraps of majolica tile, painted like Wedgewood china, clinging yet to walls otherwise naked. Before the Allied bombing in '43, the entire sanctuary had that glorious finish, a white detailed in garden colors. Henry also made sure I didn't miss the bullet holes, pocking an outer wall of the cloister. Some guerilla ambush during the street fighting.

My favorite run-in with him came late one afternoon on Spaccanapoli. By that time the wives were out, thronging in search of dinner. The center's rhythms sink into retard after lunch, *riposo*, and then pick up anew as the night takes shape. Folks add to the crowd just standing there, taking the air outside a doorway. Then too, by 1970 the street had been designated *senza traffica*, but it would be decades before anyone followed the rules. Fiats nosed their way through the hustle, a few at least the tiny 500, as well as three-wheeled trucks and scooters (the riders often a pair of cold-eyed teens). Zigging and zagging, stop and go—as sundown nears, it's the tunnels of an anthill.

So Henry and I bumped into each other. He must've been rushing to a service, and I had a funicular to catch.

"John!" He stepped back, with a wave at the surrounding chaos. "What are you doing, risking your life in the middle of the *street?*"

Good one, Brother. Good one, though with the least nudge, the question turns serious: What kind of a life was this, with everyone out in the middle of the street? Could it be the good life? And was that what I hoped to discover, whatever my age?

As for an answer, that might be staring out from a photo of my father.

This was my father as I never knew him, before marriage and Manhattan. He's not yet out of his teens, roughly the age of Henry and I, though the youngster in the old black-&-white is already a combat veteran—so I've learned. Over in the States, the picture was in an album. My older sister, younger brother, and I often showed the page to friends: our earliest picture of Pop. It catches him downtown, mid-stride, center-frame. It's as if the others have fallen into phalanx behind him. They're not on Spaccanapoli, the slope suggests instead a cross-street, at bright midday. The shadow puddled at my father's feet presents a stark contrast to the white of his open-necked shirt, and in the encroaching shade the other figures are a blur. A woman frowns at a storefront, a man grins around a cigarette, but my father stares into the lens, mouth just ajar, head just cocked, one hand deep in its pocket and his stride shifting. He's wary. Switch out the face in Photoshop, and you've got a still of some tightly coiled screen urbanite, Johnny Boy in

Mean Streets or Omar in *The Wire*. But then, my father himself was screen-worthy. This took me a while to accept, to put together that broad brow, "Roman" nose, eyes sloped in bedroom shadow. His shirtfront is V'd to mid-chest, and there are curls showing, on his arms too; he wears his sleeves rolled to the elbow. The shirt's loose, as are the slacks, and with the hitch in his stride his hips and crotch tip provocatively. Half a century and more after the photo was taken, my daughter reached an age when, looking it over in a parent's hallway, she knew what she was seeing.

"What a hottie," she declared.

But while my Vera studied the picture on a wall, I never did. Not through my early adulthood anyway, the double-decade away from Naples, between my late teens and early midlife. From '70 to '90 and then some, the photo lay out of sight. About the time I left for college, the album went into a closet in a box, labeled "Misc. Maggie & Enz." Still, once I'd seen the picture, I couldn't shake it. It stayed with me on those late-adolescent trips, as I took advantage of the lower cost of living, the good fortune of which I had no clue, and then later too, at 40 and beyond. The image of my father in the *centro* seemed to leave a trail, drift-marks on the tufa-stone. I ambled alongside a ghost.

* * *

So, Spaccanapoli, what did you have for me and my shadow?

Often enough I came across leftovers of high accomplishment, signifiers of a city that mattered. These could be vague, such as Via Benedetto Croce, one of the five names along Spaccanapoli's route. I had only the foggiest notion: some philosopher, years back. Croce had talked trash about the Fascists, I knew that much, and at some point between 20 and 40 I tried his *History of the Kingdom of Naples*. I needed an English edition, the arguments were so clotted and ornate, and I couldn't imagine how Mussolini took offense. But Croce's palazzo overlooked this urban Equator, and there hung a plaque, more legible than my great-uncle's. The Brown Shirts kept the philosopher under house arrest, and when the Nazis took over they had him ticketed for the camps. Naples had an active anti-Fascist underground—a few may have worked with my family—and Croce was hustled to safety farther south. Nevertheless, he returned to city center as soon as the uprisings of September '43, had driven out the Wehrmacht. To Croce the address was a point of pride, previously the home of Giambattista Vico, a deep thinker of the 18th century. Myself, both c. 1970 and 1990, I tracked down Vico's tomb, on one of the narrowest nearby *vicoli*. Even as a university undergrad, I'd heard of him, his theory of history. Everything goes in cycles: that theory.

At 20, at 40, I kept checking the urban canyons for echoes, if not my own father's then the city fathers'. One sidestreet was distinctive, curving away from the central *spacca*, rather than crossing it at right angles. Did I ask Brother Henry? Did I, decades later, do a Google search? One way or another I learned that the alley followed the oval outline of a long-gone amphitheater. The performance space had been built for Nero, bang in the center. The Emperor had to play Broadway, even after he abandoned Rome. He wrote all his own material, naturally, and he had his own Siren, Poppea. Together they embraced the ways of the Greeks, refined, sophisticated ... *sybaritic*. Now, that part, the erotica, I didn't have to research. One of the perks, when you're a bookish boy. I got the picture: these curved walls had worn Imperial bling, and the city had served as a playground for the star, the Don, *il capo di tutti capi*.

Up north, though, the man went on making enemies. *Nero Plays Naples* wound up having a short run. The man's last words: "What an artist dies in me!"

Delusional to the end, and a creep from the get-go, this guy too turned up along the streets on which I was trying to find myself. In my head, that final cry had a sneering echo: "What an *artist*." Still the vocation wouldn't let go, whether I was a bookish boy or a grownup with a library. The library made for lot of work, once I found a new place following the divorce. Yet at 40 I felt if anything more determined than at 20: I was going to add my own books to those shelves, books as beautiful as I could make them. This served as a cornerstone to my reinvention. And in Naples, half a globe from my failures, I might be half a block from some benchmark in my culture, or closer still to the ruins of some bankrupt aspiration. Some reminder of an Emperor who wore no clothes. The view might be chilling, or might be bracing.

But Spaccanapoli also served ordinary purposes, like buying and selling. Together, this street and its uphill parallel, Via Tribunali, might've provided the model for the expression "a confusion of shops." The ghosts of antiquity never interfered with forking over today's cash. As an undergrad, I first came to know the street vendors, forever in my face with cigarettes, hawked tax-free out of a shoebox or purse. The *negozi* required more discernment. Each had its specialty, so if I were looking for household goods, a detergent for washing socks and underwear at my aunt's sink, it was a matter of finding the right hole in the wall. Another featured meats, another breads, and twenty years further on, when I sought a miniature mandolin as a gift for my kid, everyone directed me to Via San Sebastiano, the uphill from Santa Chiara.

The best-known market, San Gregorio Armeno, was crowded with Nativity handiwork. The stuff of the crèche, the *presepe*. Back in greater New York, my father and I had an annual routine. I'd build a cavelike stable, papier-mâché, and set up the Holy Family; he'd supply the Peaceable Kingdom of animals, shepherds, and potentates out of the East. All were the same kiln-fired terracotta as I saw off Spaccanapoli, and I recall in particular the Moorish king. He came in coal-black, his servant in fudge-brown.

On San Gregorio Armeno, the stables ran far larger than the one Pop and I had built. The Naples *presepe* had ground-floor wings and upstairs rooms. Beneath dangling angels, they branched out into elaborate miniature cities, where you found butchers, fruitsellers, pasta chefs, all paired with their tools, from hunks of red meat to bright silver spatulas. Also the figures in waiting included a politician or two in suit and tie. Often I couldn't identify the caricature—too often really, after I came back in middle age. Keeping up with the Italian news was supposed to be part of the project, Domini Redux. But in some displays the only figure I recognized was Sophia Loren. Her I couldn't miss, even in the modest country dress she wore in *Two Women*, and so too I spotted the great comic actor Totò, with his cocked bowler and hooked nose. In one of those shops, however, I learned that Totò was also a writer, composing songs as well as scripts. At my surprise, my interest, the doll-maker pointed out another figure, more regal in bearing. *Il Grande Eduardo*, he said. Who?

Stranger still were the places that sold prayer offerings. Gold and silver handicrafts, intended to encourage God's help, these too have a nickname, *ex-voto*. Signs along Spaccanapoli, however, prefer the full nomenclature: *oggetti votivi*. Most take the form of pint-sized body parts. You see double hands folded in prayer, single hands spread wide, arms and legs and handsome heads. Alternatively, as a conjure against addiction, a supplicant can buy a syringe, in silver-plate or gold, rendered with the precision of a catalogue. Believers tack these hollow forms to the walls of favorite chapels, or hang them from the reliquaries of patron saints, or even scatter them on church floors. No better than sanctified bribery, really, yet they left me staring, whatever my age. In Spaccanapoli's perpetual stone twilight, behind the black steel grid that protected the shop windows, the hammered high sheen of the *oggetti* appeared to float. They constituted a second, half-secret urban landscape: a city of whispered hopes, turned by some enchantment to artifacts. A city where faith was polished to a greater glow by the overlap of one iconic belief system after another: first the Olympian Hera, later the Christian Mary. Among the *oggetti*, you noticed especially the array of hearts, a dozen different shapes on which to pin your prayers, from the anatomically correct to the flame-crowned Sacred to the sorrowful valentine, cracked down the middle.

Elsewhere, to be sure, I'd grab a bite. Boy or man, my choice wasn't always pizza, but any menu that matched my wallet didn't list much else. I found as well *insalata di mare* or *frutta di mare*, misleading names both. The dishes had more meat than fruit or salad. It arrived with an upturned centerpiece coil of octopus tentacle, like a lavender crown of flesh, and was otherwise garnished with nothing more than a sprinkle of herbs and a dollop of oil, a wedge of lemon on the side. Yet I got a full-bodied meal out of either *insalata*—and out of the pizza as well. The latter came alive with a brick-oven crackle and redolence; at each chaw, it delivered a whole-mouth workout.

* * *

The most common local pizza remains the *Margherita*, and till I returned in midlife, that woman remained a mystery. Who was she, and how'd she wind up in ovens all over town? Then there were the other women, flesh and blood, out in the streets. In their case, even now I wouldn't claim I know the full recipe.

The faces, in chiaroscuro, recalled that photo of my father at my age. I thought of the others in the shot, half-revealed at most. The smoker gave no more than a hint of a grin, and the window-shopper kept a poker face, yet they both got across the notion of *la bella figura*, a good show. Now before me, in living color, in a hundred flickering, head-turning glimpses—a cheek, a shoulder—the scene suggested birds of paradise in a coop too small. I'd never seen, for instance, such shoes: busy with tassels and stitching and buckles, buffed as brightly as the *oggetti votivi*. Italian footwear was part of *Il Boom*, the economic surge of the 1950s and '60s that lifted the country from Third-World to First-World, and I could see the results right through the end of the century. I marveled at how the women got around on those heels.

But the shoes were only a surface distraction. I'd never given credence to the expression "doe-eyed beauty," and yet I encountered it often along Spaccanapoli, though a deer hadn't wandered through since the days when the crowds spoke Latin. The phrase made a natural fit for more than a few young Neapolitan women, teenagers or twenty-somethings. After that they took on a beauty less showy, less dewy, but more assured. The younger mothers around the piazzas, the pairs and threesomes of Italy's career women (rarer around 1970, I should say, than a couple of decades later), possessed an intimidating command. The care they took with their lipstick was only part of the complex signal-system in every smile. A queen comes to mind, yes—perhaps Margherita, the first queen following Unification. In 1889 she gave her name to a pizza that featured that red, white, and green of the new Italian state.

Nor could my education omit the older women, the Crone stage. It wasn't that they stopped going out in the evenings, like older Americans. Rather, they too enjoyed the street, but always on a perch. Sharp-eyed, on a stool or a café chair, they gave the night its decorum. While youngest formed shifting configurations, from pairs to groups, with showy bracelets and earrings that themselves seemed to chatter, the oldest sat sentinel, often closemouthed and solitary, devoid of jewelry except the wedding ring. They presided cross-armed over a stretch of alley.

Myself, whether young or no longer young, I knew the local myths of womankind. I knew the three Sirens, and the name of one, Partenope, par-TEHH-no-pay. It was Partenope who, after Odysseus heard her sing yet sailed on by, couldn't bear the disgrace; she threw herself off her cliff top (on Capri, according to legend). Part bird, not part fish, the monster drowned, and where the corpse washed ashore, they founded a city. They gave it (according to legend) her name. Another prodigy was the Sibyl, the Elder who told your fortune, most famously in the *Aeneid*. Up in Cuma, I visited her cave, more of an underground theater, manmade. You approach along trapezoidal corridors, flat and narrow

17

at the peak, suggesting Mycenae if not some older culture. Both Sybil and Siren recall the Earth-Mother theocracies with which Europe began.

The men of city center posed different questions, and in their case too I've often got no more than half an answer. My lunch place might have a limited menu, but the staff always seemed to be adult, men with beard-shadow and paunch. Back about 1970, a boy might run errands, his outfit sometimes the uniform of Catholic school, but along the arched ovens you rarely saw the teenage help you'd find in a fast-food joint in the States. Again, come 1990 the rules had relaxed somewhat, and these changes kept on into the new century, among the workers as well as the customers. Still, all these men ... many in blazer and tie, yet unhurried ... Even as a dreamy adolescent, I knew there was something strange about the work ethic. Talking impassively, or what Neapolitans consider impassively, a pair might linger over a *mezzo-litro* and a calzone till the last moment of siesta. Stranger still were the larger lunches I spotted around the room, threesomes and quartets of overgrown layabouts. Their afternoon plainly unencumbered, they kept the waiter busy with platters of fried goods (calamari, zucchini, cheese) and rounds of Nastro Azzuro, a beer formerly brewed in town. Oh, and how about a pastry from across the street? Plus-size, they were, guys with bellies lopping over beltless slacks. They wore their shirtsleeves rolled, like Pop in that photo, but on them I often spied a scar. Or they wore a facial scar, a scimitar across cheek or temple.

Roughnecks, yet their table never lacked for attention. Even as a kid, I felt the prickle, the threat. As an adult, I made sure not to stare.

Yet even lunks like these, for all their *dolce far niente*, gave the impression of having something up. This could be the core Spaccanapoli Paradox: how hustle remained the rule. A man might not bear a scar, but he remained alert, his hands busy. He might linger over his espresso, but just to earn the moment's pause, he'd needed to be on his game. You saw the same in the women, forever in motion, tick-tock. When I returned in midlife, I found the *centro* at last pedestrian-only, the cars largely cleared away. Yet the crush had grown even more complicated, thanks to the new neediness out of Libya or Syria. Of course, if I were a Laplander, I wouldn't call the Southern Italians white, exactly. Regardless of their skin-tone, however—what were they all doing, risking their lives in the middle of the street?

Like Vincenzo Vicedomini, c. 1945, quick-footed and hawk-eyed.

Back during my first solo visits, when I was the same age as the young buck in the picture, my grandfather brought out a different photograph. Another that lingered in the mind's eye, it turned up in a fraying album my Nonno had labeled in elegant cursive: *1939-1945*. The album soon went to pieces, and the old man who'd brought it to light died before I'd finished at Boston U. Still, the first time I saw this shot, he gave names to the faces: his children and their cousins. The War generation, a group portrait. The family had taken a day in the country, and the teens sat around a picnic table—with one exception. My father perched up top, on the table. His feet, in saddle shoes, were on the plank seat, and his hands extended spread-fingered between the cuffs of gleaming white pants. The scene suggested a special occasion, and Nonno may've mentioned Easter. Still, young Enzo was hanging loose, ready to leapfrog across the countryside. A heartthrob, not an ounce of fat on him, he grinned hugely, his hair losing its comb. Was there a sea breeze? Was this a SoCal beach boy?

My mind's eye, back at the end of my teens, wasn't so crowded. Swiftly I recalled the other picture, the one of Pop downtown; it was obvious that the picnic shot hadn't been taken much earlier. My grandfather had only to turn the page, and look: the later photo. Over in Naples, they had it too. Duplicates weren't easy to come by back in the middle 1940s, but somehow they'd managed, and in the street shot Pop's face remained unlined, but he'd gone to a different planet. A place of threat and shadow.

If the Neapolitans knew some secret, when it came to city life, it had to include this secret. Whatever had happened, between the first pic and the second?

* * *

Before I could unearth a decent answer, though, I needed to understand that my Naples was much changed from my father's. The city of my late teens, for starters, had developed a new symbiosis, for a streetwise *giovanotto* like the man in the later photo. Their characteristic perch was on a Vespa in full roar.

If you saw two on a Vespa, everyone told me, they might be a threat. One to smash, the other to grab, and the bike would be out of sight before I knew what'd hit me. My goods would be sold to some Camorra broker before I saw a doctor. Even the gentle Franciscan warned me—but then there was the evidence of my eyes. Everywhere, I spotted two boys to a bike. If the banana seat held three or four, that would be a family. But during a busy hour, whether at the end of the '60s or the beginning of the '90s, you couldn't help but share the street with boys riding doubled-up. Myself, I'd stay frosty, perhaps jamming a hand down over my wallet, but I'd also try to catch what the youngsters had to say. Insofar as I heard anything, I heard what you'd expect. *She told me Piazza Cavour ... Not at those prices, brother ...* This at top volume, as once more *dolce far niente* proved full of zip. Also these players took care to look good. They didn't go a day without Mama's 24-hour laundry, even the ones most likely criminals: the prowlers in the Spanish Quarter (where Spaccanapoli began) and the Forcella (where it ended). Even they kept their shirts scrubbed and pressed, whether Naples blue or clerical white. Their shoes could rival the women's.

Any understanding of this metropolis soon bangs up against fresh *impedimentia*. What I learned about Via Benedetto Croce might be undone with a word from the old woman minding the block, up on her balcony. A man who appeared on the ball, a wheeler-dealer in jacket and tie, might prove no more useful than one of the terra-cotta politicians on San Gregorio Armeno. And even after I learned a few things, I faced new conundrums, in particular the Africans and Arabs working the streets over satchels and duffels. Come sundown they generally abandoned the *centro*, but plenty of mystery remained. As the piazza filled with a younger, whiter crowd, they flung around a gesture with thumb pressed to the index and middle finger: "you're an idiot," that gesture.

Among those who paid for table service, some kept their jewelry minimal and their children with them, truly young. An American didn't know what to make of it, these second- or third-graders out so far past their bedtimes. Back home, someone would put in a call to Child Health. Actual danger, the ragged edge of the demimonde, was never hard to spot. Prostitutes always showed off something extra, a butt grotesque in its miniskirt, a smile garish in its paint. The real eye-candy among them, the ones in Oscar gowns and club makeup—those were men. I'd learned this on my first solo visits, when one of my uncles had deemed me old enough to know. *Trasvestiti*, he'd explained, had long found business off the docks. The drag show had achieved notoriety across the Mediterranean, among both low-budget sailors and high-rolling yachtsmen.

Come midlife I was quicker at spotting the urban parasites. The addicts either suffered jitters or sat slack-jawed, tucked into some cathedral's ornamental foot; one or two might stare back, leather-souled. As for the boys out two to a bike, I couldn't ignore the once-over a few gave my shoulder tote. In my 40s, after adding a laptop to the books and papers, I started to take extra precautions. If I had the bag out after midnight, I wore it over the "inside" shoulder, the one against the wall of stores, churches, *palazzi*. I wouldn't let it dangle into the street. At certain intersections I became a child again, looking both ways like my parents taught me.

I became myself Janus-faced, on the lookout for both what might do me harm and what might afford a fresh discovery. Could Pop and I make palpable connection?

Most creatures of the Neapolitan night, naturally, posed no threat. In the States we'd call what they were doing "hanging out." Here, however, the slang for that, *intraliarsi*, was an odd bit of talk. The pronunciation alone: EEN-trrah-LYAHHR-see. All the city's conversation has its tricks, more than a few lost in translation. Local pronunciations and cadences remain a bell-clear signal of origin, one that carries an onus in Milan or Florence. It would be as if you dropped by MOMA talking like an Okie. Granted, by the turn of the millennium, some of the dishonor had washed away. The uptick was something else my father would never have dreamed of; the ghetto talk of his time became the language of Italian rock. Pino Daniele, a singer-songwriter out of a hardscrabble neighborhood known as the Sanità, changed everything.

To me, in any case, the city's accent always came across sweetly. A music rough but irresistible, it had, like *Twelfth Night*'s, a dying fall. *Mo' lo facc'*: the sound ballooned on the first syllable, then struggled to rise again on the third, fa-AHH ... before guttering out in a drawl, ch-shh ... The pattern tattooed my ear, and yet even now as I enter it into a computer, a technology that itself underscores how much has changed since I first caught the city's echo, I feel I can't get it right.

At the end of my thirties, as at the end of my teens, my odyssey had only an inkling of its Ithaca. Indeed, on my middle-aged rounds, the old city's inscrutability felt intrinsic to its allure. To stumble on a fresh unknown yielded greater riches, often, than whatever destination I'd had in mind. Then too, as I stirred up these unexpected nuggets of protein, I discovered W.G. Sebald; the U.S. edition of *The Rings of Saturn* appeared at the close of the

'90s. The novel achieved a miraculous coherence, open to any stray thought and yet coming together like a prophet's vision. It had nothing to do with Naples, yet it felt like just what I sought from Naples. Then later still, as my 40s came to a close and I brought off a juddering return to upright, this allowed me to glimpse a shape, Sebaldean more or less, in all the meandering beforehand. In all the *mo'*, the now and now again, I discerned three defining ingredients. A trio of passwords, unlocking my own secrets, my father's, and the city's. First, there's courtship and love in all its forms, second the heavy hand of thugs and crooks, and third, peculiar to this obstinate town, there's a knack for survival despite the loss of some element that had seemed, till then, vital. Partenope drowned, yet went on.

Yes—romance, crime, and the apocalypse put in its place. Those three slow the onrush and gather this metropolis into a book.

* * *

Spaccanapoli ends to the west of the *centro*, at an intersection you wouldn't call a T, rather a drunken F. My first visit to the spot came thanks to my Nonno. Him 60 and me 20, more or less, we steered through traffic to a wide hole with dented railings. The hole had no illumination either, best to visit at high noon, but down at its bottom lay building blocks from the street's first flooring. The site offered nothing more, nothing to match the layers of antiquity I've seen since, the shops and shrines still intact beneath a wanderer's feet. Back at the end of the '60s, though, all I got was this hole at the sunrise end of the artery. Still, the stones were something, mammoth blocks of tufa, the city in a single, elemental cell. The litter left by the Romans was usually smaller, the bricks of amphitheaters and aqueducts.

Of course, Spaccanapoli had been laid out before the Romans.

Back in 325 BCE the Greek *polis* capitulated to the rising kingdom on the Tiber, collateral damage in the Samnite Wars.

Officials of the new regime saw no reason to change the old layout, though they described everything in a different language. The central straightaway, running east-west, became a *decumanus*, the perpendiculars *cardinale*. Details like that rattled around my head, my library-loving head, both back when I needed my grandfather to show me the place and later, when I got there on my own. On that second visit, say 1990 CE, the hole's supersized building blocks looked the same, a fungous green under the midday sun—but then there was me. I was alone, a full-grown adult with haphazard obligations. I didn't feel nearly so solid as those stones, and maybe worse weathered, and I fell into a mental game. A math game based on my life. It'd been twenty years since I'd last stood on that spot, right? An interval easy to work with, right? This book itself will cover such an interval, a double-decade of reinvention. During that period, my father's death falls almost exactly halfway.

So there at the start of my comeback, c. 1990, I played a game of 20s. I computed how many such periods would contain just the Greek lifespan of Spaccanapoli, still underfoot. Just the first Naples, perhaps known as Partenope, and by any name a place its citizens had called home: for them too, in 20 years a boy became a man, and a man became, well, whatever he became. For them too, it marked an initiation, and how many such had passed, while the people who walked this street had considered it Main or First or Broadway: the incision that cleaved city from wilderness?

Whatever the object of my game (certainly it had no winner), it's strange how well I remember. But then the figures turned out strange, not to say haunting. The rough count came to my adult life times 15. All I'd endured since age 20, the sweetness and the worry, at 40 mostly the latter, the years lopping one over the other under a question that loomed ever larger: *where's the good life?*

All my John-journey, times 15. Just the first Naples.

I wound up running the numbers again, computing to a later date, the era of vainglorious Nero. The total this time, piling Roman bricks on top of Greek stones, came itself to 40, or damn close. In the life of this street, my own life amounted to no more than a percentile. My oh-so-significant John-journey! For that matter, I could throw in my father and grandfather, taking the journey back to the '90s of the previous century, and it would make little difference. And what if I continued to work with the distant past? Another notch in this long, long metropolitan bench would be the end of the Empire, 476 CE. The Goths had shown mercy on the last of the Caesars, a mere kid, and packed him off to relatives in Naples ...

I couldn't keep up. As I whipped through the iterations of the street on which I stood, I could conclude only that I'd encounter nothing like it in other cities of the world. A few, a very few, had their date of founding further back. A number had hummed more loudly, busy capitals of far-flung kingdoms. Yet their centers had been ransacked, their maps redrawn. Not even Damascus could resurrect, with so little as an informed glance, so many previous sensations of *mo'*. Spaccanapoli may have been in continuous daily use longer than any other urban byway in the world.

What secret might it possess, this stretch of paving stones? What had kept it so vital, despite loss, grief, delusion, and failure?

PART TWO:

'O Polpo Si Ccuoce In Acqua Su'—
The octopus cooks in its own water

MY LEARNING TOOK YEARS OF over-and-back, and as I say, now and again my father himself offered some small lesson—including a couple of times after he passed on. Now when there's no ghost to interrupt, also, I've got to admit again that there remains plenty of mystery. Plenty of ambiguity. Even towards the end of my Neapolitan changes, well into the new millennium, I still knew so little that, when I took my shirt off in a good-looking young painter's apartment workspace, all I could do was wonder.

The woman had asked me to strip down, I knew that much. The undershirt as well, she'd specified, though I was to keep my pants on. I was to pose topless, all part of session for which she'd freed up an entire summer afternoon.

Also she'd freed a corner of her two-room walkup, uncluttering. She'd set up a stool, and from that end of the place, I couldn't miss anything. Not the bed, a futon of course, right here beside the stool. Handy, yes. Wouldn't take much to clear it for action. Then there was the woman's own top, a tank top, sweat-stuck to a bra of that beige called "nude" and a stair-climber's midsection. Just reaching her place, five worn flights between narrowing walls, had taken the wind out of me. But then the painter suffered maybe fifteen years less wear and tear, overall; I couldn't miss that either. I thought of "the angel in the marble," the metaphor from Michelangelo. Maybe he could've found the angel, amid my kudzu body hair and sagging avoirdupois. As for my friend—I'll call her Anna—I was happy to have her try, or whatever she had in mind.

She was no dilettante, I should say. Her work had been turning up around the city for years now. She had a plan in mind, a series of paintings: all men, all artists, in paired panels. In one they'd appear fully dressed, in the other topless.

And what workspace did she have except her home? Her bedroom?

No place for a dilettante, Anna's lay uphill along one of the *vicoli* that crosses Spaccanapoli. The old *decumanus* has been ranked a UNESCO Heritage site, but its feeder streets often offer no better heritage than a single light every block, its wiring visible along the brick, and a hole in the wall selling pizza by the slice. In fact, as I watched the painter swivel and dip before me, I began to think that, some days, a slice might be her whole diet. This when the rent couldn't be much. In New York the building might've been called a tenement, but here the bottom floors went back a lot further than on the Lower East Side. The upper stories were more recent add-ons, slapped together with at most a secondhand notion of building codes. But then, here on the top floor, Anna enjoyed plenty of light.

At street level the *palazzo* had a kind of courtyard, packed dirt. Formerly a goat- and chicken-run, maybe a stables, now it combined space for engine repair and outdoor washing with a scrap of playground. The scruffy kids included a couple barefoot, when I arrived, and an oil-smeared "mechanic" sat grunting in one doorway. The scene comes to mind every time I revisit the sorry creatures of Elena Ferrante and her Naples Quartet. Those novels' mob-sickened blocks lie elsewhere, past the sunrise end of Spacccanapoli, in the neighborhood known as Vasto. Nonetheless Ferrante's battered strivers would've felt at home around any number of local intersections. Among them, too, would always have been those few with some gift, some reason to believe they might not tumble into the city's long-festering ruts, like Elena in the novels or Anna, here.

Her reason to believe stood stacked all around us: more paintings than she had cups and saucers and cutlery. The kitchenette in fact used one of the largest canvases for a door; if Anna sold it, the piece would have to be cut off its mounting to go down the stairs. Today, she was after something smaller; each canvas fit neatly within one of the skylight's parallelograms. Still, the paintings would mean two more sardines for the tin, by the end of my sitting—that is, if a sitting was all Anna had in mind, when she'd assured me we would have "hours alone together."

She began with serious focus, her top bunching as she prepped the first canvas. Nearby I spotted another set of shirt-&-skin, a pretty boy I'd say. Sleekly semi-bearded, he was an actor, Anna told me. She explained the lack of finish as well, the way the semi-nude turned to a stick figure below the nipples. The sitting was for the details, she said, the face and musculature. After that she took it "into a personal thing."

Personal, *amica?* The question was too much, I realized, it left a number more dangling, and I settled in quietly for the take with my shirt on (nothing formal, Hawaiian rather, splashy). My portraitist had a *fidanzato*, I knew. The word no longer meant "fiancé," but it carried weight nonetheless. I couldn't use it myself, for instance, though back in the States I was seeing someone and I nursed hopes of taking it further. By this time I'd worked through some changes, as I say. I'd pretty much completed my Neapolitan learning curve, though the woman in my life wasn't yet a *fidanzata*. She couldn't be, not so long as—a memoir can't be coy—she was still married to someone else. That afternoon, shifting on my stool, alone with a consenting adult and her mixed signals, I could only wonder.

As for Anna's man, he was older, perhaps as old as I, and he'd achieved the Southern Italian nirvana of a lasting job. *Un posto fisso*, yes, though nothing executive level. He was only a shop-clerk, but then what he might do for his Trophy Wife, if things got that far, wasn't what you'd think. In him, Anna would have more than a sugar daddy. Rather he factored into a complex calculation such as you'd expect from one of Ferrante's women, in which the key variable was the artist's status as an out-of-towner. She wasn't *Napoli*

D.O.C.; she worked without the net of parish and neighborhood. Over a lifetime, that net could suffocate a woman, but it might also save her; it might do both, over a lifetime. Thus to ally herself with a homeboy, long in place, provided Anna a lot more than help with the rent and the pizza.

Not that I brought any of this up. I perched there owlish, watching. Yet as Anna swiveled and dipped, she opened up about the *fidanzato*, admitting that he helped with the rent. It was only right, she declared; he slept over often enough.

I wondered, first, about the logistics. Getting the futon to co-operate must be tricky, and come morning, they'd have to organize breakfast … Meanwhile she finished the first painting, locked in, then broke for coffee. She fired up the *macchinetta* although by then the heat had me down to my undershirt (another portrait: *Stanley Kowalski Goes to Pot*). But a couple of *singolos* didn't take long, and then as my friend stirred in the sugar, she got my inner Q-&-A whirling as well. She spoke of an earlier lover.

Out of the blue, she brought him up: her first lover, a *Napoletano*. They'd gotten together during her first months in town. The story emerged with the speed and concentration of her painting: the unmistakable outlines of a dead dream. Life with another artist, that was the dream, because the boy played marvelous guitar and when he sang, *davvero*, truly, he was an angel. I put in a murmur or two, sympathetic I hoped, and meantime did the math. Figuring from our first encounters a dozen years previous, and from what I knew about art school in Italy, my friend hadn't been that young at the time of this *primo amore*. She'd been into her twenties, late for this day and age. Then wouldn't that put her past puppy love? Virgin or no, wouldn't she have toughened up, some? Just listening to her story, freshly espresso'd, I could see the dream's collapse. Anna's Renaissance Man turned out to have more than one woman. He'd lied and lied again, and finally—despite twenty years and more of toughening up—the woman had taken a knife to her wrist.

"Right here," she told me, hoisting her hands into the sun's parallelogram.

Truth was, I didn't see scars, though they might've been hidden under today's paint-stains. What I noticed was how she gripped her cup, all knuckles, and how she perched on the edge of her one clear patch of futon. She'd done it wrong, my friend explained. She'd slashed the wrong vein or something, and she hadn't expected so much blood or pain. She'd fainted and been discovered.

Discovered? She'd done this where she'd have company? Even as Anna made her confession, she raised more questions.

For her, though, there was nothing but certainty, firm as her grip on the cup: if she'd stayed awake she'd have finished the job.

I had to ask: *davvero?*

"My first love," she repeated. "There is nothing else to say."

As you wish, Anna. I offered what I could, condolences, plus some feeble attempt to lighten things up. When I caught myself looming too close—the stool left my legs spread before her face—I scuttled back and straightened. Her posture too was changing, regathering, and then she shook her head. Break over. My friend returned to her easel, checking sightlines and palette. I couldn't even catch her eye, as once more I struggled to understand: was she through? Was that it, whatever she'd wanted? In any case I kept my mouth shut, pulling my drenched scoop-neck over my head.

We continued in silence until her *fidanzato* called. From the first ring-tone, that descending Nokia ring-tone, a '90s staple now out of date, it was obvious that Anna didn't care for the interruption. The way she got her back up, her chest straining against her soaked T and tank, you'd have thought she was calling attention to her nipples. But she set her man straight. She'd *told* him about this session. She'd *known* he'd be at the shop. Again I did the math, figuring from the midday *riposo*. Once a business reopened, it didn't close again till 8 at least, and meanwhile here at Anna's the sun's parallelogram stretched out almost wall to wall. After lunch, she and her subjects could count on (how had she put it?) hours alone together.

"I *told* you," she repeated.

Before she closed the phone she had to wipe the sweat from its face. She swabbed her ear too, with the ham of that hand, frowning, muttering. With that I could no longer keep my mouth shut. Even now, maybe ten years further along, I can't sort out my nobler motives, like compassion, from the nastier promptings. *Baby, sounds like you need a real man* … Even now I'm sorting that out. At the time, there on the stool, at least I maintained my posture. I wasn't a rookie, as an artist's model; I knew I could talk, and she could answer. So too she continued working, frowning more neutrally, as she replied that her boyfriend had another apartment he wanted to show her. He was hoping they could see the place before nightfall.

Then she added: "We've decided to marry. This next place, it'll be our place."

The *fidanzato* had made a formal proposal. The news hadn't reached me, plainly, though it wasn't a secret among the people we had in common. As for the ring, Anna left it off when she was planning to paint. But then, I'm not sure I'd have noticed a ring, or made anything of it if I spotted one. The woman was never one for convention. Yet here she stood, sizing up my half-nakedness, telling me she and her *fidanzato* had agreed on a date. They'd marked their wedding day on the calendar, along with the day by which they had to be in a new home. And *Madonn'*, it was so much to organize! They had family coming out of the woodwork!

"You have no idea," Anna told me, "how difficult it is in Naples."

She broke off painting for another shake of the head. And then what should happen? she asked. Right in the middle of everything, what should happen?

In the middle of everything, she got a great idea. This idea, the diptychs, all men …

My eye fell on the other one, the pretty one, the lower part of his portrait still sketchy. Again I had to wonder, this time imagining a string of paintings never finished, all the boys she'd never have. All these samplings of intimacy, her own learning curve, before she settled in with a lover intended to last a lifetime.

* * *

An insight, there? A glimpse into the woman's soul? Perhaps, but my friend had more going for her, I'm happy to say. She wasn't just working in the grip of unreason, frenzied by fear of commitment. Anna saw the series through, and her shirts-and-skins came to occupy a long gallery wall. The show went up at a good time for me, I could attend the reception, and better still, I came with my new wife. As Anna was done sampling, so was I; we'd each found the central figure for the landscape of our remaining days. For the exhibition, she did without her Domini Diptych, but I've found the painting online: *Scrittore Italo-Americano*. It might be a wedding gift, I suppose, except I gave her a better one before I left. At the end of the afternoon, back in my shirt, I declined her offer of a beer and instead flipped through her racks of canvases. I bought a double-canvas with a wildly different subject. A fat and faceless woman in gym gear, a blob in the first piece, in the second leaps high; all at once, she takes flight.

Looking over the piece now—my wife likes it in the dining room—what occurs to me is that my Neapolitan midlife put me through the reverse. First the mysteries of family and city had me wheeling around in Zero G, the vertigo worse at 40 than at 20, and then I wound up back on earth, with steady work and a sustaining marriage. The stuff of Pixar? Maybe, but it'll do for a thumbnail, and by the end of the process I'd also parceled my Neapolitan experience into three handy bundles. To repeat: the city gave instruction first in romance—the theme of my Afternoon as an Odalisque—second in living with corruption, and third in the awareness that all could be lost, at any minute, around any corner.

Before I go any further, though, I've got a more pressing concern. I've got to ask, *what's the problem?*

A metropolitan Italian background, in particular southern Italian, can leave a person with terrific resources. I mean, my father could cook. His ragù gives me my title: his word for what, in proper Italian, would be *sugo* or *salsa*. As for "ragù," the root might be French, but what did Pop care? The French were in Naples for centuries, weren't they? For a quibble like that, he had a ready laugh, a playful shrug. The same spirit carried over into playing Horsie or kicking around the ball, a/k/a, first lessons in soccer. Nor did we kids see anything less affectionate when he turned to Mom. The two of them were quick to pick up a dance rhythm and take a living-room spin. They'd have fun with the steps, improvising. Years later, after Pop had passed, my mother joined millions of other American readers in devouring Ferrante's Neapolitan Quartet, sharing I think two of the novels with her book club. Yet when these women asked, or anyone else, she'd insist: "None of the Neapolitan men I knew behaved anything like that." Ferrante's boyfriends and husbands forever threaten violence, often erupt, and besides that betray their loved ones with cold indifference. They leave terrible bruises. But though the stories held my mother spellbound, to her the men's cruelty seemed utterly alien.

The nature of that difference, just what set my father apart from, say, the vicious Solaras of the Quartet—well, I could write a book. And haven't I already brought a few pieces of an explanation to light? Haven't I sketched one subsection of Naples society, if not two, and shown where my family fit, with their music and their politics? Those explanations will go on, to be sure, but for now what I mean to emphasize is the benefit an American wife and family derived from this particular Neapolitan. He "modeled behaviors of love," as they say around the parenting workshops. Myself, right through adolescence and beyond, if I sat down with Pop, nine times out of ten I'd see more of the same. So what's the problem? Why pick at old scabs, pinching out connections to latter-day troubles? For his entire half-century in America, my father left the worst of his experience in the old country unspoken. And whatever my re-entry into his home and his whole truth reveals, it hardly obliterates the better angels of his nature.

Yes, earlier I used the grim phrase "sins of the fathers." But are those the immigrant's most significant legacy?

The answer's obvious: No way, Parteno-pay. Yet just as obviously, since I recognize the good my father did, I need the full story. I need to confront the Shadow—isn't that the name for it? The essential work, according to Carl Jung? If I don't know the shadow, the light my father shed will be imperfectly understood and vulnerable to rot. Then too, centuries before Herr Jung, in Naples they understood that everyone's some part darkness. The city's folk sayings, a motherlode for Italian publishers, grin knowingly at humanity's base elements. No one's evolved much beyond the donkey or the chicken. Even a saint, *"pure San'Antonio,"* even the ascetic St. Anthony, *"s'annammuraie d'o puorco"*: even he can fall in love with a pig.

On my visits I kept notebooks, and I jotted down both the refined locutions of people in power and the broken Italian of refugees. The murmurs across a couple of deathbeds, too. But the notes that bear an asterisk are mostly the "proverbs," carnal, savvy, and full of brio. The best have a double edge, simplifying matters even as they expose an all-too-human muddle. You'd think Lao Tsu had spent time in town. Hence my chapter titles, each another side-of-the-mouth Koan. The aphorism I've selected for talking about women and romance is heard frequently across Naples, but rarely anywhere else: *'O polpo si ccuoce in acqua su'*, oh POHL-poh see KWOH-chay in AHH-kwa soo. "The octopus cooks in its own water."

Surely even a celibate can see how the quip's congenial to the moil of love. The octopus stands for the object of affection. In this chapter I'll be speaking of one woman in particular—not Anna— and among the things I understood first about her was the need to let our feelings for each other simmer. Nevertheless, when a Neapolitan deploys the expression, it speaks to a richer ambiguity. Around the Gulf, the *polpo* can be had cheaply. Pollution and overfishing threaten the entire Mediterranean, no question of that, yet throughout my adult visits to town, I could always find a salad crowned with coiled purple tentacles. As a result, the saying turns up in all sorts of combinations. One day the cephalopod might be a *Camorrista*, a capo whacked by his own hitman, and the next its tentacles stretch across global *Realpolitik*, as lingering poison out of the Third Reich continues to seep across the Euro Zone. Whatever the context, the force of the proverb depends on the local abundance. The octopus is everywhere, and just one fruit among the region's profusion. Think of the famed mosaic of Mediterranean life, salvaged from Pompeii, now in the downtown *Museo Nazionale*. A decoration for a villa floor, the piece doesn't miss the least notch of a fin or a gill, its creatures vivid in lighter hues against Homer's wine-dark sea. The octopus provides the centerpiece, and it too is about to eat, some sort of arthropod in its grip. In Naples as in few places around the world, the feast goes on and on. *Abbondanza!*

Also the parable requires that you know how to cook. A chef with a fresh catch, still dripping—an old kitchen hand like my father, cracking wise as he wheels from stovetop to counter—will sauté in oil only. He may throw in a dollop of wine, certainly some garlic, but no water. *Polpo* doesn't need it.

Now, if the recipe prompts a metaphor, it also risks stereotype. The city, in what's become a media cliché, ranks as "the most densely populated in Europe." Naples proper houses perhaps two million souls, and the count rises threefold if you throw in the *perferia*, on the Metro line or the funiculare. Among all these, though the thought must set my father rolling in his grave, a fair number don't cook at all. The men and women of Partenope occur in the same variety as anywhere else. Still, were I to generalize, I'd say that in the kitchens hereabouts, more people than not keep their menus under control. They recognize not just their abundance but also the limit it imposes. Their meals and homemaking, their love-making in all its forms, re-enact the paradox of their setting. This is at once a land of plenty and a place of severe constriction.

No one would ever deny the loveliness of the scenery: the volcano, city center, and long sweep of the Gulf. Nevertheless, the metropolis occupies a tweezer-slice between calcareous headlands, and this confinement defines the entire region. "The Crater," some call it, suggesting jagged heights around a yawning mouth. When I look at a map, however, I see a crescent moon. The horns are each bordered by a river (Volturno north, Sele south) and scarred by a volcano (north, the so-called "Burning Fields," south of course Vesuvius). Also both tips of the moon end in an island, up top Ischia and below, the more celebrated Capri. Celebrated for love, *si sicuro*: you can hear Capri stories sung with a mandolin or see them onscreen in the multiplex. Myself, though, I had far too flimsy a wallet for those girls. Insofar as either island contributed to my redevelopment as a lover, it was Ischia. There a woman or two knew the best beaches, the best pasta and clams, and, overall, how to make the most of our *appuntamento*. They had the knack for finding a comfortable nook.

* * *

Now, to begin with, I should say that if anyone's picturing a bikini yanked off behind a sand dune, they've got the wrong romantic education. That would be the 20-something, not the 40-something. An older hand like myself prefers, for the moment, to get back to the volcanoes.

Both the two that frame the city are live. Naturally, the threat everyone's heard of is the dromedary to the south. Vesuvius has loomed large in European arts and letters since back when it had a single peak. You see the smaller model in Pompeii's *Casa del Centenario*—a fresco intended as an *ogetto votivo*, a prayer to

Bacchus. Also the grumbly mountain, along with places like it, may have fired the imagination behind *The Odyssey*. So insist two more recent imaginations, Samuel Butler and Robert Graves. Both writers claim that prodigies like Scylla and Charybdis, as well as the Sirens, must've been inspired by the perilous beauties of southern Italy. What's more, they believe the poet was a woman, a well-born Greek. Myself, reading *The Authoress of The Odyssey* (Butler's title from 1922), I think of Susan Sontag. Sontag never wrote a better novel than *The Volcano Lover*, set in Incandescent Naples, when Mozart was at the opera house and Pompeii was first excavated. Or, switching genders, I think of Nietzsche: "Build your cities on the slopes of Vesuvius!" The challenge (in *The Gay Science*) sounds worthy of an epic, though in fact the slope remains user-friendly. A visitor can catch a bus after morning cappuccino, drink in the fumes at the summit, and then be back down at the base in time for a midday *mezzo-litro*. Still, Nietzsche's rant had nothing to do with rock climbing. He spoke, rather, to the place of Naples in humanity's self-definition as a social being, a city dweller.

Homo is *sapiens* in part because he's *urbanus*, a natural correlation. Yet most early cities, like the Ur of Gilgamesh, are now little more than heaps of rock. Indeed, never mind the Big Apples of the Bronze Age; think of Detroit. Gotham, I'm saying, remains a fragile construct. To trust it'll hold requires Nietzschean *hubris*. One shift in the weather and the land goes barren. One cross word to the wrong visitor …

May as well build on the slopes of a volcano. Perhaps the secret to the longevity of Naples, then, lies in that it's built on two. You'll find the lesser-known across the city from Vesuvius: no mountain, but a sulfurous lunar landscape. A sick-gray badlands with pus-yellow fumaroles. Yet the "Burning Fields," *Campi Flegrei*, has also played host to legend. Here Odysseus sought advice from the dead—and come to think, it seems telling that this hard-bitten warrior summons up his mother first, and second his grandmother. It does suggest a woman's touch. Then later the Fields were home to the oracular witch of Vergil, the Sybil who foretold the rise of Rome. In her smoking trapezoidal lair, she could've been a throwback to the Minoan queens; when I first explored the Cave, around 1970, it was still consecrated land, the sanctuary of a woman saint.

All this caldera underfoot, I should add, has its benefits. It hatches the nutrients fortifying Sorrento lemons and the mozzarella-milk of the buffalo. It yields miraculous building material and, stacked up to either side of downtown, spectacular views. The best is an easy funicular ride up from Spaccanapoli, in the Vomero.

Here on the heights, as in other cities, you've got prime real estate. You've got better than down in my father's home piazza, Borsa or Bovio, and so the Vomero was where he set us up, when he moved the family to Naples for a year. This was the visit back before I had body hair, when Pop tried making a go of import-export from the Italian side. It left some stubborn memories, helpful with my later walkabouts and more. In particular I recall another ragged spray of bullet holes across one nearby wall. "The war," said my grandfather; my father just shook his head. He preferred a sweeter angle in our hilltop oasis, the viewpoint outside the former monastery of San Martino. There you get the famed panorama, the inner crescent of the moon, the packed downtown and the glowering volcano. It's the view that launched a thousand postcards, and it's all about fragility: a city at the mercy of history, tectonics, an ill wind.

* * *

Which brings me back to Ischia. The island is itself one immense dead volcano, Mt. Epomeo, and the *appuntamento* I have in mind occurred during my first year or so of Naples re-entry. I was full of questions, interesting questions it turned out, for a woman who taught middle school. Pietra makes a good name, solid, and she took me first to the museum in Laco Ameno. Hardly more than a roomful of scraps, nonetheless the space had me taking notes. Considering we were visiting c. 2000 AD, it was pretty impressive to see "c. 1000 BC." This set Pietra smiling, eyes going wide, and she told me what the Greeks had called their settlement: *Pithecusa*, "Monkey Island." *Ah si*, I said, a name that takes you to the rainforest. Think how this land must've appeared, verdant and lush, if you'd just arrived from rockbound Achaea …

Exactly, she said, and did I know where the name "Italy" came from? Did I know the Greek root meant "land of cattle?"

Ah si, talking ancient migration patterns, Lesson #1 in *How to Score With Chicks*. Actually that wasn't any part of my thinking. My guide hadn't sent any such signals, strictly courteous, and she had nothing like Anna's honed appeal. Of course, my visit to Anna's walkup wouldn't come for years yet, but though Ischia too demanded plenty of stairclimbing, Pietra retained a certain heft. Her curves, granted, had me wondering about some kind of local Loren gene. Her outfit was nothing special, vacay, but when her eyes went wide, her pretty eyes, you noticed. When her tone warmed, too: no longer a museum docent, rather another wounded warrior. I'd heard she was divorced when we'd been introduced, and we'd consoled each other about sharing custody. We shared further commiserations as we browsed the ancient geegaws, complaints about teaching. Reopening my notebook, I showed her the class plan I'd outlined, and she got it. Even on break you had work.

That was why, she went on, this weekend she'd set up a staycation, right here on the island. A generous friend had arranged a discount at one of the resorts.

Not only did this woman look nothing like Anna, but also my experience with her strikes me, in retrospect, as the opposite of what I went through with the painter. I believe I knew what was up as soon as Pietra mentioned her weekend's pampering. I knew just how to sigh and say the place was one I'd wanted to see. More than a hotel, with pools and a spa, it was rumored to be a favorite of Russian gangsters and their girls.

Pietra's laugh, too, proved easy to read. She couldn't help me with the gangsters, she said, but she could get me into the spa.

Soon enough, I was seeing her in a bathing suit, no bikini but a compliment to those breasts. After that, back across the shadowy lawn, she slipped into a robe, a shorty, silk. I was asked to wait on the deck of the "cottage," out where my only light was one of her room lamps, on the other side of a gauzy curtain, and again I understood. Pietra was keeping the *appuntamento* in shadow. She'd asked me to arrive at an hour when most of the patrons were done with the pools, out at dinner or elsewhere, and we confined our dip to the one designed as a secluded lagoon. Thereafter we avoided the restaurants. Her minibar, she assured me, had everything we needed—including condoms, I discovered. We had a three-pack of the Settebello brand, and we got through two, as the rich-kids' playhouse and its splits of champagne helped us steer clear of self-consciousness. I was always aware that I could've fumbled my end, killed the moment, and she appreciated the care I took, at least with our opening caresses. As she set the pace, she set the limits. Pietra could keep the playhouse shuttered, while within she enjoyed a night, finally, as Loren. She pranced in a silk shorty.

The Italian for "affair" is *storia*, the same as "history." It suggests complication and weight, and I wonder if either of us was up for that. Whatever it takes to follow up on a night together, even one that went off without a hitch—I wonder if we had it in us. From her side, my visitor's status was most likely part of my appeal. The fact that I wouldn't stick around might've mattered more than how well I came off as a man of the world. Even as I played the part, with a lippy smile and slow strokes, I discerned our boundaries. It may've taken me a decade-plus to articulate the details, but that night revealed its shape from the first. I could glimpse even my wee-hours departure, putting me back at my *pensione* as the dawn birds raised their clamor. It's not as if Pietra was lying, when she claimed that if I slipped away quietly it would be best for her friend, the one who'd arranged the cheap stay. It's not as if our final kiss didn't stir fresh chuckles and groping. Nevertheless we both sensed the smallness of our zero-gravity pocket. A few days later, about to leave the island, I asked our original connection to pass along my best, and soon after that my phone rang. Pietra, and she spoke freely. She didn't avoid mention of the night at the resort, *una notte bella*. But she also termed it *fortunata*, lucky, and she spelled out why we couldn't make our goodbyes face to face.

"The island," she said, "is much too small for that."

* * *

The island, and also our wounded hearts. Struggling for recovery, both the schoolteacher and I couldn't help but protect ourselves. Some years later, I heard the same from the Neapolitan woman who came to matter most to me. After the collapse of a recent relationship, she told me, she'd fallen into the sack first with one near-stranger and then with another. Before long, however, she'd come up against some interior Do Not Cross, barbed wire or worse.

"If I'd kept on like that," my friend told me, "I'd have wound up the saddest person in the world."

Now, I wanted this woman myself, no denying, but for the moment I had to snuff out any jealousy. I had to pat her hand *e basta*.

To put it another way, my father isn't the only element in my archeology that raises the question: *what's the problem?* Romance, too, my romantic rebirth—even with Naples involved, it's not headline material. I had no predator in the family, leaving scars across my notions of love. My memoir's got the Mafia, it's got Nazis, but none of the internecine biting and clawing of myth, the slaughters that generally begin with a woman wronged. If the

Sybil's Cave suggests the palace of Agamemnon, it also recalls the Queen who killed him. Clytemnestra did a better job than the entire Trojan army.

So too, as soon as the emigrants out of the Aegean unpacked their shallow-draw craft, they sited the location for a temple to the Goddess. The land of cattle must've looked to them something like Golden America did to their hungry descendants, centuries later, but in the ports of *Magna Grecia* they put up more than one Lady Liberty. The outstanding case in point stands down on the southern border of my crescent moon, along the Sele River. I mean Paestum, which once ranked as the capital of greater Parthenope. That was half a millennium before Christ, and the city lasted a good millennium more. Romans, Goths, and others came around, rattling their armor, but the Greeks tended to work things out, *civilized*. Instead, Paestum succumbed to hordes of mosquitoes, after the Sele shifted its banks. Till then, its territory was consecrated to Hera the Queen.

Her temple stands yet, burly, Doric, ghost-gray, large enough to contain a pair of New England churches (perhaps the steeples would poke through the roof). Compelling testimony to Mother-Worship, the place was at once dubbed "the basilica" on its rediscovery in the 1770s. Long before, though, Hera had won a place in Catholic iconography. You'll spot the connection at once in the Paestum museum. The most common token of worship—not to say *ex voto*—is the Queen of Heaven on her throne, at her breast the sacred pomegranate. The fruit promised resurrection, plump with seeds: plump as the baby Jesus, in the lap of the Madonna.

Hera's temple is one of three still standing, the smallest a sanctuary to Athena, at the opposite end of town. Between the two, we peek into an Easter egg that goes back long before there was an Easter, on a site that extends across an undeveloped plain. Ruins in Syracuse or Agrigento have high-rises looming, but here south of Naples, beyond the temples there's nothing but shortgrass and sea. When Chateaubriand paid a visit, he declared the place "the last horizon of an enchanted sky." Yet if Americans have heard of Paestum at all, it's for something more, shall we say, cosmopolitan. A few Americans at least know the frescos from the Tomb of the Diver.

These adorned the burial chamber of a young man, still sowing his wild oats. He went into the crypt about five centuries before Christ, and came to light again in 1968. So recent a find makes you wonder what else slumbers unearthed, nearby, and I can't resist adding that, on the dig, the overseer was named Napoli. In any case his discovery has provided Naples with a new bestseller postcard. The picture, like all the Diver paintings, brims with sensuality enough to make you whistle, all incontestably gay. The four walls depict young men in terrific shape, some white and some brown, in long skirts that show off their abs and pecs. One struts around naked, as does the serving boy, not much taller than the wine krater. It's a party, a *symposium*, not unlike the one in which Aristophanes and others bandied about their notions of love. At the Paestum affair, most of the recliners are shared by a pair of bros, and you'll find one of those pairs on the new top-selling postcard. These two can't keep their hands off each other. They're either fluffing a sea-thickened head of hair or fondling a well-knit chest, with a finger extended to tickle a nipple. The faces draw close, lips puckered for a kiss.

I sent that postcard myself, in 2005, on a day when the Italian papers carried the news of a court decision over in middle America. Even in Kansas, the court had ruled, homosexuals had the right to marry. This when I'd come to Paestum, that spring, hoping that I might soon marry. I had the woman with me. Though she herself came from middle America, she'd risked a journey to my cockeyed notion of a rehab clinic, with Anna's portraits on one wall and the Tomb frescos on another. And didn't that prove the rehab had worked? In another year, wouldn't this woman become my wife?

On this June morning in '05, however, the big story was the court decision in Kansas. The occasion seemed to demand that postcard, the two Greeks on the verge of a kiss. Together the woman and I found one that wasn't too sunburnt. As for the recipient, we'd known that as soon as we'd seen the news. My wife-to-be had an old friend long out of the closet, a man who'd suffered for his honesty.

We wrote: *Over here, folks have known about this stuff for 3000 years.*

* * *

A touching moment, and our friend responded in kind. In retrospect, the exchange offers another long look down into that hole at the end of Spaccanapoli. It's the shock of history, once more, as our own aches and pains shrink to a smudge on the stones. This wasn't the city's only gift, not by a long chalk, but as my visits mounted up, lessons like that took on a fond familiarity. I enjoyed the same when I learned that these days NATO troops are headquartered out roughly where the legions of SPQR had been based.

21st-century Naples remains—how do the politicians put it?—"significant for American interests?" It's as if September,'43, with its bloody crawl north from the Salerno beachhead, left as profound an impression on the US military as it did on so many Neapolitans. Eighty years later, there's both the Consulate down by the waterfront and, an hour to the northeast, a fully-stocked military base. The place resembles a California suburb, and indeed *Campania felix* could've been the original model for Paradise California. The Borbon kings liked the area as well, and in Caserta they put up their country palace, "The Versailles of Italy." Still, lately the ground has gotten poisoned. Around Caserta, these days, the topsoil and aquifer have tested toxic, in yet another of the controversies that keeps Naples in the news. The garbage crisis of '08 and '09 wrought its worst havoc in nearby Casal di Principe, where the mob set up unregulated waste dumps. In *Gomorrah*, Roberto Saviano calls Casal di Principe "the capital of the Camorra's entrepreneurial power," and the town lies a stone's throw from the center of operations for the US Sixth Fleet. A very Neapolitan irony, that, very Vico. Those who rule by the gun have found their own kind.

Am I just playing more mind games? A clever connection like that—what good is it to a traumatized veteran of local street combat? And among my contemporaries, my family, how does it help them contend with the thugs of "The System"? The Camorra and its depredations, the War and its injuries, had everything to do with what I learned in Naples. The damage was impossible to overlook, so long as I'd done my homework, and yet behind it, through it, I always caught a better glimmering, more enriching. There's a wonderful book by Peter Gunn, now out of print, titled *Naples, a Palimpsest.*

Whenever I pull out of downtown on a ferry, headed for the monkey islands, the retreating urban landscape looks like a palimpsest: a tattered sedimentary buildup. The heights west of the docks present a stipple of ridges and colors, a slope known as *Pizzofalcone*, the falcon's hood. I can just see it, the bird in its hood. Or maybe not (what do I know about falcons?), and anyway this quarter too has more than one story to tell. A number of these precipitous blocks are now among the wealthiest in town. The *palazzi* gardens can tantalize, sculptured around external staircases ("scenographic") behind monogrammed gates. Among the more spectacular is the home of the extended Degas family, cousins of the famous Edgar, another visitor. Before he grew infatuated with the Paris ballet, Degas tried his hand at Naples cityscapes. These days, the place is scrupulously maintained, and the contemporary owners tend to shop at Gucci or Ferragamo, along the local version of Rodeo Drive.

At the base of Pizzofalcone, a woman will eye herself in the shop mirrors as if preparing for dinner with Silvio Berlusconi. Her sandal straps, calf's leather, lace up to the knee; her décolletage is calibrated for maximum pop. I won't even get into the makeup. In the days when I was thinking I'd settle in Naples, when my pain was nine parts loneliness, one of my cousins suggested I open a business in this neighborhood, teaching English.

"All the wives on Via Chiaia will sign up," he told me, not quite joking.

"But, wives?" I asked. "I thought the idea was to find someone for me."

"Eh, don't worry about that. I'm speaking of wives in a certain sense. The women of the richest businessmen in town, every one of them just beautifully taken care of. Goddesses. They've got plenty of time for classes, for private sessions ..."

* * *

Cousin, I appreciated the concern. I got it, warmhearted, joshing, though throughout those trying early visits there remained much I didn't get. Right from the beginning, no question, the trips felt ameliorative. Even when my "bedroom" lay behind a folding screen, it felt like a way station on a new John-journey. But I had no idea, for instance, whether I'd make that journey alongside another wife and partner. I had only half-answers for the inevitable question, *Why Naples?* I'd first talk up tourist pleasures, "most Americans have no clue ...," and after that those of my father's language. My deepening fluency brought me, in particular, to two special talents: Elena Ferrante twenty years before her Quartet, and Roberto Saviano when his *Gomorrah* was still newspaper work. Different as they were, these two set off waves of inspiration that swept away my bruises and cynicism. They invigorated my writerly determination, that one setting for my sextant. Whether I got where I wanted to go, I suppose I'll never know, but I know I'm closer thanks to encountering both Ferrante and Saviano early and in the original.

In time research like that also garnered a practical benefit, namely, something to write about. The assignments I wrangled always had to do, one way or another, with the arts. One piece that mattered especially considered both the Vomero, the moneyed hilltop on which I lived when I was 11 and 12, and the Spanish Quarter at its feet. The two neighborhoods lie a single funicular stop apart, and if you're on foot you can climb a daunting switch-back staircase, cracked and weedy. Yet when it comes to class or economics, the two stand on opposite sides of an intraversable chasm. The bottom blocks were laid out during the heyday of Spain, about the time Ferdinand and Isabella funded the sea-ventures of Columbus. In Naples, the Viceroy needed *Quartieri* for his troops; as a result, the neighborhood is all tight alleyways, the feel distinctly Arab. Though picturesque, it's nonetheless a slum, its hardships detailed back in the '70s by Thomas Belmonte, in *The Broken Fountain*. Belmonte's downtrodden families antici-pate those in Ferrante, and only on my most recent visits to the Quarter (years after the end of this book's events) have I seen signs of gentrification. Back in the '90s, most inhabitants wanted nothing to do with an inquisitive outsider, and so my best sources were theater people. These constricted blocks may be home to the oldest theater in Naples, though that's another fluttering tentacle of detail, difficult to catch.

Now, my host Vicedominis, with the guest bedroom behind a folding screen, lived a couple of stops out on the commuter line. As an alternative, I began spending nights in a Quarter hotel that, despite its squalid surroundings, enjoyed a reputation as an artists' lodging. Show folk at the level of indie films and regional theater stayed at this *albergo*, as well as musicians on tour. It occupies about the same place in Southern Italian bohemia as the Chelsea used to around New York. The proprietor was happy for any US exposure; he gave me a break on the price, and I got a base down-town. There I found the stories most likely to turn a buck, having to do with performance or painting or poetry, if not all three. If in those days I made myself over as some kind of artist—awfully late in life for a man of any sense—this was in part inspired or validated or something by the way Naples made itself over as a center for the arts.

The 1990s saw the closest thing to an urban renaissance since the War, if not further back (only in the late 2010s, it bears reiterating, did I witness a similar upswing). The prime mover was Antonio Bassolino, nominally Communist, elected mayor in '93. Like most winning politicians, his pitch was simple: Naples would once more become a destination, "the most beautiful city in the world." Local charms began to enjoy fresh promotion and support. Pedestrian zones, among them Spaccanapoli, were finally enforced, and more were created. The piazzas of the *centro*, which for decades had served as Camorra-run parking lots, were cleared and cleaned. Bassolino also worked out alternatives for the unused city-center real estate, the deconsecrated churches. More than one was turned to a museum. Soon enough the foreign press took notice, and the usual comparison was to Rudolph Giuliani and the way he changed Manhattan.

Over those same few years, too, Neapolitans were making the best movies in Italy. Americans might know a film or two of Mario Martone, in particular *Amore Molesto* (*Troubled Love*, '94), based on an early Ferrante novel. Martone set up a production company, handling both film and theater, and this outfit remains busy. Tucked into an upstairs-downstairs space, at the base of Pizzofalcone, the office shelves heap up treatments and scripts in file folders, DVDs and books higgledy-piggledy. There's even a couple of wide racks of film-reels in cans. The outfit also claims one hometown boy made good, Paolo Sorrentino. Celebrated first in Cannes and then in Hollywood (the Oscar came for *La Grande Bellezza*, 2013), Sorrentino got his start in that cramped Neapolitan space. That's where he and I wound up sitting together.

I stopped in regularly, with the excuse of drumming up an interview for a Stateside assignment. Anyway the company's daily agenda was catch-as-catch-can, though the decision makers upstairs claimed to keep an appointment book. Whenever I dropped by, too, I'd give another poke to the slumbering possibility of a move. Maybe, in Naples, I could be born again as a screenwriter. Then came the afternoon in '96, perhaps '97, when I staggered in wounded. I'd been lucky to escape with my life, following a meeting with one of those La Chiaia women, scrupulously put together. She and I had met at a nearby café, enjoying what might be the city's most expensive *gelato à limone*. Not three bites in, my date had established that I was divorced, a father, and a freelancer. With that, the ice was no longer the coldest thing at the table. Not even close, and soon I staggered away. In Martone's office, at least, the espresso would be free and the assistant would have a kind smile.

Ah, il Americano. Always a pleasure, said the woman at the desk, and she introduced me to the other guy trying to catch a break. Paolo Sorrentino, then wearing his hair shoulder-length, sat under the shelf of film reels.

He was eager to talk—to vent, no less. Well into his first movie, that morning he'd had to break off shooting. He'd had to hustle over from one of the old-center *vicoli*. Actually it sounded as if Sorrentino had come seeking the same thing I was, some sort of pick-me-up. Whatever he had in mind felt pressing but vague; perhaps the right phone number would make it jell, or perhaps some piece of machinery. So far as his directorial debut is concerned, I'm sorry to say, the result's a disappointment. An update of De Sica's *Gold of Naples*, the movie shows intermittent promise at best. Still, when he was young and trying to find his way, Sorrentino profited from the local artistic ferment. There were ideas in play, connections to be made.

As for the size of his talent, that afternoon I had no clue. All I could be sure of was his commitment, as he kept bringing our conversation back to the movies. He wanted to hear an insight I'd had about Fellini.

And wasn't I eager to talk, myself? I argued that, to appreciate Fellini, you had to see how he stood apart from the other greats of European film, among the first generation following the War.

"The others," I said, "you can see at once where they came from. Bergman came out of theater, Truffaut and Godard out of the Hollywood *gialli*, the detective movies. But Fellini, his vision, it came out of nowhere."

I very much doubt Sorrentino recalls this meeting. My notebook from that summer includes an ".it" address for him, but I don't believe I followed up. What I remember is how he liked what I had to say, nodding with eyes narrowing.

"He took the greatest risk," I went on. "A complete reinvention."

Now, I find myself reluctant to say what came next: him asking about my work. I find myself reluctant, because I don't want this to be a story about a celebrity encounter. Famous People & How I Impressed Them, that story, no. Rather, I'm saying I found a like-minded stranger. We shared something of our struggles.

As for my assignment, that summer, it was hardly Hollywood stuff. I was trying to write about Naples as a livable city.

"Ah," said Sorrentino. "So it's science fiction."

* * *

A small incident, yet I'd say it encapsulates my own larger story: in a livable city, a like-minded stranger. A woman turned up, while I was trying to start over, seeing what I might salvage from the old family recipe. She was Neapolitan, yes, but nothing like the *donne di Ferragamo e Gucci*, rather a compatible sensibility, and our paths crossed thanks to the citywide efflorescence in the arts. In her case it was the plastic arts, painting and sculpture and such. New exhibition spaces made a natural complement to Bassolino's vision, a better use for the abandoned buildings of the *centro*, and before long the city had two such venues, one in a sketchy zone behind the Duomo. Come 2005, Naples was featured in the *T Magazine* as a world center for contemporary art. To be sure, this status has proven spotty, and more than one gallery was shuttered by the financial crises of 2008, particularly damaging in Southern

Italy. So too, Bassolino no longer looks like a savior. A number of his improvements remain in place, but many Neapolitans see him as just another front for the mob: the man who handed them the contracts for garbage disposal. As the muck lined the streets, early in the new century, Bassolino appeared to line his own pockets. One of my cousins, during an evening of ugly revelations, raged about the former mayor.

"Bassolino," my cousin snarled, "is the biggest crook of them all."

A hard night, that one, maybe my worst in Naples. But it came a dozen years after the halcyon mid-'90s, when the city administration kept sponsoring concerts, theater, and art exhibitions. At one such event I met the woman I'll call Nunzia.

I took the initiative. She was striking, strong cheeks and whittled chin, her pout defining a natural thoughtfulness. The eyes were Loren, lined and shadowed with unapologetic drama, the outfit Goth Madonna. She wore black lace-up ankle boots and a high white collar, its trim frilly. While her neck didn't get much sun it had darkened enough to create contrast, and actually she appeared to revel in her contrasts, including an outsize silver-and-black crucifix. Then there was her hair, rich, blacker still: she had to be Neapolitan, and despite the crowd I found a pocket of quiet and confirmed it. We went on to speak of the show, the evening, and I pulled off a decent quip or two. Half-Neapolitan by blood, far more by inclination, I took the initiative.

I'd already noticed this about Mediterranean women, that they expected a good show of interest. Yes, I realize how that sounds, suggesting women elsewhere don't like attention, and lumping the millions who inhabit the greater Neapolitan crescent into a single "they." The arena of romance is nothing if not stippled with ambiguity. Still, by the time I met Nunzia, I was again a single adult, and my lovers and close calls had been adults. I'd had my better days, though my ambitions as a writer excluded books like *How to Score* ... I'd noticed that (most) American women preferred to be (sort of) the aggressor, both in the initial signals and (if there were any) the follow-though. In Southern Italy, on the other hand, the object of desire established a distance and a man had to transgress (sort of, etc.). For a Neapolitan, that is, an attempt at a kiss didn't put an end to conversation. Rather the woman took it as a part of the discourse. And wasn't this in keeping with the Italian notion of personal boundaries? A far more permeable notion? The mindset might even owe something to that pomegranate crushed to a woman's breast, crushed and bleeding, or for that matter to Caravaggio, his flesh aglow with divine illumination. One of Caravaggio's best is right off Via Tribunali, and by the time I met Nunzia I'd also encountered D.H. Lawrence, *Sea & Sardinia*: "The women of Southern Italy send one's heart straight back to pagan days."

Then Nunzia delivered up a miracle, a bench apart from the crowd. Throngs were the norm, during the most densely populated resurrection in Europe. When I at last got off my feet, and got a decent breath, it occurred to me that I might've trespassed this woman's boundaries even if she hadn't—why not go whole-hog at first glance?—called to mind an alternative life abroad. Just look at the name I've come up with, from *Annunziata*: blessed art thou among women. The Neapolitan I might become, that's what I glimpsed in her, beyond the striking, sultry externals.

I brought off a couple of quips, a passable insight or two, and so began to discover that her wit went deeper than her fashion sense. She had intelligence and sensibility, an artist herself. She had an artist *fidanzato*, too.

At the moment the man was lost in the crush, and I'll call him Guglielmo, Elmo. He was networking, chatting up potential clients, but for a number of years he remained a part of the picture, the part that made my heart sink. As for whether Nunzia and I ever took each other to bed, I'll say it again: a memoir can't be coy. I'll confess there came a night of extended kisses and heavy petting, as heavy as it can get when both parties lack protection. Bear in mind, too, that in this Catholic country most women learn how to work around contraception. And isn't that all I need to say, concerning the two of us naked together? Doesn't the absence of a latex sheath matter less than the presence of a battered heart? The inner Do Not Cross, strung with barbed wire? It was Nunzia, after all, who articulated the danger of going through her days as the world's saddest person.

I'd argue that, since our needy one-off, the relationship has gone on deepening. Our physical give and take is conventional, a double-cheek kiss, but Nunzia has become the Neapolitan outside of family on whom I count the most. Whenever I've had enough of my relatives, my first visit is to the studio this artist shares with Elmo. For starters a *fidanzato*, after some years he became simply a fellow *artigiano*.

* * *

Their space is a single ground-floor room, a long rectangle without a window. It suggests the shotgun apartments that, at pavement level, line the downtown grid: the notorious *bassi*, ventilated solely by the street door. When that stands open, it's as if passers-by are invited to dinner. In the *bassi*, only the front room's large enough for the family table. Yet Elmo's and Nunzia's studio, though squarely in the *centro*, isn't on the street. They've taken advantage of Neapolitan inner space, the air pockets amid the chockablock. The studio is on a courtyard, inside what was once a baronial palace. In rooms like these, a noble family housed its animals and their tenders; lower down, in the cellars, the cask of Amontillado …

As for the artists' workspace, it must've housed some smaller animal. It's got too low a ceiling for a stable, but at the base of one wall runs a drain trench, sloping down to what would've been the cloaca. Since then someone's installed a sink and toilet, and Nunzia, behind her folding screen of a bathroom wall, also keeps a bucket and plunger. Still, if there's a smell, I've never noticed, not with the kiln set up at the uphill corner of that same wall. The heat's what hits you, under a low ceiling with a stand-up egg of a kiln, its buffering minimal. Yet Elmo and Nunzia keep busy; their confabulations range across the walls. The smallest call to mind a coffee donut, the largest a law-school diploma in its frame. *Abbondanza!* Terra cotta of course is a challenge to paint, and colors tend to the stark: carnal red, fiery gold, bone white, funereal black. The slash of Goth again. Shapes however challenge geometry in a hundred ways, the implied borders of each piece broken by stylized lips or wings, by a scimitar or halo. I've thought of the critic Achille Bonito Oliva, who argues that recent art out of Northern Europe and America relies on right angles and machine forms, whereas the Mediterranean artist still sees things in biomorphic terms. He's got a point, to judge from what Nunzia and Elmo are up to, always at work with fleshy elements, even the octopi.

Other media, paint and photography, occupies other walls. The crammed bookshelf includes sketchpads and journals. But it's what the woman can do with baked clay, the detail she makes dance on the head of a pin, that knocks me back. I'm a teenager again, slack-faced before the *ojetti vottivi.*

Before arriving, to be sure, I'll stop at the closest bar for an espresso to go. With sugar, thanks, though in Naples one doesn't need to say so. You speak up only if you want it without, *amaro,* bitter. Once the sugar's stirred in, the top capped with aluminum, the plastic cup makes just the sort of gift a friend should bring, and Nunzia's former chicken coop or whatever of course has a table, though usually she needs to clear away the latest project. There are chairs, a stool, even a battered futon.

My friend has slept on that futon, every now and again. The workspace, unlike Anna's, wasn't designed to serve bedroom duty, but in Nunzia's case the collapse of Bassolino's promise, the City Built on Beauty, overlapped the collapse of what she had with Elmo. The partnership extended back to their days in the *Conservatorio,* but it lasted only about five years into our friendship—when I was about halfway into my 20-year renewal. With a single furious affair, Nunzia at last countered her man's many infidelities. The breakup, however, sprouted price tags; she and the *fidanzato* had depended on each other. My friend wound up spending nights on her couch, and some days she relied on folks like me for more than a cup of coffee. She never asked, but to offer a pizza took no more than a wave of the hand, and once or twice I let her use the shower at my hotel. The staff at the front desk would give us a look, sure; the woman's a good dozen years younger than me. But then, as I often reflected, trolling the downtown for the man I might become—everyone was younger than me.

And one evening in there, yes, her need spilled over into in my own. Whatever else she felt that night, her fingers on my skin must also have sketched the unforgiving math of her monthly expenses. Not long after, she and Elmo worked out some sort of rent, perhaps a commission on sales. He moved back into the studio.

A bitter concession, no doubt, the arrangement has nonetheless allowed Nunzia to hold on to her space and her vocation. She's cooked in her own water. The gifts she's nurtured extend, I must add, beyond the striking shapes out of her kiln. One afternoon early in the 21st century, she told me there was a writer out of France I needed to read. She opened one of her notebooks to make sure I got his name straight: Michel Houellebecq. No one on either side of the Atlantic beat Nunzia to that discovery, and around Naples no one seems to have a better knack for stirring up a cultural brew. Around her courtyard now, all the ground-floor spaces have become exhibition spaces and studios. It's a *cortile dell'arte*, throwing regular events.

Mover and shaker that she is, too, the woman's opened my eyes in other ways. Once, on a walk from her apartment to the studio, she sketched the recent immigrant flow through a block of neighborhood *bassi*. Most of the street-level space these days had been taken over by Africans, she explained, and the reasons were largely predictable. Cheap rents, check. Low expectations, check, along with what we in the States call "white flight." In the *bassi*, however, the vanguard of the dark-skinned new tenants turned out to be prostitutes. Girls from Liberia, from the Sudan, found the units tailor-made for business. They offered both easy access and, in the back, just privacy enough. Also a shower-bath, also a fridge for booze and medicine. As for the landlords, they had two forms of payment to choose from, and if they preferred cash, there'd be a nice bump up for their discretion.

Even the most successful of these "houses," however, experienced high turnover. More unforgiving math: a girl got sick, or got deported. Then too, better options could turn up, decent employment. Sex workers aren't entirely without resources, family or friends or even, once in a while, a client or madam. The same in Naples, Nunzia told me, as anywhere else around the world.

We were standing midway, just then, on this brothel-block not far from her apartment, and she took the world's measure with a two-fingered gesture that I might've seen on a Grecian urn. Then she was back to her city and moment, pointing out a crucial difference hereabouts. Around Porta Capuana or over in the Spanish Quarter, should a few women achieve the wherewithal to quit the sex trade, their line of work might change without any change of facility. Space was at a premium in this town, *capisce?* If you had a good space, best keep it and make it over: a shoe shop, a tailor, furniture repair. By the time Nunzia took me down the street, it was nothing but working black families. Nearly all had documents of some kind.

The only problem now, explained my friend and muse, was that some of the old customers still came around. Some were from out of town and hadn't heard.

She pointed to a door, a hand-lettered sign. *NIENTE PUTTANE*, no whores here.

* * *

If I've done right by this woman, if she's not coming across as a fantasy, that speaks well for my re-entry into the bruising arena of romance. It suggests that, during those years, I wasn't such a blockhead as I thought. Inevitably, too, it summons up my model, my Neapolitan father. For him, love and marriage were never merely "solid." He and Mom always showed us something more, dancing after dinner, slinging round happy innuendo. Years further on, as I say, Ferrante's men left my mother baffled, but when I read the Quartet I noticed the exception to the rule. The narrator's father, I noticed, took real pleasure in his wife's company. Every now and then *Mamma e Babbo* fell into suggestive biplay, and even bookish Lena had to chuckle.

So, amid the wreckage of my divorce, I began my mending with this notion in mind: marriage as a love affair. Of course I had a lot of other stops on the learning curve. I needed to reconfigure my notions of a grown man and, maybe most of all, a good father. Still, for me these obligations dovetailed with romance, and the very idea that dating and kissing should coexist with raising a daughter, that the lover could lend the parent a hand—such a collaboration, I came to believe, must've been born in Naples.

Certainly the teachings of the old city had a bearing in my new one. I lived then in Portland, OR. As my wife and I divorced, our child Vera was entering her teens, and we worked out shared custody. At some point in there, lurching after any bit of help I could grab, I signed up for a weekend men's retreat.

Our "center" for the retreat was woodsy, hilly, Oregonian. It couldn't have looked less like the urban mazes in which, later that same year, I'd first encounter Nunzia. But I was glad to head up into timber country, and not just for the good it might do me. Also I saw my participation as sustaining the illusion of stability, for my daughter. I was joining ten or a dozen guys who belonged to the same church that she and I attended with my now-ex. A church on the liberal end of the Protestant spectrum—that matters. The minister for instance asked me for help with an early-'90s mission statement, and I got the committee to approve the words "welcoming and diverse." When I sat in the congregation I felt among friends, and some Sundays I felt more. Some mornings a spirit was palpable, the hymns and prayers mushrooming into a nimbus that seeped up and out through the wooden ribs of the ceiling. Once I was invited to deliver the annual lay sermon, and though I spent a quarter-hour ruminating on Kafka, nobody objected. On the retreat, likewise, these men avoided harsh prescriptions. Nothing out of Paul's letters or, worse, Leviticus.

Rather, I could speak openly of the counseling my former wife and I had gone through, entirely secular. These sit-downs had helped us salvage a couple of better years. We couldn't arrest the widening central schism, the difference in how each of us pictured the good life, but we could sort through final details. We worked with a legal mediator, rather than lawyer against lawyer, and after we filed the documents I could summon up the phrase "a good divorce." That ritual scarring of my late-life initiation.

A scar, yeah, itching and oozing—and what did it reveal about my 20 years of marriage? Had I been so incomplete, so incompetent? I felt as if I were in for a talking cure without end. On the retreat, before long, I'd had enough of my "good divorce." I was glad our facilitator had prepared a few group exercises.

As you might expect, a number of these had to do with fathers. The activity I recall, the one I'm still working through, asked us to consider how our fathers defined manhood. We could use the old man's actual words, of course, but more commonly, explained the facilitator, a group would explore "the behaviors modeled." All of us on the retreat had to compile a list, pencil and paper, in which each item began "A man is …"

The words that followed, around the circle, were often the same: *responsible, ethical, caring, handy.* I too had these or the equivalent, but then came an anomaly.

"A man," I read, "is sexy."

Now, as I say, I sat among friends, solid folks. These guys were neither the cartoon bohos of *Portlandia* nor the gun-totin' cowboys that many Italians still believe make up the population beyond the Rockies. They may have lacked my artist's wiring, but they had their creative sides and, what's more, any honest artist realizes he's got no fundamental superiority over a broker, a lawyer, or a candlestick-maker. I can't go claiming any high ground. I can say, though, that though our mission statement read "welcoming and diverse," the church sure looked White Anglo-Saxon Protestant. The signup for the retreat was full of names like Dunham and Scott, and Vicedomini's definition of manhood, or this part of it, knocked everyone sideways. Gesticulating, gaping, they placed me squarely back at the center of attention.

I struggled to clarify. As soon as I knew what sex was, I said, I knew my father and mother were having it. They were enjoying it, and often. I could see it in how they danced, I said, and I could hear it in their jokes.

Jokes? My friends asked. Your father told *jokes* about sex, in front of the kids?

"Ahh …" Here in the woods of Oregon, I could've been back in the *vicoli*, their daytime shadows. "He had limits, sure. But as far back as I can remember, they'd cuddle and kiss, and meanwhile they'd be chuckling, they'd be making little jokes."

This didn't sit well either. "If I came into the room," said someone, "and my folks were in an embrace, they'd break it off. We weren't supposed to *know*."

"Ahh." I suggested that differences were only to be expected, on the far side of a continent on the far side of the Atlantic. "For a Neapolitan, sex is more the bread of life. The pleasures of life, everyone enjoys them, and that includes the women, too."

"All the women?"

"Well, adult women. You know, friends."

"You're saying, your father made jokes about sex, with other women? Other than your Mom? You saw your father *flirting*?"

The facilitator, I expect, eventually took a hand. I can't be sure, not with the gap left in my memory by the discomfiting give-and-take. Understand: I still feel warmly towards the crew on that retreat. Any time I'm in town, I'm happy to meet one of them for a pint of craft brew (Beer-Vana, that's Portland). Nevertheless, the workshop raised questions I needed to answer. When I bought my father's act, what else was in the package? As I looked for a better partner, what did I offer, by way of "love"?

Pop began his American life in lower Manhattan, like many and many another Southern Italian, and he also shared the post-war yen for the suburbs. His wife was the true New Yorker, but she felt the same. By the time I was old enough to have the least understanding of love and sex, we were out in lower Connecticut. Of course the region has its pockets of Italian-Americana, in New Haven, in Bridgeport. Still, those circles didn't much inter-sect with ours. The older immigrant communities mattered for my father's work, but his social circle was more mixed. The reasons are complex, and include the unusual extent of Vincenzo's educa-tion, for a boy born down by the old Seaman's Chapel. Also he didn't share his hometown's shrugging acceptance of its criminal culture, and on top of that he'd suffered whatever the war put him through. For now, though, what matters is that, even after he and my mother abandoned the Five Boroughs, they moved in a cultured crowd. Maybe not the Van Doren crowd, with "Bunny" Wilson and like that, but people who'd found a place in the greater metro systems of education, publishing, and journalism. These be-came my parents' friends.

You know, friends. Adults, women as well as men. And yes, by the time I was old enough to recognize it, I saw my father flirting. Or something like that, taking another woman on the living-room dance floor, punctuating what they had to say with a smirk. As he served a scoop of salad, he'd share a wisecrack about the other night, and sooner or later every woman at the party would be referred to as *cara* or *bella*. This included the occasional actual Italian, in particular the vivacious wife of an art teacher, a woman I'll call Chiara. Chiara had more than a touch of the artist herself, and on a few evenings in southern Connecticut, she spoke of her family's apartments on Ischia. Years later, when I began to reconnect with Naples, I discovered this woman had divorced and gone home. Back on the island, she'd made fresh connections; she put me together with Pietra. In the sea-view apartment of my parents' old friend, dangling from the ceiling of every airy room, there trembled a handmade butterfly, wire and fabric and a feather or two. Every visit, these never failed to fetch a smile.

As for Chiara's husband, back in Cheever country, the story I'd heard was that he took up with one of his teenage students. Not that I asked, out on Ischia; we talked about her children, in Switzerland, in Central America, and about my parents, in particular my father. Something else that never failed to fetch a smile. For Chiara, past 80 now, the mere mention of my father's name …

* * *

I read that smile correctly, I'm sure. Also I trust my memory of those potlucks, with their soundtrack out of Motown. Yes, my father had an easy way with women, "Continental charm" and a rhythmic gift, plus a dozen terrific recipes. But there's no predator here. Just the opposite, the man was a rock, when it came to wife and family. For confirmation, I hardly need to consult the Great Mothers of Campania. Here in the U.S. I'm surrounded by women quick to speak their mind, my sister and mother at the top, and in the 20 years since his passing I've never heard a whisper about an affair. Pop liked a lively dinner party, but he knew the difference between that and, to choose a Naples reference, the orgiastic Feast of Trimalchio.

Indeed, I remember as well how much my father enjoyed Fellini's version of the Feast, in 1969. Now *Satyricon*, as you might expect, presents a free adaptation. Possibly the most far-out Fellini (though the competition's fierce), the movie actually played the big suburban houses, in those days. My father and I could watch together, and the run lasted long enough for a second viewing. The *Maestro* was a realist, if you asked Pop. Granted, Fellini could be freakish, but he had nothing on old *commedia dell'arte*, and in Rome he'd started out as a cartoonist (that is, the films didn't really come out of nowhere, as I imagine Paolo Sorrentino knows). Still, according to Pop, the work onscreen amounted to a faithful depiction of *Italianità*, as it endured the challenges of the '50s and '60s. The later *Amarcord* eventually ranked as my father's favorite; he knew all too well the Fascism it portrays, at once ludicrous and menacing. But he maintained, as well, a nodding respect for *Satyricon* and its insights.

"Exactly," I remember him saying. "People applaud the golden hand attached to the stump of an arm, and they forget all about the man who got cut to pieces."

This refers to an early scene, the public mutilation of a thief, but while my father's interpretation seems right-on, the incident is only a sideshow. The sin most prominently on display is lust. Insofar as *Satyricon* has a narrative, it's driven by desire, both homosexual and hetero. A comely young man, rarely shown in more than a loincloth—he could've stepped out of the Tomb of the Diver—travels the collapsing Empire in search of a cure for his impotence. Finally he's brought to a sumptuous demon woman. African, entirely nude, this creature seethes with such sexual power that she's kept tied to a bed. She never fails, her handlers assure the boy; that's why she carries such a high price. But our hero has the money, and as he pays, leaping flame and shadow stroke the woman's heaving body. Hungrily she licks her lips.

Well, problem? My father was hardly the only filmgoer to consider *Satyricon* a masterpiece, and by the time he treated me to a ticket, I was nearly out of high school. I was no Make-Out Master, but I wasn't unfamiliar with a woman's excitement. I'd seen both skin mags and, around Times Square, the skin trade (this was, of course, before Giuliani got out the scrub-brush). Does it matter that Pop himself occasionally browsed a *Playboy* or *Penthouse*? By the end of high school I'd come across a couple of those, neither out in plain view nor hidden. Out on city sidewalks, meantime, or in department-store aisles, I'd long since noticed that he had an eye for a pretty girl. Eventually he noticed that I noticed, and at that he might make some offhand wisecrack. "She's got quite a wiggle, doesn't she?"—that's one I remember, lighthearted, rated G. He made a crack and then we moved on. If my mother was around, she laughed.

My mother's laugh in fact strikes me as the best frame for my father's picture of the romantic life. It's a laugh alert to complexity and free of monsters. The most illuminating case in point concerns the night Pop told me the facts of life.

I was 11, for that sit-down; Mom's amusement erupts ten years later. Ten years, or thereabouts: that's how long it took for me to give them back this man-to-man talk. Before then, I lacked the necessary self-possession. To tell my folks what Pop had told me, after all, was an assertion of my own adulthood. I must've been 21 at least when I tried out the story on them. Before then I'd worked with lovers and friends, a rehearsal process. Eventually I had it whipped into shape, the whole show, *Pop Teaches the Facts of Life*; I knew how to land its best line, just two words. So I told my parents, on a weekend visit home, and my mother brought out her laugh, and the result was something like a family legend.

None of which is to say that, back when I was 11, Pop did a bad job. Not at all—I was a lucky boy, to learn about sex from Enzo Domini. If some Time Machine could shuttle the facilitator from my men's retreat into that night, he'd concur. My father modeled the right behaviors, serious but never scary, thorough but never lascivious. Ten years further along, when I was able to speak to my parents as an adult, my doing so owed a lot to how Pop had talked with me earlier. At times the half-century relationship between my father and me feels as if it comes down to a few brief conversations, head-to-head. This book features just three, and this one's the first.

Pop took me aside during the year we spent in Naples, up in the Vomero. The setting was our kitchen, nothing medieval, nothing you'd find in the *bassi*, rather an artifact of '50s Italy and *Il Boom*. "Populuxe," its Formica shone like pudding under the fluorescents. On the stove, the squat cylinder of the espresso *machinetta* was already set up. My parents had made preparations, in other words; they must've seen something in the preceding days. That night they worked together, whisking my older sister and younger brother out of the way, though the apartment didn't have nearly the size we were used to in America. Not that my father required special consideration, as he set out the details, intercourse and its consequences. He worked briskly but with sympathy and, as he wrapped things up, he put the final emphasis where it belonged. This was a healthy pleasure, he assured me, an *abbondanza* available to anyone.

Then he added: "But if you ever drop anything in there, if some girl ever shows up and makes an accusation, well then, you deny it."

The line that, ten years later, burst into family legend.

"*Deny it.*"

My mother put on such delicious mock horror, when I at last shared the story.

"Deny it, because who knows who she was with the night before."

Ten years further along, stepping up as a peer and a raconteur, I chose a weekend when my sister and brother were back at our table as well. They too gave my performance good reviews, my sister rocking in her chair, my brother howling "No *way!*" My mother's response was the best, though: that mock horror, that parody of a reproving outcry, and then at last the laugh, exasperated, delighted, deep in the throat.

As for my father, raising his chin and grinning, he brought off a riposte.

"You told yourself," he put in, "this is where I *come* from. This is the old man, the old country ..."

It was Naples, certainly, this approach to the birds and bees. Over in Connecticut, among grown children at the dinner table, Pop took my recollection in stride. He wasn't about to spoil the party, to growl or sink into his cups, not when his oldest son had turned out pretty well. If the *primogenito* could poke fun at his father's inverted commandment—Thou Shalt Lie, and to thy lover's face—he'd turned out well. Besides, aren't such rationalizations part of the defense system for any Mom or Dad? None of us has better than a vague notion, ultimately, of how our parenting will turn out, in a child's recollection. I'm not just talking about our mistakes, our failures. More than that, things said and done with the best of intentions can, over time, prove trouble for the growing person on the receiving end. Each child cooks in its own water. With that in mind, that and my mother's laughter, I don't see much use in passing judgment on the old man. The better option seems to be taking his advice, thinking about where he came from. The way Vicedomini learned it, to "have his fun" meant hooking up with whores.

* * *

In a piazza down by the docks, the Sailors' Chapel, working girls find their target demographic. Men come off the boats pent-up, short-timers with cash. In my father's case, he must've still worn the short pants of *scuola elementare* when some older boy first explained. After that he could no more have overlooked it than could the recording angel of another old seaport, as he gathered his *Leaves of Grass*:

*The prostitute draggles her shawl, her bonnet bobs on
her tipsy and pimpled neck,
The crowd laugh at her blackguard oaths, the men jeer
and wink to each other ...*

Now, although Walt Whitman's seafront puts its sex workers
on display the same as young Enzo's, the poet's description also
helps define what's different about the Vicedominis. In *Leaves* the
narrator declares himself bottom-rung, "one of the roughs," but my
Nonno had government work (so long as he toed the Fascist line),
and my *nonna* an honored name (or its residue). They claimed
accomplished relations, clerics and musicians, and so while their
economics were at best middle class, in other ways the family dwelt
on a higher social stratum. The niche was precarious, and rare, but
they weren't the only ones to strike such a balance. Among the
others was a skinny young thing from Pozzuoli, Sophia. Her last
name remained a mystery, you never saw her father, but the girl
had obvious culture, as well as a sweet face. She turned up at the
same gatherings as Enzo and his brother: the teenage Loren, of
course. My father recalled that they used to call her—oh, irony—
Sticchina, "little stick."

In her home as in his, kids grew up with books in the house.
The Vicedominis claimed an 1867 *Divine Comedy*, paper vellum,
with the famed engravings by Doré (copies of course, but not
bad). A hefty tome, it requires two hands, whenever I pull it from
the shelf above my desk. On Nonno's shelf, in Naples long ago,
it meant something even for his wife and daughter. Both women
had some schooling. My aunt's, however, largely excluded the arts
of love. That was a man's business, in a good family, and given the
possible consequences, everyone made sure he learned early.

Myself, I wasn't quite 12 when Pop sat me down, there in
our Vomero kitchen. Decades later, reading Andrea Giovene's
thinly-veiled autobiography *Sansevero*, I came across this: "I was
nearly 12, a time of life when ... many boys are knowing." That's

how the translator puts it, *knowing*. The meaning's hardly obscure, not when Giovene lays out such lush detail, and his time setting overlaps my father's childhood. Indeed, so far as I can see, every Naples book set in this era features boys who lose their virginity before they hit their teens. The scene's a staple of the brief, oneiric novels from Erri De Luca (in particular *The Day Before Happiness*), and you find an outsider's confirmation, cold-eyed yet sensitive, in a memoir by Norman Lewis, *Naples '44*. Lewis served with the British occupation force, and his wartime diary ranks as a masterpiece—but then what am I doing, poking around the library in order to talk about my father's sex life?

Trying to bridge a lifelong silence, that's what. Pop never said a word, never an explicit word, concerning how he'd become so at ease with women. According to my mother, by the time they met, he was already a model for the value *A man is sexy*. Now her, I know that as of 1946, she was still a virgin. I know that in college (also in greater New York, and matriculation came early because of the War) there'd been some serious necking. Indeed, many years later, following a party at which my siblings and I met some old family friends, Mom grinned and identified one man as her "first big, sexy kiss." She was likewise frank about the flasks of gin that fueled some of those kisses, and about her worldly circle of friends. These included a woman then called a "Negress." Also Mom liked fast cars and physical challenges, a Title IX girl before her time, and she crossed the Atlantic on a decommissioned troop transport and rode to Southern Italy in a British Army lorry, on her way to doing what she could for poor and orphaned children. All that I know, and I'd heard much of it before my little talk with Pop. His own intimate life, however, remained under wraps. Granted, other than that year in Naples, we grew up a long way from his home turf. Still, most immigrants live with the same, and so they'll show off scars or put up photos, to make sure their children know just what Mama or Papa went through. But my father limited his sharing to things like a ten-minute recipe for *un bel ragù*. He dug up a couple of classic Neapolitan songs.

As for the girls with whom he'd first heard those songs? The yearning and experiment that takes up, what, four-fifths of a teenage boy's mind? I'm left digging and sifting, rummaging first though my library, then thinking back to my own initiation at age 13. The girl came from across the Atlantic, where else? She was Danish, though, an au pair working for a neighbor. She wasn't out of her teens herself but, four or five years older, to me she loomed as all-knowing, all-powerful. I wouldn't have been surprised if she had a temple somewhere. Yet after she'd gone back to Copenhagen, what lingered with the boy from New York was something less awestruck, more like conviviality. I'd had an adventure with a friend, a great time but nothing that ought to change my life. Which is to say, I caught my first breeze off Ischia, my first glimpse of Pietra. The Danish version, Inge, was no more heartless than the Neapolitan, but she too insisted on restraint. She used a Britishism: "You mustn't go making assumptions." When a postcard arrived, it was addressed to the family and bore just two words: *Warm greetings*.

Methinks I see my father, once more, a few years further along. I was 18 then, back in Naples for the summer of my first solo walkabouts. The old man's ghost emerges behind a woman for sale.

Throughout the visit—what I'm about to describe didn't keep me from extending my stay—I lived with the Vomero family. The grownups in the house swiftly picked up the locust-thrum of my teenage hormones. Even in the better, hilltop neighborhoods, apartments are small and a boy can't keep a book over his lap forever. The family first arranged a date for me, an affable young lady but out of synch. She arrived dressed as if for a cotillion, whereas I was heading for a Be-In. She took me to Capodimonte, the city's loveliest park, and up there we indulged a bit of cuddling, but neither of us expressed an interest in following through.

With that, my uncle took a hand. The man rated himself Head of the Household, now, though the place was also home to my Nonno. He was half the size of his son-in-law, however;

the two of them, bantering, suggested Laurel and Hardy. Also the older man was retired while the younger one had parlayed Italy's boom into a sweet *posto fisso*, a job for life, in the local bureaucracy. He was one of those lordly suit-and-ties I would see downtown, holding court over lunch. Long after they'd finished their pizza, they'd keep on talking, smoking. A pack a day was my uncle's speed. In his case, though, lunch tended to be at home. He'd do the cook proud, whether it'd been his wife or his mother-in-law, mopping up every dollop before he sat back with a flat and satisfied smile. Afterwards his *riposo* would stretch almost to an hour, and before he returned to the office he could count on espresso.

If I sound like I'm poking fun, okay, some. The man is best understood, though, as a product of his times and city. If we grin, we should keep it respectful.

By local standards my uncle was generous, giving up his *riposo* for me. Instead he escorted me downtown, offering some pretext like a shopping trip. Nor did he waste time coming to the point, only a block or so out of the funicular, and in hindsight this tells me that we'd reached one of those distinctly Neapolitan junctures of slum and finery, perhaps where the Spanish Quarter abuts the base of Pizzofalcone. I found myself steered towards a corner portico in which stood a girl about my age. A chunky girl but not unattractive, and I suppose there must've been lipstick and eyeliner. What I noticed, though, were the hands: one jammed down her unzipped jeans, the other up at her mouth, where her lips fastened around an extended middle finger.

Disassociation, I've learned, is the word for it. A word I picked up from my daughter or one of her therapists, it describes a separation within, *Spacca*-psyche. A person face to face with some walloping trial will, for sanity's sake, sail off as if across the Atlantic. As for this woman in the doorway, this still from *Satyricon*, she stayed put, and so did my current Head-of-Household. As the moment stretched on, even a dissociative case couldn't help but get the message. The girl's hand wasn't just down her jeans but inside her panties, a dark Italian pink, and the man who'd brought me struck a pose likewise easy to read. His chin was up, his frown regal but benevolent, and he held his suit-coat folded back behind one arm, with two fingers of that hand inside his front pants pocket, indicating his wallet. Yet I was elsewhere as well, thinking of how my uncle's pants needed to be let out. Thinking how keeping the wallet up front was a Naples trick, a way to protect your cash. In borderline neighborhoods like this, you got the thieves with quick hands ...

I was the one to move us along, with a half-nod that left my head down. Not that I had a clue where we were headed, on our so-called errand; I moved.

As to why, sure, I get it. I was shocked and she was dirty; I was leaking emotions all over and she might've been a zombie. In short, I lacked the nerve. Over time this left me so ashamed that, before I flew back to the States, I spent much of the cash I had left on one of the government-sanctioned prostitutes up in Amsterdam. One of those tourist attractions dancing between red curtains: she and I were famous for fifteen minutes.

Down in Naples, too, it's possible that I sensed the girl's pain. It's just possible—as I stared, I got some inkling of the blows she'd caught, behind that door. A sensitive boy, right? In any case, I had subtler stuff at work in me, as I dropped my head and moved on, and that's the stuff I'm writing to discover. It's the difference between the adult American self my father constructed and his own early models for manhood. A transformation critical to his children's shaping, yet one I'd never have grasped if I hadn't so often gotten back to the family's native home.

* * *

Back when young Enzo's hormones had him off his rocker, perhaps even with the help of some worldly uncle, the boy would've gone through more or less what I did. *Puttane* must've loitered close by; before the Allied bombing, many Naples whorehouses had been in place for decades. It took an eruption of Vesuvius, after all, to shut down Pompeii's *Lupanar*, the bordello with the frescos (one depicting a pair of men). If a boy couldn't get in without a recommendation, a family like the Vicedominis would've known whose coat to pull.

My father's own father could've handled it, since I remember the man as a *bon vivant*, a witty master of gesture and aphorism. Nonno may've been the first to tell me the octopus proverb. Another time, he described one of his wife's snobbish family as "the sort of person who scratches their left ear with their right hand," meantime coiling an arm around his head. So spry an old man had no talent for naps, either. He and I often remained on our feet through the siesta hour, enjoying a gabby *passeggiata*, keeping to the shade. Talk about Laurel and Hardy! For an American college boy I was size Medium, but beside my spidery Nonno I was a bull. My curls raddled out, I was headed for a Be-In, but he remained the true radical. To him the Socialists up in Rome looked flimsy as cardboard. Still, as Nonno spoke of poking his fingers through them, those poster politicians, the rant seemed amiable. The things he found to snigger at all shared some root absurdity, the human comedy. If our stroll crossed paths with a pretty girl, and most days it did, he'd sigh and moan, *come si soffre*. How we suffer.

It's easy to imagine my Nonno playing the same prank on his son that my cousin played on me, a couple of decades further along. By then, one of my first adult visits to the city, our grandfather was gone. Back in Oregon my marriage was in its final throes, and though I hadn't yet met Nunzia, every time a pretty girl passed—how we suffer. My cousin didn't fail to notice. He arranged for me to meet *una persona interessante* at one of the cafés inside the Galleria. A chi-chi setting, the Galleria: the mall as Fabergé egg. It rises four stories to a girdered glass dome, and across the floor, the marble mosaic depicts a wheeling zodiac. It's a stray piece of *fin de siècle* Paris in a metropolis otherwise dominated by the Baroque and Medieval. Filmmakers are forever poking their cameras in, and the space provided both setting and title for a visionary novel of the War, *The Gallery*, by John Horne Burns. There I was set up with one of the downtown drag queens, the *trasvestiti*.

The prank, to be sure, depended on the illusion lasting a while. Ideally I would remain ignorant until, along about the second cup of coffee, my cousin sprang the truth on me, giggling and wagging a finger. No dice, homeboy. You should've tried me when I was 18. Every once in a while, booklearning comes in handy out on the street, and anyway this particular cross-dresser had gone over the top. He'd done himself up like RuPaul. Indeed, he proved the same color as RuPaul, beneath the cosmetics, and I spoiled my cousin's fun further by turning the encounter into an interview. I asked the man if many of his clients came from across the Mediterranean, Africans like himself.

His answer provided the only moment, that evening, when I felt like a chump. *Dai, caro*, he said: Come on, honey. It's the white man's got the money.

It's business, honey, however colorful its raiment, and no doubt my father took his place in the local economy. Now that I've completed my archeology, too, my significant discoveries include another Naples prank, not unlike the one my cousin attempted. The perpetrators in this case were my mother and father, and their victim someone I never met. I heard the story several times, though. For Mom and Pop, the recollection had a sweet taste. It took them back to their first happiness, when they were barely 20 and working with children in a camp near Sorrento. Young Enzo had quit another career, far riskier, though the work had improved his university English. At the camp, he was the one to welcome the counselors from overseas, including this "Maggie." *Hello, Americans,* my mother recalls him saying. She was still clambering out of the lorry but she noticed that sonorous, smiling *hello*. Not long after, the two had grown close enough to cook up a practical joke.

Their victim was another colleague, a virginal Midwesterner with some formal Anglo name, let's say George. George tended to pontificate. Name any crisis across the Continent, this sinkhole of festering ills, and he had the solution. He had a plan in two parts: 1) contraception for everyone, and 2) European unity. With these policies in place, claimed George, even poor, benighted Italy could begin to approach the power, the glory, of the United States. He said so every time he got the chance. Then one day the camp's Neapolitan liaison declared he'd found a group of people that George wanted to meet. Their organization followed precisely the precepts he recommended, 1) contraception for everyone, and 2) European unity.

Enzo urged the young American to come by. Tonight, why not?

With that—while his wife-to-be remained behind with the other counselors, chuckling—my father took this church boy to an international brothel. Girls from all over the Continent and abroad.

The story tickled my parents no end, a fond look back that became part of my own childhood happiness. Nonetheless the prank had a more serious implication, one that eluded my sister and brother and I for years. Our father knew the address and what was on sale. Women for hire were part of his local abundance. In the international brothel, in the first years after the War, the girls from overseas would've been tragic cases, but their country of origin would've been just another factor in the fee. The menu would've been easy to consult, tacked on the parlor wall. A single shot or a *doppio*, a half-hour or hour, each with its price. Such lists still turn up around Naples, tin placards that resemble our country's Depression-era diner menus. The best I've found was in the office of an aging bookseller. His wrinkles stretching into a wide smile, he found good light for me to study the piece, under towering double-windows. The only rust it showed was around the tack-holes, and the lettering was unscratched, easy to read as ever.

My father however grew cold to such reminders, over his decades in the States. Every once in a while he could even sound like his old victim George, and late in '76 he wanted no part of *Naples '44*. Lewis' was one of the first books I reviewed, a *Boston Globe* assignment, and Pop made a gratifying fuss. He took time with my 600 words. Afterwards though, between a couple of claims in the review and what I went on to tell him face to face, he pronounced the British author just another blue-eyed insensitive. Especially galling to Pop was what Lewis had to say about Neapolitan women. An intelligence officer, the Englishman circulated enough to encounter prostitution at every level, from roadside transactions paid in K-rations to well-born girls tricked out to the Allied command. In one spectacular incident, the Camorra blackmails an officer with the help of a sophisticated lady out of the international brothel.

"A thing like that," my father insisted, "I never heard of it! I was there and I knew *plenty* of girls ..."

He caught himself, not much past 50 at this point, still gingery enough to get himself into trouble. The next sentence emerged more slowly.

"I would say I never witnessed anything of the kind."

* * *

My dig turns up more as I sift through my father's early business trips. Back before his children reached their teens, he visited Italy perhaps half a dozen times. Generally the product was food, but he also spent a week or so working with a moped manufacturer. In other words, he traveled solo. Mom became a regular companion only as the two of them reached the far side of middle age. Yet one evening following Pop's first heart attack, out of the blue my mother announced that in nearly a half-century of marriage her husband had "never touched another woman."

As I fumbled for a response, she went on: "Not unless it was some whore in a hotel room in Naples."

That last was put across with the same quaking honesty as the rest; the first attack had unsettled us all. My father had nearly died, though he'd only reached his mid-60s, and he'd achieved a comfortable semi-retirement along Florida's "First Coast." He still liked to dance and he cooked many of the meals. For his grandchildren he brought out the toys and crayons, and he hadn't touched a cigarette in years. Nevertheless his heart gave out, and the family was left badly shaken, wondering what could've taken such a toll. Myself, I rushed to St. Augustine from Portland (spotty employment has its benefits), arriving while Pop was still in intensive care. That night, over a late round of wine and pasta, Mom made her unasked-for declaration, confident yet rattled.

In another moment, she turned defensive: "Why shouldn't I be proud of that?"

Naturally I came back with assurances, happy talk. It wasn't much longer before I was folding open my sofa-bed. Yet as I tried to get comfortable I found myself wondering. Once more I studied a vivid and familiar fresco, a set-piece gesso'd on the wall of memory. This dated back to a night in my early 20s, in a Southern Connecticut roadhouse. I'd discovered my father with a waitress in his lap. Or perhaps she wasn't in his lap, since recollection too plays its pranks, but only coiled close around him, leaning into him. Pop sat at a table over a glass recently drained, counting out what he owed, and the waitress sagged so close that her long and youthful midsection pressed against his ribs and arm. Youthful, yes, my age or a hair older. She had one arm around his neck, one hand dangling over a shoulder, and one breast (the uniform Sears-&-Roebuck, white over pink) against his cheek.

My father kept his eyes down, on his bill and his cash.

Often he carried a sizeable clip, though this had nothing macho or Mafia about it. Along the Italian-American spectrum, you'll find Tony Soprano a long, long way from Enzo Domini. My father carried cash because his primary business was food. Who deals in cash if not restaurants and groceries?

He wasn't the Godfather, and she wasn't in his lap. Not exactly.

As for Mom, she'd sent me out to get him. She'd known the place. When their nest began to empty, my mother went back to school for her M.Ed., and soon she had lesson prep and after-school duties. That night, they'd been expecting me, but dinner was just getting started. In another twenty years, if not sooner, cell phones would render such pickups unnecessary, but then, I'd wanted to see the guy. I'd long since taken down that sign on the bedroom door, *No Adults Allowed*, and I'd come back south along I-84 in order to hang out. So here was my first sight of Pop in months: thumbing through fives, tens, and singles for a working girl.

Recollection too plays its pranks, wicked one moment and saintly the next, and so I'm glad to have reconnected with my father's native city. Having studied the frescos of Paestum and Pompeii, that scene in an American bar-&-grill looks nothing so erotic. Rather, it's Pop's equivalent of a long lunch on Spaccanapoli. He was unwinding, at the start of the weekend; outside was summer, and so his drink would've been Campari and soda. I may even recall the lemon twist, down in the dregs. So too, now that I've walked his former stomping grounds, I notice the rest of the roadhouse staff. Everyone hung back, playing along with the charade, the Sheik and the Harem Girl.

Certainly Pop never showed embarrassment. Much less remorse, on a night decades before #MeToo, when the waitress was only bucking for a tip and he'd hardly been caught *in flagrante delicto*. As soon as he noticed me, standing there staring, he broke into a wide grin, entirely genuine. I expect he pulled an extra couple of dollars from his billfold, and as for the girl, she pretty much vanished. My recollection turns her to the Cheshire Cat, nothing but a grin on the air, and Pop and I headed off. If I had a question, an objection, my home's odor of simmering onion and garlic would've smothered it. Then over the meal my parents would've vied with each other, poking bilingual fun, touching hands and wrists, as they ping-pong'd though anecdotes about recent suburban silliness. Perhaps they had a couple of friends over. I wouldn't be surprised if my father put on solo Diana Ross, Diva Diana, and got my mother up to dance. And that girl half his age, with her boob in his face? Over in Naples, for centuries, the brothels have been known as *case chiuse*: closed houses.

* * *

Is there a problem here? The map my father was given for the arena of romance, granted, included spots marked with an X. In those places, women were used and forgotten, annulled as if by church decree. To call the girls slaves wouldn't be far off: see the *Lupanar* or (changing genders) Tomb of the Diver. If you think about it long enough, you arrive at Berlusconi and his pretty young things. Indeed, at the end of the '90s, there were rumors that Berlusconi had a girl in Pizzofalcone. Back in the '30s, you would've heard the same about Mussolini. Il Duce, so his Brownshirts claimed, had a different woman every afternoon; it helped with the *riposo*.

Stories like that would've come up in the first conversations Pop and his pals had about sex, and over the decades that followed he never entirely buried the Gangster Of Love. His wife caught a glimpse every now and again, and she understood how, on a night far from home, the old creep might've re-emerged. And hadn't he offered a kind of confession: *this is the old man, the old country ...*? As for his New World children, once in a while we tripped up on such ugly remains, losing our balance. *Vabbè*, okay. Still, as bad parenting goes, all this hardly leaves the starting block. When it comes to love and sex, anyway, what father isn't facing a different direction from his kids?

What matters for Pop, I'd argue, isn't just that he spoke out of "where I come from," but that, over time, he could speak for different places. Confronted with a radical new design for home and family, he could make adjustments. By the time his oldest son had learned how to unhook a bra, after all, the docks by which Pop grew up had shrunk. They'd lost most of their business, and his home piazza had a new name. None of this, however, left my father sighing over what he'd lost. He liked *"Torna à Surrientu"* as much as the next *paisan*, in fact he'd heard the Roberto Murolo original, but as I say, he fell happily under the spell of Diana and Marvin and the rest of Motown. More than that, look at my sister Amy. She's raised two kids to my one, Amy, and another sort of Italian father would've claimed that defined her. In another family, she'd have been *la Mamma, e basta*. By nature, though, Amy was Pop's match as an entrepreneur. She showed him promise far beyond any Old-Country roles, though his response recalls an Old-Country line. He let her cook in her own water. While her brother scuffled on freelancing, she came up with a better place for people's money: Domini Social Investments, Investing for Good. In his American daughter, really, I find the best evidence for the distance covered by the former Vincenzo Vicedomini.

Pop likewise found fresh resources when his two oldest took a bad hit. Mine was the first divorce, but Amy's proved more protracted and costly—so much for Having It All. My father however didn't care if his child needed help out in Portland or up in Boston, where Amy lived. He never responded as if back in Naples. He and Mom even took on extra babysitting.

Besides, if the Vicedomini School of Romance left me with a couple of fringe notions, a surprise or two concerning what "a man is," most of the time I made my own trouble. My slip-ups tended to be undramatic, Aspergerish. Then when my wife and I really began to fail, I found a pair of coping mechanisms that, together, seem significant. On the one hand I began taking church seriously, joining the men's group and delivering a sermon. On the other, I retooled my writing skills to turn a pretty dollar, by betraying the very values that a good church teaches. I took on ad work and PR, lucrative stuff, though full of spotty truths and cracker-thin promises. Still, the money was great, so long as I could kid myself that it would save my marriage. So long as I could ignore how viciously my workdays opposed my Sabbath. The schism strikes me as very Neapolitan—I saw something painfully similar as the Vicedominis struggled with the Camorra—and after a while it proved too much to bear. After a while, I quit the hustle. Within another year my wife and I had filed for divorce.

* * *

Not that I can play the martyr, either. Lots of people lose the stomach for advertising, just look at *Mad Men*, and the change in career doesn't mean the end of everything. For my wife and me the problem lay elsewhere: we were plain wrong for each other. Our wiring was fundamentally different, when it came to adult work and why we do it. The partnership was bound to collapse, at least in our America, mad for self-fulfillment. The flaw's so glaring that it illuminates another Naples connection.

Despite its aggravations, my first marriage never drove me to infidelity. No, not even a whore in a hotel, and not even in the southern seaport that the business had so long found congenial. The material turns up in my Naples notebooks from the first, my re-engagements of the early '90s, back when Pop was still alive and I was still in couples therapy. Decades later, I've no trouble finding the entries, interspersed with question marks and exclamations. There's research both into prostitution as my grandfather and father knew it, and also into recent developments, given the changes in technology and demographics. A number of locals assured me (though, you know, I don't recall worrying) that there still existed high-end brothels. In those days phone sex offered the most common alternative, and later came others, but none of them eliminated the demand for a few pretty young things lounging around a comfortable parlor. So too, a posh address still made a difference. In the Chiaia, you got the blondes out of Eastern Europe, the ones cut loose by Victoria's Secret. Word was, Berlusconi …

Actually, the *Cavaliere*'s local plaything was Italian. Noemi Letizia, still in her teens, had a nice smile and parents eager to curry favor. The story broke internationally, it helped to bring Berlusconi down, but for less headline-grabbing material I relied on informants closer to home. In particular, I had my two closest cousins. Both are men, and neither fits the stereotype. Neither throws around his weight for the Camorra, or idles away his days fine-tuning the family ragù. One's a doctor, I'll call him Marcaurelio, and the other, Nando, works as an engineer. So far as I can tell, judging from what amounts to months of sleepovers now, both are loving and sensitive with their wives and children. Still, concerning the skin trade, both proved … knowing. Marcaurelio was the one to pull the stunt with the *travestito*, and Nando made sure to point out the women along the roads of the periphery. Never mind that I'd have to be blind to miss these girls. Outlined before a bonfire, their cleavage Wonderbra'd, they posed in heels all wrong for the roadside gravel. Yet my cousin, him with the infrastructure projects in the Middle East, made certain I noticed.

Look, he said, *all African, these days.*

Mm, Nando, interesting. I mean, as a journalist …

If I wanted to get all Cotton Mather about it, I could accuse these two of the same witchcraft as my uncle had practiced, years before. Weren't they letting the lonesome American know where he could find a few minutes' relief? And roughly what it would cost? Yet just as my father had grown and changed, over in his adopted home, in Naples my cousins had come to adulthood in another way. Given their generation, their education, when they were younger they got it for free—and only with consent.

As for later, after they were married, one of them seems the more likely candidate. He's suffered such upheavals at work, demanding so much time out of the city, even overseas. Still, a girl in a hotel room in Kabul has nothing to do with my Naples experience, my re-entry. Throughout those years, Nando and Marcaurelio made up part of a chorus. An oratorio, in which first some cousin or friend would notice, perhaps over espresso, what was up with me. They'd notice my glum silences, while I devoured the girls with my eyes. Then they'd confirm their suspicions, it's divorce, *ah si*, and with that, with a sigh, everyone would start to talk about alternatives. These included the *puttane*, yes. The mere mention afforded me a glimpse into older conceptions of a love-life, in particular before my father's War. But on the verge of a new millennium, the suggestions didn't stop at sex-for-hire.

The chorus had its recurring phrases: a man my age (*my age, age…*) shouldn't be ignorant (*ig-no, no…*). But its primary theme wasn't the *case chiuse*, but rather simple company. My friends and cousins urged me towards the sort of intercourse that took place without removing a stitch. A date in which I paid some café cashier, rather than the woman with me—this was held up as a more healing alternative. As for sitting around feeling sorry for myself, *dai*, come on, a man my age, age, age …

I liked the tune, much as I recognized its dangers. I realized what a quick snack some beauty might make of my self-esteem. At times, too, I was left uneasy by my cousins' talk about other women in their lives. You know, adult friends. Both spoke of meeting for *aperitivi*, off in cities up north or on the Adriatic. Whenever Nando and Marcaurelio shared such stories, they kept a tight rein on details, instead making vague claims about "a sense of worth outside the family." *Vabbè*, cousins, but I notice you never talk about these women when your wives are around, and I can only draw the same conclusion: one of them, maybe, under harsh and lonesome circumstances.

As for adultery, explicitly, I heard about that from Nunzia's dodgy former *fidanzato*. He never lacked for a smooth line of talk, with expressions like "fresh energy" and no hint of apology. Toxic stuff, yes, smoking fumaroles, but I could visit safely. Besides, Elmo used an aphorism I enjoyed: *Chiodo sciacca chiodo*, a nail drives out a nail. The quip exists in Spanish as well, and it may be left over from the city's century or so of Spanish rule. But the metaphor also appears in Ovid, *The Art of Love*, and anyway, whichever culture claims it, they had me. They convinced me. The old generation's solution, a battered girl in a dark door, would've left me beating a quicker retreat than when I was 18. But the new encouragement to get out and try, this appealed to me. What was my alternative, the grim forecast of my men's group?

Out in Portland, they offered cold consolation: *It's going to hurt a long time.*

Much as I'd come to enjoy their company, these guys, I didn't care for their advice. *Best you get off by yourself. That way no one gets hurt …*

At which I'd think, *alla Napoletana*: My friends, one thing we can be sure of—we're going to get hurt.

* * *

One of the men's group went so far as to offer a cabin up by the Mt. Hood timberline. For a couple of weeks, I could've gone all Henry David Thoreau—or should I say Cheryl Strayed? Strayed however was coming out of a very different breakdown, and seeking a fix in very different places. If I went *Wild*, for instance hiking the woods above Paestum, that evening I got the best of the woods' mushrooms: *pasta con funghi*. Granted, if I'd stayed in my friend's cabin, my expenses overall would've been less, but I was learning how to win small grants, in Humanities or the Arts, and to line up travel articles. I had my people in Naples, too, which through most of the '90s meant the family out on the *periferia*, an uncle I'll call Gigi. This uncle never introduced me to a girl with a hand in her pants. Rather Gigi and his wife, the parents of Nando and Marcaurelio, set out a full dinner on the nights I joined them, and the next morning I got *caffé e cornuto*.

Lucky man, the American cousin on a Neapolitan menu. Lucky too, having these women of Southern Italy sending him, all harmlessly, back to pagan days. I had to laugh at myself, I'm saying, coddled even when I camped out on a sofa. I did a lot of laughing, actually, for a guy no longer young and newly single. To think of it recalls an essay by Gilbert Sorrentino, in which he claims Italians grasp "the essential idiocy of living." Gallows humor thrives, in Naples. Case in point, a prank involving a drag queen.

Speaking of cousin Marcaurelio, he arranged other diversions. One night he and his wife shanghai'd me off to a concert in a restaurant above Sorrento, a performance of "Reginella" that seemed to scrub the soul. I'm eternally grateful for their woman friend, laying a lovely hand on my arm while she sang along to the song's final chorus. As for Nunzia and Elmo, they took a likewise joshing turn as Cupid, while they were still a couple. They set me up with an acolyte of theirs, a younger woman, forever stopping by the studio. From out of town, she saw possibilities in these urban canyons, their shadow and sun and low cost of living. A painter, name of Anna.

She and I had great times, dancing, exploring. Anna accompanied me on my first descent into *Napoli Sotterraneo*, the spooky network of cisterns and waterways beneath the inner city. This was the infrastructure first carved out by the Greeks, after they discovered the near-magical properties of Campanian stone. In the earth, certain strata are so soft, you can pick it out with a fingernail, but after exposure to the air, the same material toughens enough to support a temple. It's cool in summer, warm in winter, and helps keep the skin pliant. On my first visit to the *sotterraneo*, alongside Anna, our guide explained that he'd begun exploring these tunnels and reservoirs while still a teenager (that is, long before the city set up formal tours), and the man had a lot of teenager in him yet. His smile popped his cheeks. He never looked more like a moonfaced Archie, though, than when he revealed his age: 63.

Meanwhile, his halogen lamp led us to spaces retooled by Mussolini's engineers. Starting about 1940, basins from the Classical era had been squared off and made over into bomb shelters. Electric lines were run downstairs, and the toilet facilities installed were the finest most of these Southern Italians ever knew. The fixtures were plated in germ-resistant gold. Not that disease much concerned the Neapolitans who huddled so far underground, as first North Africa and then Sicily disproved Il Duce's claim of *Mare Nostrum*. When I told my uncle Gigi about the new *Sotterraneo* tours, he pulled a long face. Down in the Piazza della Borsa, he recalled, the sirens had gone off almost every night. After so much time down there when he was young, the last thing he wanted was to pay a visit as an old man. Sobering talk, *Zio*. Talk that started me wondering, as well, about that friend the Vicedominis had hidden in their closet. A Jewish musician, another standout at the Conservatory—that was really all I knew. Even so, I ought to have thought of this. Once the bombing began, what did my family do about their refugee? With all the risks of exposure, to them as well as to him? I shouldn't have needed my uncle to bring these questions to mind.

What answers I found were a long time coming, but on my first visit to those shelters, there was no mistaking the prayers for help. The Madonnas on the walls, the angels' wings, called to mind the *ogetti votivi*. Also I saw a familiar doodle, anti-aircraft taking down a B-17; I'd drawn the same, but as a dream, an escape. Our guide however didn't dwell on such nightmares, he was out to give us a good time, and before long he turned our attention to the obscene graffiti. Many a downtown baby, he assured us, came to term nine months after a scary night in the shelters. For Anna and I, he had a mock warning: no sneaking off into unlit corners!

So why didn't we, my date and I? Myself, I imagined such getaways. Anna wasn't long out of the *Conservatorio*, in those days, and if anything more fetching than the lean and hungry woman who later painted my portrait. Even in my fantasies, though, I had trouble picturing just where the two of us might find a place. Like me, Anna often had to make do on someone's couch, while scraping by as waitress, barmaid, whatever. Had we found each other irresistible, our best option might've been to get a car and motor up to another clifftop, the *Parco della Rimembranza*. Dedicated to the War dead, the *Rimembranza* loops through tall palms and fallen pillars and commands a breathtaking vista. Out over the sea, Ischia's volcanic exoskeleton dominates, inspiring deep kisses. Then the lovers duck into vehicles wedged nose-to-fender along the access road. In Fiats and Beetles—if you can afford a SmartCar, you can afford a hotel—couples grope after their own feeble abundance. As for privacy, newspaper usually serves, plastered across the windows. Crumpled leftovers litter the drive every morning, and the hilltop has been dubbed with another catchy Neapolitanism: *Parco della Gravidanza*, "Pregnancy Park."

Whatever you call the greenspace (on most maps, it's named after the poet Vergil), Anna and I came nowhere near. Doesn't the nickname, the word *gravidanza*, suggest something other than heedless rutting? Especially in a park that honors the War dead? Both elements take us to consequences, and ten years later the painter told me just how painful those consequences could be. *My first love. There is nothing more to say.* Now that I've heard, and I've done the math, I believe that when Anna and I went down into the *Sotterraneo*, she was either still in that hurtful affair or struggling to recover. So much for fantasy.

One afternoon during those same early visits, I found myself up on those heights alone, watching the sun fatten to orange out over the Tyrrhenian. Unexpectedly I caught a glimpse of the couple inside one car. A Fiat 500, it looked no larger than an overturned bathtub. Within, the man was a shadow, but the woman emerged clearly, covering the windows with double-pages of the day's *Mattino*. Before the newsprint hid her face, she revealed a concentration intense enough to knock me back a step. Her fire-engine lips might've been intended for a club, but then there was her frown. One look, and I sensed something other, something greater, than a quick and grunting satisfaction. Naturally this threw me back on my own solitary place, here, wondering if I'd ever again be up to the effort: to "making love" with all its ramifications. Yet as I recall the incident I see my father alongside me. I see an old-world figure with brains and soul enough to work through a romantic transformation of his own after he'd left that first home, so rife with whispers out of long ago. He'd changed so thoroughly that during his last years alive, my mother honestly didn't care whether he'd once slipped back into hoary macho prerogatives. Her response seems the most sensible, really, the most humane. By now I've solved most of my father's mysteries, all more important matters. As for this smirking question, it either doesn't deserve an answer or has its best in the son he raised—one who wanted no part of such usury.

* * *

It wasn't in Naples that my child and I had our facts-of-life talk. That took place in Portland, rather, in the late '90s, in my latter-day bachelor pad. Anything but a swingin' pad, with my rack upon rack of books. At that point Vera and I had worked through about a year's worth of adjustments, following the final decrees, and as for our conversation, I shouldn't exaggerate. She'd learned the basics already. Her mother had taken care of that, she'd brought home a book with illustrations, and I shouldn't deny credit where it's due. On this evening, however, I had arranged a dinner for three: me, my daughter, and another woman. A lover.

This was the first woman I saw seriously following my divorce. There would be others, during these years when the Siren City kept up a song only I could hear. Pietra turned out to be one of a number of casual encounters, *fortunato*, and with two or three others the connection went deeper. In Chicago, for about a year, one woman and I set up housekeeping. That didn't work out, but as I say, the latest has; I've remarried. These days, insofar as there's a song on the air, it's all through with the verses about lonely nights. My challenge wasn't to score a lover, but to love as an adult, and over time I've learned how this second coming-of-age followed the trajectory of my father's, back after he'd traveled the other way. Pop's own second go-round came in greater New York, but from my perspective it looks awfully familiar. He wised up about the old school, the "love" that was always down the block and then at once wiped from the books. He moved beyond the glee he radiated from his perch on a picnic table, in the older photo, a glee verging on the smug. Not long after that picture was taken, he was hit by all sorts of changes—first combat hand-to-hand, then a baby in his arms—and he came to understand that his best self demanded a mature commitment.

His learning curve too seems to occupy about 20 years, '48 to '68, but whenever he got through it, he made sure to take the lesson back to the old country. His brother Gigi's last words to me, when I visited his bedside during the final weeks of his cancer, were in response to a mention of my mother.

My uncle's head remained sunk in the pillow, but his eyes flared. *"Una donna ottima,"* he said, or whispered.

Ottima: optimal, and the sense speaks not just for the woman herself, the *donna*, but for her effect as well. She wasn't the whole story, of course, when it came to forging a new, improved Enzo, just as Nunzia was only one of my Vergils, leading me through spirals of Naples to a better self. Still, I got somewhere, and one of the first landmarks along the learning curve came one evening in Portland, when I set out penne and sausage for my 13-year-old (or was it 14, by then?) and my first lover to matter. After the woman left, Vera and I talked.

What I recall most clearly from our give and take, wouldn't you know it, concerns her romantic life rather than mine. We spoke a tiny bit about her sexual orientation. We made the allusion, also sharing a significant glance, and for a 'tweener and her father in the wake of a divorce this counted as talking it over. High time we did so, too. This weekend again she'd worn floppy corduroys from Friday to Sunday, a button-up long-sleeved shirt and a hand-me-down suit-vest, a fisherman's cap and high-top Converse. Nary a lick of makeup. Come to think, before that evening, the last time I'd seen my daughter in a dress and lipstick had come over in Italy. I'd funded a recent trip by working with one of those educational tours, shepherding a bevy of teens around Florence and Rome, and once or twice Vera had allowed a couple of the older girls to doll her up. Such innocent young Americans, I should add, were allowed nowhere near Naples. A slum like that, full of crooks and Africans, offered nothing for nice girls from the 'burbs. Only after my charges were on the plane back to the States could I get on with my own education. I caught the Intercity south and spent an additional ten days, with the help of Gigi and others. A postcard for "V" everyday, as always. Then on my return, my daughter greeted me at the airport in her usual shapeless androgyny.

Not that the look didn't work for her. You saw Kurt Cobain in what she'd put together, the grunge ethos that persisted in the Pacific Northwest. When she broke with those conventions, too, she did so with a certain flair. When V wore a cap, for instance, it was often one I'd brought from Naples, in carnival colors, maroon and black and green. Still, the outfit delivered a message, the same as my daughter's lack of interest in boys. A guy mattered only if she might jam with him on guitar. The posters in her bedroom were women, young but hard-hitting, their voices burly with a turmoil she must've found sympathetic. Madonna was the one you'd expect, but she also put up first-wave rappers like Mary J. Blige and Salt-n-Pepa, plus riot grrls like Bikini Kill and L7.

On this particular evening, however, she was no riot grrl. Following dinner my lover had given me a kiss goodbye, demure but definitive, which left my only child at the far end of my bachelor's sofa, her knees to her chin. And a father can't be coy. I strove instead to follow the trail my own father had laid down, long ago in that undersized Vomero kitchen. Frank yet sensitive, speaking of love and the shapes it can take, eventually, finally, I brought up those who my Vera might, in future, happen to love.

"I always figured you'd be heterosexual," I remember saying. The cumbersome *heterosexual*, I remember distinctly. "I mean, given the family, the Italian family especially, I thought you'd be straight. But if you don't like boys—"

There was the significant look.

"You're still going to enjoy it, V. You see what I mean?"

She's young, I was thinking. Her family's just gone to pieces.

"I mean, you're one of those people who *gets* intimacy. You're one of those people who, whatever your, whatever you …"

Also I couldn't be sure she'd come out to herself, yet. How much, really, had this child allowed herself to know?

"You like an intimate relationship, that's all. To you, love like that, it's what's good in life."

The look flashed again, and she offered one adolescent word: "Yeah."

Recollection keeps changing the names on us. *Virgiliano, Rimembranza, Gravidanza* … In this case, this conversation, memory takes me from my father's voice to an entire hubbub, all the close and informative babble of the ancient port, all revivifying, as if the Hydra's heads preferred to nuzzle rather than devour. As if encouraging me to additional salty wet samples, more mysteries of history and persona. One striking instance comes to mind, one day in the mid-'90's when a sharp and cosmopolitan creature sat just across the room: a grown woman nothing short of gorgeous, and fully dressed, and in sunlight—and out of reach across the room—yet she feels as much like a lover as anyone I knew throughout my long stretch solo.

I'm speaking of Nunzia, to be sure. On this evening we sat in the studio she shared and shares with her edgy, undeserving Elmo. We'd known each other for not quite three weeks. The following morning I was flying home.

I'd found her place on my own, picking up directions along Spaccanapoli and Tribunali, in the process proving something to us both. I'd shown her, I'd shown myself, that I had more on the ball than those Heart-Italy types who don't even read the papers. Nor was this the first time I'd provided proof of authenticity. I'd sussed out how strapped the couple was for cash, and I'd read between the lines concerning Elmo's occasional long absence. One night he arrived too late to share a pizza with Nunzia and Anna and I, though the appointment was at a legendary *fornaio* and the American had promised to pick up the tab. The boyfriend glossed over his delay (and I must add, he has much to recommend him, Elmo: a sculptural gift, a sardonic *Realpolitik*, a vulpine charisma), and though I could read between the lines, I confined my response to another significant look, fleeting, with Nunzia. So too on my final evening in town, alone with her in the studio, I felt the erratic shudder of a long love affair starting to crack.

My sense of doom, I'm sure, would've had another name on the men's retreat. The facilitator would've called it projection. For me, that evening in Naples, the whole notion of romance remained in pieces; I'd only just begun my rehabilitation. Okay, doctor, but my left ear still itches and my right arm is about out of its socket. My presentiment wasn't wrong, I'm saying, when it came to my friends. The pleasure of strolling into that studio, a detective who'd caught the *femme fatale*, got tamped down at once by the woman's end-of-day blues.

Her body language didn't lighten up for my sake. She'd been working with a severity unlike her, mechanical, and it took two or three sips of my gift espresso for her shoulders to lose their steepled fixity. She'd spent hours alone with the kiln and, I was about to learn, she hadn't sold a single piece, yet still she had to hang around the studio, waiting while Elmo wrapped up another *appuntamento*. The gloom out of Nunzia's inner life reached across the baron's former animal pen so palpably that, after the double-cheek kiss hello, I didn't touch her again till I got back to Naples the following summer. Still, the coffee helped. I saw her relax, and, abandoning the piece on the table, she unplugged the kiln. Throughout, though, she kept her distance. She spoke with me but prepared for her lover. First Nunzia washed up at the trickly sink-tap, then before a scarred mirror she retucked her shirt and adjusted her beltline (at that I folded my hands: the prayer of the infatuated), and then, with the mindful strokes and touches of an artisan, she set to work on her face. Foundation and blush, lipstick and liner—yet as the coverup went on, my friend revealed more and more. She told me that she'd sold nothing that day. That day and several previous, she told me, and they'd fallen behind on their rent, because in this city, "Everyone's trying to get the most they can for the least." When I ventured that the same held true over in America, her response was little more than a cluck of her tongue, and yet this too brought home how close we'd become. In time, thinking back, at my desk under my Dante or on the sofa across from my child, I got it: this was intimacy. This cluck sweetened by *caffè normale* yet combined with a cold-eyed stare at the studio's drying racks, forever dusty, forever spattered, and then the weary growl: "You have no idea how difficult it is in Naples." With that there could be no mistaking it, no misreading the code of cosmetics and hanging out, not even on the shaky tectonics of middle age, and though it would be years before Nunzia and I shared any serious kisses, there and then we sank together into intimacy, like an abundance to which the soul itself aspires, and now when I think of that evening off Spaccanapoli I believe firmly that I haven't yet wrung it of its last learning and final good.

PART THREE:

Chi Chiagne Fott'À Chi Ride—
The one crying is in bed with
the one laughing.

Y ET ANOTHER PAIR OF BOYS on a scooter, they swing into the street downslope. We're three, on foot, two women and myself, and already we've had our chatter cut off by a few night riders. This latest hoves into view with a wobble, climbing our way more slowly. Of course, here the paving stones could make anyone wobble, and the lamplight's spotty. On the approaching machine, it could only be teenagers, neither bothering with a helmet; on foot, we navigate past dumpsters, buskers, canoodlers. We fall into single file, and my women friends drop back five steps, six ... With that these boys rev up. As they gun past, I'm left flatfooted; it takes a moment to turn and frown and shout. Is one kid pawing a breast? Plucking at a purse-strap? I might shout, but the real noise is out of the young men, a howl, a cacophony, and for a beat or so the scene might've been a comedy: the teens flailing, the machine wobbling, the women dumbfounded. Only as I swing into my first full stride uphill does a friend's voice emerge.

"*Aiuto,*" this is Nunzia, her smoker's throatiness. "*Ai-uto,* John."

My first stride, my second, and the scooter changes direction. They abandon the attack but keep up the outcry. A savage outcry, they'd like to think, Apache or Zulu, but of course both the boys are white and European. As they roar away I focus on my friends. Their mouths might've been stretched and dried on a coat hanger.

I look to their clothes, their purses. Everything remains in place—good luck, though little more than luck.

"You see?" shouts Nunzia.

This is her city, her time of night, a summer weekend between 11 and 1. We've just left a place the papers call the city's living room, Piazza Bellini, *in pieno centro*: bang in the city center. You'd think we wouldn't need to keep eyes peeled, the way my father had in his Portrait as an Urban Blade. Yet his photo might've been shot on this very street. My friends and I were hardly the first to suffer a near-hit.

"You *see*," says Nunzia, "how hard it is to live in this city?"

I try reminding her that there's street crime everywhere.

"Everywhere? Everywhere they don't have the Camorra."

I try to argue that these boys weren't in the mob.

"Oh no? And if they'd got my phone, my phone from my purse, John, I ask you. For them that'd be money, my phone. And I ask you, who'd give them the money?"

I don't have an answer, though by that night I'd come to know the city well. Eventually she adds: "The Camorra will always be with us."

Nunzia, my friend, my sometime muse—man, was I sick of that line. By then I was 15 years at least into my Neapolitan recovery, and this could've been my least favorite of the local conversational tics. *The Camorra will always be with us.* Not that Nunzia was wrong about the rest. "The System," as it's called, did lurk behind these boys on their bike. They must've known a guy, and if they came to him with a phone or a piece of ID, they could count on a cash payment. An ordinary mugging, on a 21st-century summer in Naples, can raise daunting complications.

A few weeks before this, no one had stepped in to prevent a similar attack on my aunt. My uncle Gigi's wife, mother to the two cousins I knew best, she'd long since earned the title *Napoli D.O.C.* But then, so had Lena, the narrator of the Neapolitan Quartet. Yet Ferrante's protagonist too, though she'd seen her city improve, suffered a mugging: "beaten and robbed by two kids." At that point, also like my aunt, Lena was well past 40. Still, both fell victim to a *scippo*, SHEE-poh, carried out by a pair of *scippatori*.

If you found the word in an illustrated dictionary, the picture alongside would be two teenage boys on a bike. In my aunt's case they swooped down out of a cliché, in broad daylight. She was spared any blows to the head, but the hand in which she'd held her purse came out badly. She needed a splint and went on painkillers. According to her doctor son, Marcaurelio, Mama never could do without the meds thereafter.

So far as her purse was concerned, the only thing for that was another shrug. *Scippatori* don't leave a paper trail. Most snatchings would never play on *Law & Order*, even when the crime scene is one of the tourist attractions, a World Heritage site like Spaccanapoli. Weekenders and sightseers too have endured the thuggery. The summer of '03 the news gave a lot of play to an attack on a couple from Barcelona. The swag was ordinary, a camera and jewelry, but the victims had some of the best lodgings in town. They'd booked one of the waterfront swanks, where their balcony looked out over Vesuvius and the Gulf. Pastel showplaces like that, put up at the turn of the previous century, have names that are supposed to set them above the fray. Brittanique, for one: a name to reassure an out-of-sorts Englishman. But the place proved no haven for these two. The headline in *Il Mattino*, above a photo that featured the dazed and bleeding wife: "Never coming back to Naples!"

Whenever the *scippatori* got busy, Italian media likewise swooped down. Papers from both the left wing and the right gave major coverage to the Neapolitan *micro-criminalità*. A poor name for it, I'd say, since the crime hardly feels "micro" to the person on the receiving end. Still, I had to smile at one editorial: "We face the worst crisis of our time!"

Hyperbole? Yes, but the same half-decade saw the Secondigliano Wars. In '04 and '05, this turf battle among Camorra clans in the northern suburbs left dozens dead. Just about all were mobsters, naturally, but fresh gaps in the criminal chain of command had encouraged younger wannabes, including even a few freelancing *scippatori*. With the head cut off, the rest of the snake thrashed and bucked: such was the argument of most journalists, and my friends and family didn't disagree. My father was gone by then, but he too would've recognized the pattern. He'd have explained that, to keep the hotheads in line, a crew needs its *guappo*, GWAH-poh, the OG at the top. The term is so common among southern Italians that, around the immigrant ghettos of the US East Coast, it may've given rise to the old slur *wop*.

Back in Naples, a hundred years later, the Secondigliano Wars prompted fresh euphemisms. People spoke of *the situation*.

"For shopping, take just one bag," a cousin might say, "given the situation."

Or: "That *funicolare* stop, at that hour, eh. The situation."

By this time Bassolino was out of office—and under investigation for cutting deals with the mob. The current mayor was the first woman to hold the job, Rosa Iervolino. Reaching out to Rome, she arranged the transfer of 90 federal officers, and *the situation* began to ease. Come *Ferragosto* '05, tourist numbers weren't too terribly down. Later that same August, however, the bustle around Porta Capuana erupted into knife-play. A young man was stabbed outside an international call center, and before the night was over he'd died of his wounds. This was Ibrahim Diop, 24, a laborer from Senegal with all his papers in order. The murderer, according to witnesses, had been about the same age, but white. He'd been on a bike, riding with another boy.

* * *

Compared with that, what's a near-miss, near-*scippo*, for an American visitor and his two friends out past midnight? *É niente*, really: nothing but one more measure of the chasm between my experience and that of so many Neapolitans. Once again I came and went without a scratch, as I have even when bedding down in some dubious *zona* like the Spanish Quarter or Secondigliano. In other words, Nunzia may have it right, and my father as well, warning me with his stare, in that photo from '44 or '45. As I say, I've heard him speak when he wasn't around—after his passing. So I believe, and in any case he and my artist friend seem to agree: I have no idea how hard it is to live in Naples.

The tragedy of Ibrahim Diop would be the extreme, the ultimate hardship; not much better, too, was the outcome for his killer. Gennaro Caldore, 19 years old, was brought to justice with startling efficiency. In less than a week, they had him. Credit is due in part to the *Associazione 3 Febbraio*, an outfit that works on behalf of immigrants, and in particularly Africans. They encouraged a couple of witnesses to step up, and so helped steer police to the Adriatic side of the peninsula, where Caldore was camping with family. He was taking a *Ferragosto* vacation, all of a sudden and on the cheap.

An apprentice hoodlum, child of a family in the *malavita* (the "bad life," one case in which the simplest translation works best), Caldore had caught the cops' attention before. He'd had a chip on his shoulder, a rep to build, and the night of the murder he'd been the go-along, riding the back of the bike. No doubt they'd geared down outside the call center because they knew its clientele: nine-tenths foreign-born, many with less legal standing than Diop. Many new arrivals have *lavoro nero*, "black work," a phrase that's got nothing to do with the laborers' skin color. Thousands are recent arrivals from Africa, granted, but what's truly *nero* is the contract, in shadow, off the books. A young white tough would know what this meant, in those days before everyone had a cell phone. Many in the crowd at the call-center would be *braccioli*, "arms," paid in cash. They got an envelope, not a check. The boy riding shotgun, that night, must've figured that he and his friend would find an easy touch.

But when they tried to shake down young Diop, he'd blown them off. He'd made it a matter of honor, for Gennaro Caldore.

The boy's sentence, "not less than 14 years," sounds lenient to an American. Granted, that's hard time, "not less than," and Italy too allows plea bargaining. Nevertheless, I can see why Ibrahim Diop's brother and sister keep calling for the investigation to be reopened. Both claim a legitimate work visa and live up by Venice. Once the first of these siblings found a stable situation, the others used him as a kind of carabiner, in order to clamber up the rockface from South to North. The process is common, among arrivals from Africa; most claim some connection in-country, and following Ibrahim's murder the Naples authorities had no trouble finding his closest relations. The brother met with Madame Mayor, an act of civic remorse impressive for all that it was a dog-and-pony show. Yet the surviving Diops have kept up their complaints. They know there was an accomplice—a second white boy on the bike.

Gennaro's companion had never expected, when he headed out that evening, to wind up accessory to homicide. Still, he knew the drill, smash-&-grab. What's become of him, then? The brother and sister haven't stopped asking; from time to time one of them turns up in the press, often with a member of *Associazione 3 Febbraio*.

Myself, too, I've spoken with the attorneys of *3 Febbraio*, mostly pro-bono. I've attended meetings of Dedalus, an immigrant-rights cooperative, and spent hours in 'O *Pappacé*. That last is a store just downhill from Spaccanapoli; it features Arab and African goods and, in keeping with a name that translates as "the worm in the apple," it's a space for those who feed beneath the surface. The shop even offers counseling, legal and more, and I've sat in on one or two sessions. I've found out what I could about the kind of *clandestino* who used to rely on call centers.

Naturally, I've met some who wanted no part of the ofay. Once I tried to buy a suit out of Ghana, one of the gaudiest things in 'O *Pappacé*. The tailor had good English (the colony was British, after all), and her wrapround tops and drawstring pants exploded with green, gold, and berry-red. You could see where Rasta got the idea. I couldn't find my size, but I told this woman I'd pay for custom made. Her gaze was skeptical, there beneath her turban, but after a bit of back and forth she shared a phone number. A number she used for business, she claimed. My follow-up, however, got nowhere. The woman backed out, explaining that the order would be a one-off—more trouble than it was worth. Some truth to that, I suppose.

Years later, in Jenny Erpenbeck's compassionate novel *Go, Went, Gone*, I read about a retired German professor struggling to understand refugee Africans in Berlin, and he made similar missteps. Regarding Ibrahim Diop, I guess I learned more than most white boys. Regarding Gennaro Caldore, I knew more from the start, and I've no trouble spotting the filthy stickum of the Camorra. Caldore's pal looks to have been very much in the driver's seat. He looks to've been better connected, which got him the better of the favors exchanged. As he was kept off the police radar, too, the arrangement included a couple of sweeteners for the boy left exposed.

For starters, in exchange for quietly taking the fall, Gennaro would get friends on the inside. Prison conditions around Italy can be so hellish, they've attracted the attention of Roberto Saviano. This Naples journalist stirred up such trouble with his mob exposé *Gomorrah*, he now lives under police protection, but he continues to write. A few recent *Repubblica* pieces offer a radical change of perspective, investigating what happens after Saviano's former targets go to jail. It can be ugly in there, terribly maintained and full of guys whose problem-solving tends to fist, stick, knife, gun. A new boy needs friends, protection. More than that, Caldore had always wanted to claim such a community—to call himself a made man. Wasn't that half the reason he pulled a knife, half at least, outside the call center? Didn't he know the mob could always use a killer?

The System depends on its thug novices, eager and otherwise out of options. For them there might be the occasional perk like a Suzuki fresh off the boat (and come to think, how *did* Caldore's accomplice score his wheels?), but in general the work at entry level proves tedious, not to say numbing. Most kids begin as sentries, keeping an eye out over a local drug market. At the first sign of interference, they have some pre-arranged signal. Still, in a time when over a third of Italian young people go without a job—and the worst numbers are in the south—the latest rate for lookouts is eighty Euros a day. Eighty cash, every day. Thus everyone stays at high alert, perpetually, and this is what makes the Caldore family vacation, in August '05, look so pathetic. Whatever plans Gennaro's people might've had, they were also hustling their boy out of the city, but once the police got a lead, nobody in Naples so much as raised a finger to alert the runaways. Nobody risked any violation of the exchange of favors, worked out in the shrunken circles of clan and *guappo*.

As word of the arrangement got around, to be sure, it traveled in code. The Caldore neighbors might even have used another aphorism, earthy and quick: *Chi chiagne fott' a chi ride*, kee kee-YAHHN-yeh FOHHT-ah kee REE-deh. "The one crying is in bed with the one laughing," more or less.

More or less. The expression could also be translated the way you'd hear it from a schoolmarm, "He who complains shames he who laughs." Or there's the embittered inverse, "Anyone who's laughing messes with the one crying." Yet any translator satisfied with such a simple rendering has no idea how hard it is to live in Naples. The quip pivots on that verb *fottare*, for which the most direct translation is the most obscene, fuck, and to fuck of course takes two—as it does to connive or bamboozle. All these concepts factor into what it might mean, every time one group sets to laughing and another to crying.

I must add, too, that no interpretation rises to the level of the tragedy that engulfed Diop and Caldore. No. A pointless tragedy, a muck as yet no more than halfway clean, the murder's unhappy implications reach to skin color, they reach across continents, and they can never be summed up in a gutter proverb. The saying, like most you hear around the old city, comes across with a certain lightness of heart, despite its dark sagacity. I can hear my father tossing it off with a grin: *Chi chiagne fott' a chi ride*, over the sweetness of simmering peppers and onions. Nonetheless, the one-liner serves us as the password into a criminal culture deeply ingrained; it embodies a nasty turn of thought that also shapes my perceptions Stateside. The expression doubles itself, deconstructs itself; Derrida would've had a field day with Neapolitan "grammatology." For myself, though, the quip will never lose its taste of blood and injustice.

* * *

The murder outside the call center can play like a blues classic of the Sirens, a clash of cultures, inevitable. Ibrahim Diop worked at dirt-level, yet he was noble in his commitment to building a new life with his brother and sister. Gennaro Caldore was born to slightly better comforts, but such a wreck of a man that he'd stick you with a knife to defend his narrow stratum of privilege. One had wagered his life on a system, the other on a System, and either way their small sobs and groans are subsumed into a greater echo of heartless laughter.

For a closer look, read *Gomorrah*. Saviano's reporting of course takes us to larger wickedness, the worldwide reach of the underground market, but his bestseller never loses sight of the micro—including *microcriminalità*. The author grew up in Secondigliano, which he identifies as the headquarters of the mob's ruling "Directory." Early in the book he takes his Vespa around this northern suburb, more like an outer borough. As Saviano cruises his old turf, it's easy to picture him crossing paths with either Caldore or his eventual victim. Many a *bracciolo* shares some cheap digs around this bend of the periphery, if not in Secondigliano itself then over in Scampia, on the other side of the Naples airport. Both neighborhoods, according to *Gomorrah*, are drug emporiums: "Via Baku is always hopping. Clients arrive, pay, collect the goods, and leave … The narcotics squad reports that on an average four hundred doses each of marijuana and cocaine are sold here every day … Via Dante also brings in astronomical sums. It's a thriving market … and the pushers are all young kids."

I've seen those kids. 12 years old or thereabouts, one rung above lookout on the mob's employment ladder, the first I noticed was easy to spot. He took cash for a block of hashish, and the black rectangle changing hands likewise posed no mystery. It was no candy bar. Yet whenever I visited Via Dante, I tagged along after my cousin's wife, shopping for dinner. The street's also a market in the more ordinary sense.

One of the few leftovers from old Secondigliano, Dante recalls the *mercato* that once served the surrounding farms; it follows the S-curve of a footpath. The neighborhood has an origin story too. Locals claim that, somewhere among the nooks and crannies now dotted with drug pushers, a Borbon king of the 19th Century received one of the first inoculations in Italy. The shot was for smallpox or for syphilis, depending on who's telling the story, and the injection was made in what would then have been a startling location, on the Royal Person—back where it tore him out a second anus: *secondo ano*.

Shaggy-dog stuff? The Borbons are better known for their flaws; in Sontag's *Volcano Lover*, the ruler of the Two Sicilies comes off piglike, Trumplike, and the author doesn't appear to have taken many liberties with the historical record. Still, these kings embraced cutting-edge culture and technology. In the first decades of the 19th century, before Garibaldi swept away the old regime, the dynasty treated its city to a brief *Belle Epoque*. Naples saw the first railway in Italy, as well the first gas lamps, telegraph, and undersea cable (as for the Galleria, that went up later). Then too, on the map of the greater metropolitan moon, Via Dante lies more or less at mid-point between the waterfront Palazzo Reale and Caserta's Italian Versailles. Such details suggest the story's not entirely apocryphal, and in any case, it's the postcard Naples that comes to mind while you slip in and out of the bead curtains along the sinuous alley. The women could be picking up dinner for one of those culinary tours, pausing to chat outside a *fruttivendolo*, with nothing further from their minds than drugs or guns. My cousin's wife took no extra care with her bags. She even trusted one to her American in-law, though he kept glancing around like a startled rabbit. It wasn't that she didn't see the cash-for-hash, quick as Three-Card-Monte. Rather, eh—don't they play that game in America?

Regarding cannabis, most Italians shrug, laissez-faire. The resin product, hashish, was after all first developed just across the Mediterranean. It turns up in classics of Continental lit (Baudelaire, anyone? Colette?) and I found a more illuminating reference closer to home. My father smoked. The evenings my father and I shared a few tokes, I don't mind saying, remain among my happiest memories of him. In and around New York of course we had marijuana, nickel bags and dollar joints, but it came out that, over in Naples, he'd used hashish. Some of the details remained a secret, as ever, but he explained that back during his career as a midfielder, playing soccer in a semi-pro metro league, he and the rest of the team used to pass around a bit of hash before a wintertime game. Took the edge off the cold, Pop said.

Among my happiest memories of him. As his buzz settled in, my father became a Buddha, his creases deepening, color weathering ...

More recently, all over Italy, even in a clean, well-lighted place like Perugia, a weekend night will offer plenty of nooks and crannies redolent of hash and tobacco. Down in Naples, I've never had trouble catching a peaty whiff, or cadging a toke. In winter the city's more traditional stay against the cold is the Vesuvian red Aglianico, but a single glass may be all that the wallet allows, among folks out for *intraliarsi*. The fortified cigarettes, however, keep circulating for hours, as friends help each other endure the ever-chillier stone. *Spinelli*, these smokes are called, though I prefer the slang term *mezza-mezz*, half'n'half (alas, the expression has fallen into disuse). Whatever the name, though, I'm far from the only American to partake, in-country. Often I think of that miserably unlucky Seattle girl Amanda Knox. In the travesty of Knox's 2009 conviction for murder, a ruling it took six years to overturn, none of the so-called "evidence" against her was more laughable than the fact that she and her Perugia boyfriend liked to share a *spinello*. The city's a university town, one that the best book on Knox's case, Nina Burleigh's *Fatal Gift of Beauty*, calls the "Italian Amsterdam."

Naples can't be far behind. I've spotted the kids peddling hash in neighborhoods other than Secondigliano. In the Spanish Quarter, for instance, the *vicoli* cluster so tightly, there's no place to hide. Yet I've also heard intelligent Quarter-dwellers, family folks with straight jobs, assure me that the Camorra clans of the neighborhood have an agreement to keep their streets free of hard drugs. *Niente eroina, niente cocaina,* they tell me. I've no evidence to the contrary, either—certainly not that junkie I stumbled upon once when I turned down the wrong alley. I was on the slope out of the Quarter, that afternoon, feeling my way over towards the luxe boulevards of the Chiaia. The addict was just coming out of his crouch. He'd lit a cigarette to moderate his lift-off, a cigarette or a *mezza-mezz*; I didn't stick around to get a whiff. The white of his shirt caught the sun, no doubt Mama kept it spick and span, and he had both sleeves folded back Euro-style, but one was shoved up higher so he could tie off. The narrow rubber hose dangled from above the elbow. He'd begun to hum, too, through bared teeth, his lips peeled back, eerie. The moment he spotted me his instinct for denial kicked in.

Rubber hose, what rubber hose? What did I know, a mere buttinski? All of a sudden he was a tour guide, chattering and pointing with his cigarette arm. The arm without the paraphernalia.

I needed no encouragement, as quick to move on as I'd been with my uncle and the girl for sale.

* * *

Uncomfortable as that encounter was, of course, it's not evidence. It doesn't mean the Camorra's not keeping its promises, in the Quarter. At the far end of Spaccanapoli too, in the shadow of the *Università Orientale*, I've happened upon a kid curled over his works. The site embodies what's best about the city; it's the oldest center for Eastern studies in Europe, dating back to when "Oriental" signified Sidon and Tyre and *The Thousand & One Nights*. Still, I came around the wrong corner and put a damper on somebody's high. The point is, just as a Seattle girl on Junior Year Abroad could easily score some hash, the slow suicide of stronger drugs is hardly limited to so-called "criminal neighborhoods." On the contrary, check the blossoming streets of Portland, OR, or the scrubbed stoops of Chicago's Ukrainian Village …

The reality is so ubiquitous that it leaves me irritated with a staple of most reporting about the Camorra, a well-nigh obligatory scene: the reporter's visit (accompanied by a cop or three) to *Le Vele*, the Sails. A housing project from the '80s, put up in Scampia, just ten minutes by Vespa from my cousin's place, this stood for the better part of four decades, a landmark to the trade in killer opiates. The structures suggested sails, and the open spaces between them an inferno of lost souls. For each addict who sank down against a wall, a dumpster, another staggered up. *Le Vele* provided a central setting to the film and TV adaptations of *Gomorrah*, and foreign reporters found it irresistible. A writer would get a walk-through, accompanied by police who knew better than to waste an arrest on these end-users, and then scurry back to his hotel and his lunch. I mean, *Vanity Fair* recently ran a Camorra piece—imagine the lunch. Imagine the clichés, too: "junkie twitches" and "dead eyes."

Needle Alley isn't news, I'm saying, no more than scoring a joint. It's the same old "Algebra of Need," a phrase William Burroughs coined back in 1962, for the introduction to his *Naked Lunch*. "If we wish to annihilate the junk pyramid," Burroughs insists, "we must start with the bottom of the pyramid: *the Addict in the Street.*"

Le Vele themselves are no longer news, either. At the end of the Twenty-Teens, they at last came down. The current urban planning looks a bit smarter, but in any case the whole sorry episode mattered little to Marcaurelio and his family. So too, though Roberto Saviano claims, "no substance gets introduced on the European market without first passing through Secondigliano," whenever I've passed through, I've enjoyed the local shopping. Corso Secondigliano is Broadway, once part of the king's highway. The boulevard has reaped the benefits of recent grants for infrastructure, and though God knows some *guappo* got his percentage, the throng feels nothing like a crowd down in the Seventh Circle. A couple of blocks from the intersection of Via Dante and the Corso stands a legendary pastry-shop, notable for its colorful racks of cookies, surprisingly American. If you want an oyster-shaped *sfogliatella*, though, white with powdered sugar, they've got a trayful. The espresso on the side shimmers gold. The man who serves it, meanwhile, sneers at the full-page article in today's *Repubblica*: a summit meeting in Rome, a special commission against the Mafia. He shakes a finger at the picture, the suits and ties around the table.

"There's your Mafia," the barista announces.

Which is just how it happened, one morning. For this visit I'd again hammered out an assignment, and that day I'd seen the photo in the paper, the anti-corruption team. I had the bright idea of going man-on-the-street. Bright, bright idea: Signore, the real crooks are up in Rome. Here in Secondigliano, look around, life is good.

The neighborhood even boasts a pizzeria run by one of the Sorbillo brothers, the most respected family of *pizzaioli* around.

The summer I turned up with the woman I would marry, my cousin swiftly read the signals between her and me, and his gift for us was an afternoon at Sorbillo. In time, too, a number of apartments along the Corso have converted to B'n'Bs. Now and again the street has featured a movie house, in the cozy European style. None of these have managed to stay in business, unfortunately, like many of the other professional offices, open one year and shuttered the next. An exception, lasting for decades now, would be Marcaurelio's *studio medico*.

His office takes some getting used to, for an American. In our country we expect a temple labyrinth, with the doctors off in some sanctum sanctorum and, outside, the stalls of the money-changers—sorry, the administrative support. Italy's government-funded health care allows Marcaurelio to handle everything out of two small rooms. His staff consists of a woman about 60, with a ledger-book. Also the doctor carries a bag, an actual barn-shaped, top-clasped bag. Within are stashed such classics as a stethoscope and a blood pressure gauge, and there are days when my cousin takes the bag on the road, on a house call. Should he require an x-ray, he sends his patients a couple of blocks down the Corso. For bloodwork, that's a block the other way.

All in all, the quality of life could seem to justify a wisecrack from the '90s, one I first heard from a city official: *If it's the Mafia that's run Italy, then my compliments to the Mafia.* In my cousin's case, he made his home in the most reliably constructed and secure of the local complexes. A quadrangle of apartments above a parking level, it had a gate with both an electronic lock and a deadbolt, and the center lay open to the sky. Families enjoyed something of a courtyard. From the street side of the apartment, looking down on the intersection of Dante and Secondigliano, the bustle could seem supernatural. As evening came on, as the streetlights brightened, the crowds turned peacock. In quality threads, strolling hand in belt-loop, couples sampled the sidewalk foods and each other's kisses. The laughter sounded free from worry.

The wife, I'll call her Serena, would join me. "You see what we've got here?" she'd say. "The good life? Everything we need, right on the street."

The last time I heard that kind of thing was years ago now, before '04 and '05, when the free-for-all among the clans forced them to move.

* * *

The Secondigliano Wars didn't result in the kind of homicide levels you'd see in the U.S. Gun violence, in Naples as in L.A. or Detroit, took the greatest toll, though a couple of car-bombs went off as well. Still, the murder count came to just 78 in '04 and fewer the next year. Not that these figures aren't terrifying, if you can hear the gunplay from your front windows, overlooking the Corso. Not that my cousin's comings and goings—and those of his wife and preteen son—didn't take him past the occasional homicide site. The wet of blood and viscera, the way blocked by police tape, these became a regular part of the … *situation*. The carnage drew substantial attention from the media, including that piece in *Vanity Fair*. This article, however, served primarily to kiss the Don's hand. *VF* stopped just short of calling the capo a "criminal mastermind."

Myself, I'll give the man this: he had a good run in the bad life. Paolo Di Lauro, born and raised in Secondigliano, had emerged a winner from the last significant Camorra squabble. That one erupted in the early '80s, following the worst local earthquake in half a century. The disaster freed up millions of *lire* for reconstruction, and with the clans so big in the building trades, it was only a matter of time before they started swapping bullets. Di Lauro helped broker a peace, an exchange of favors. He enabled the criminal aquifer to open up fresh runnels and sinkholes, giving rise to the abuses detailed in *Gomorrah*. Nothing so fuels Saviano's outrage, in fact, as how long this went on; nothing did the city such harm, he argues, as allowing the crooks to set the balance of power. Still, Di Paolo couldn't hold out forever against the twin pressures of the cops and his rivals, and in 2002 he tried to cut and run. He handed control to his son Cosimo, and in so doing proved himself a long way from a "mastermind." The son turned out to be a thug and a moron, happy to start a war.

Despite the best efforts of the other clans, too, neither *padre* nor *figlio* died in a mob ambush. Both Di Lauros were collared by the police; both never got out of Secondigliano, unable to conceive of life beyond the neighborhood. The point is, the gunplay of '04-'05 should never be reduced to a one-man show. Rather it's a bloody round of Musical Chairs, and though the former head of the Directory may sit crying in a jail cell, his sobs find an echo in the laughter of the latest kingpin.

The true loser is always the same: the people with decent jobs and functional families. Among those, in Secondigliano, many looked up to a certain doctor. Marcaurelio stood out as one of the few successful straight folks along the Corso. But then, my cousin too suffered a setback, at the start of the Wars.

His specialty is physical therapy, and by the mid-'90s he and a couple of others had set up a rehabilitation center. Another of the ventures along the Corso had collapsed, and Marcaurelio's group bought the building. They set up a full-service facility, with examination offices, stationary bikes and stair-climbers, medicine balls and jump-ropes. A winning concern from the get-go, the PT center looked to enrich its co-owners in a way still rare in Southern Italy. Naples, as I've suggested before, has never known much social mobility. Here the usual ticket to wealth is the right name in the parish records. But my cousin soon bought his first boat. He kept it down in Paestum, where Serena had family. So I discovered the temples to the Great Mother, the Tomb of the Diver. So too, whenever I rode the *Circumvesuviana* south, I was treated to long days on the water, even jaunts over to Ischia. One happy summer, my daughter joined us. Yet before the decade was over, the boat was gone and my cousin's stake in his *studio* had shrunk. He'd been busted down to some sort of consultant, and his schedule grew busy with freelance assignments. He had to work out of his bag.

By then I was well into my Neapolitan re-entry. I'd spoken with everyone from the mayor to *clandestini* who wouldn't give me a name. I couldn't miss the stench of the mob, in my cousin's losses, his changes, and I had to ask.

The Camorra? replied Marcaurelio. They'll always be with us.

Now, the man loves to talk, to ramble—it's something in the DNA, clearly. Also he's got a tinkerer's energy, his hands busy whether with the stethoscope, a *telefonino*, or some recipe item. Once he started shaving his head and watching his cholesterol, he looked like a flyweight boxer. It's Marcaurelio who's provided a lot of the detail in these pages, including alternatives to my father's ragù. Also it's he who, faced with chaos north of Naples, blazed a trail south. In Paestum his son finished both middle school and the *secondaria*. Not that my cousin established a *studio* down that way, more than an hour's drive from the office in Secondigliano. Not that he cut back on the consulting he did around Naples, or sold, at what would've been a steep loss, the old apartment. Most weeks he spent two or three bachelor nights up in that apartment, with its double locks at parking level, while off on the far side of Vesuvius his wife handled the childrearing. A family-fraying arrangement, it must've been hammered out under duress. Still, insofar as my cousin bothered to explain, he'd bring up Serena's brush with ovarian cancer. The disease had more to do with the move, somehow, than the Wars.

Nor was my cousin reluctant to sing the praises of his new address. Close to the beach and the ruins, in the heart of the mozzarella ranchlands: *Every time I come home I go on vacation.* Besides, with in-laws in town, he had a pied à terre to start with, the upper half of a duplex. At ground level lived his wife's parents, and they weren't getting any younger, were they? To speak of this brought on his gift of gab, mulling over future possibilities, the way the in-laws' might be converted to a B'n'B. He and Serena could even take over the abandoned place next door …

Ten years along, a couple of these dreams have come true. Turns out I'm not the family's only *fortunato*, and these days, tourists in Paestum can enjoy a capacious new B'n'B. In the heart of the mozzarella ranchlands. Marcaurelio and his wife even get repeat visitors, again proving he's got an eye for a promising situation. Yet when we speak of the rehabilitation center up on Corso Secondigliano, where after all he still keeps regular hours, he sounds as if nothing has changed since the '90s. As for '04 and '05, the shots outside the windows, you'd think he'd never heard a thing.

Chi fott' à Marcaurelio? Who was messing with him?

* * *

Concerning the relocation, I did have someone else to ask. I had the son, a trim and sunny boy I'll call Rikki. In those days Marcaurelio's only child wasn't yet a teenager. One afternoon we shared the walk to the beach.

When I asked, the kid brought off an adult shrug, *Napoli D.O.C.*

"Eh. It became impossible."

Over summer, Rikki darkens to the point that an American would call black. On that walk, he recalled an interrogation in a Memphis police station, c. 1936: a Negro suspect between two imposing white cops. *Yassuh. Nawsuh.*

"The *zona*, impossible. The situation."

It'd been his father's decision, Rikki declared. "Papa heard something, or he saw something. It was Papa who put it to us, one day. *But why don't we leave?*"

This sounded familiar, and indeed the question echoes back and forth across my reconstruction project, my Twenty-Year Itch.

Why not leave? The words play on a loop, as the decades themselves loop over. If I were writing about Berlin, I'd call it a *leitmotif.* But in this case, walking with Rikki to the beach, the phrase resonated more closely, somehow, and the sensation nagged at me for the next couple of hours.

Hours in no way a nag, themselves. This was peak vacay, under the family umbrellas. Within their preferred lido, Serena and her sisters maintain season-long rentals side by side. Each circle of shade comes with its own pair of recliners, though the women often show up with an extra. It's mostly women and children of course, brightly keeping up their rounds of *intraliarsi.* Everyone's got a magazine, and every mag has its summer sex poll. No shortage of things to talk about, and then the women need to assess the pros and cons of the goods on sale at the beach. Africans walking the sands offer an astonishing array, racked across their shoulders: beachballs and sunglasses, the bead jewelry gaudy but nothing compared to the drawstring pants, green and gold and berry-red ... And if there's lunch, if a group of us don't stroll back to Marcaurelio's, it's chewy homemade panini, as farm-fresh as the melon or plums that clear the palate. If there's wine, you couldn't find better than one of these women's *vino della casa.* The lido bar has a fine selection, and its kitchen offers catch-of-the-day, but why bother? We've got better in our cooler. The best-stocked is the one that's come the farthest, the cooler that belongs to the sister I'll call Carmela. She often brings two and always packs plenty of ice, since her home's so far up in the hills.

A palatial spread, actually. Carmela's patio commands the kind of view to which Shelley would've dedicated an ode. Outbuildings include a gym with weight machines, and the in-ground swimming pool extends far enough to have kids at the shallow end and swimmers at the other. Along the roadside, the property's bordered by a curving brick wall, chest-high; its gate has a callbox. Once you're let in, once you're down through the first loop of the driveway, there's a second gate, more ornamental, operated by hand. From that point it's still a good hundred feet to the house.

The husband, my cousin's sister's husband, finds this place getaway enough. He's *proprietario* of a vast hardware store by the train station (imagine the biggest Home Depot in the mall, except downtown), and it's obvious he can set his own hours, but I never saw him on the beach. For family, he prefers entertaining up at the house. Not everyone's comfortable about visiting, though. One of my aunts, in particular, erupted at the very mention of this in-law. This was Marcaurelio's mother, his and Nando's, *Napoli D.O.C.* One evening at her place I spoke of Carmela's husband, and my aunt turned ugly. She spat out some obscenity, Neapolitan, and as she flung herself across the kitchen I caught the word *disgrace*. After that she focused on her ragù.

Down on the Paestum lido, under the umbrellas, Carmela covered for her absent husband amiably. She spoke of *lavoro*, and indeed the gang on the beach rarely included a family breadwinner. If one of the fathers did show, say on a Sunday, he'd spend most of his time on a recliner. Around him the raillery continued but, covering his face with the newspaper, he'd contribute no more than a rumbly aside. A guy like that could leave me feeling ashamed, actually. Feeling as if my job as freelancer deserved another title—*freeloader*. What gave me the right to such summers?

Anyway, Carmela's husband never seemed to take a day off. I never saw him visit her parents, either, in the home my cousins later took over. At get-togethers like that, the wife made excuses, and she proved likewise understanding when others in the family offered their excuses, in order to skip an event up at her house—the compound, would you call it? Marcaurelio and Serena, however, had no problem with spending an afternoon around Carmela's table. I came along perhaps three times, and what impressed me most about the head of household was his inability to relax. A big guy to begin with, square-headed, he held his upper body in a permanent clench. Maybe it was the weightlifting; God knows, he never had a trainer.

On a winter visit, a February Sunday, his wife threw herself into daylong preparations for a hearty *pasta Genovese*, a dish invented, despite the name, in Naples. The husband and I found ourselves alone on the patio, warming ourselves with Aglianco, savoring the poetry of the view. What little he shared came out flat-mouthed, and with his head sunk between hunched shoulders, he made me think of Richard Nixon.

Vaguely he alluded to business besides the hardware store: *construction, real estate …*

Then come summer, the day of my interview with brown young Rikki, the man's wife was once more on the beach. As for the boy, no sooner did he reach the lido clubhouse than, *ciao cugino,* he was done with Secondigliano. The vague answers he'd given me would have to do. He found a friend and a ball, and myself, I wasted no time trotting down the hard-rubber corduroy of the walkway, avoiding the hot sands. I was greeted with adult playtime, *chiacchiera*, chatter, in which Carmela never missed a beat. Handsomely tanned, her beach jewelry limited to a piece or two, she's alert as well to the teenagers' mating rituals (first games in the surf, then gelato at the lido bar). The day I interviewed Rikki, one of those teens picked up a new mood ring. Just the sort of geegaw you could rely on to while away a few hours, starting with the banter over the price, as soon as the beach-walker unhooked it from his rack. On the girl's finger, the toy flushed vermillion with passion. *Ah ha!*

I ventured a brief solo, in this *Dolce far' niente*. My accent lacked the music, but I made a quick quip, meantime thinking over Rikki's line, his father's line: *why don't we leave?* Trying to remember, to pick up the thread of some recent connection …

* * *

When Southern Italians speak of the sea, on a good day, they like the word *morbido*. "Soft" would be the dictionary definition, but this doesn't begin to convey the magic. Soft, yes, well-weathered by the odyssey from the gates at Gibraltar. Out in Oregon, the Pacific was barely approachable, and even on the other side of America, the beaches I'd seen along Cape Cod and Long Island, those too were dotted with warnings: undertow, riptides, sneaker waves. Ah, but on this ancient shore, no sooner did I hustle across the scorching sand than the Tyrrhenian rewarded me, coddled me, offering a kind of massage. Once I was in above the ankles, a massage, and then later when my toes kissed the sea-floor goodbye, it invited a loll. I eased over into a float. With that the waves might reverberate with the din of my youngers, the children with their floats and the teens at their mating, but to a father half a world away from his daughter that clamor too seemed a comfort, a role-reversal: the kids sang a lullaby. They sang reassurance: I wasn't a freeloader, or a bad father. I'd moved on into a loamy realm whose nutrients I could bring back to feed the people I loved.

Another summer came the opportunity to treat my wife-to-be to a dip. I made sure the sea was part of her first jet-lagged day in greater Naples, and how'd she respond? "You never want to get *out*!"

It's another happy quirk of Vesuvian geology, the look and feel of beaches here. They're among the very few in Italy that resemble what an American would have in mind, an unbroken crescent of sand and sea. Elsewhere, you tend to get gravel. Here the waterfront makes up part of a national park, the Cilento, which extends far up into the mountains. The hills have their towns, but the authorities resist development, just as down in Paestum the beach clubs are single-story with dirt parking. There's always a free beach as well, and wherever a person spreads out their towel, even on a weekend in August, he or she can find zen. Every lido marks the outer limit of its swimming area, a string of red buoys on a cord, and with a hand on that cord you can ride the waves' chuckle, ears underwater. *Morbido*, yes, especially if you roll over into a Dead Man's Float, blinking down through the mottle of shadow at a sea-floor not far off but distant enough to drown in, squinting down at a scrap of red that might be Roman brick, or at a bottom-feeding white blob: the stinging jellyfish, *la medusa*—from where I lay, it couldn't have felt more natural to drift into poetry, a piece by my contemporary Jay Parini, the man-of-letters grandson of a Neapolitan immigrant:

> *When all is said and done, undone,*
> *it's rock and water*
>
> ...
>
> *When war and peace,* folie à deux,
> *have found each other*
>
> *wanting and gone home, at last, for good,*
> *it's rock and water.*

"Morbid," the threat in the word, can itself grow mottled around here; it can look like "acceptance." I mean that acceptance, not to say *resignation*, swiftly set in among my favorite family over in Naples, when it came to the *malavita*. No greater tragedy had afflicted the Vicedominis since the last World War; midway into the first decade of the new century, the bad guys had muscled my cousins into steep cutbacks and a difficult relocation. What's more, by that juncture in my Neapolitan double-decade, I had no trouble spotting the Camorrista at the dinner table. The man's dirty money must've paid the rent on our lido Fantasyland. Up in his walled fortress, while I've never seen any guns, I imagine he knows just which drawer or closet.

Now, if I asked a psychiatrist, wouldn't he say the *goal* was acceptance? Among the Naples folks I'm closest to, so many joys remained, not just the toy jewelry but also the pearls beyond price, the affection and support that oozed from these people like the milk that leaked from their farm-fresh mozzarella. My compliments to the Mafia.

Out at the border of the lido's swimming area, in my Dead Man's Float, I could study a flake of brick on the sea floor, perhaps three years old or perhaps three thousand, and whatever had left that home a wreck, it too had long since turned to flotsam, broken down under tides of crying and laughing. If it wasn't rock, it was water.

So the question came back to me: *But why don't you leave?* It came like the lapping of these soft Tyrrhenian waves, in many voices, but especially my dying father's.

* * *

Marcaurelio and Nando grew up in that apartment out along the commuter line. Another "suburb," Soccavo, it has its own train station. More than once I reached that station after midnight, on the last train out of downtown, and then had to walk several long, half-lit blocks up the local main drag, Via Epomeo. The hike to my relatives' place could stretch to 20 minutes, but this arm of the *periferia* is no Jungleland. Uncle Gigi also had a sea view, if a distant one. The building was, like my Vomero apartment, one of the tighter products of *Il Boom*. At the end of the 1950s Fellini turned a cold eye on the era's excesses, in *La Dolce Vita*, and there's also the chilling *Hands Over the City*, 1963, set in Naples. But no such scandals blew up around Soccavo.

The layout, for Gigi and his boys, afforded delicious cross-ventilation. From the balcony the sea fluttered, a far-off ribbon, while the kitchen's utility porch (the fire escape) afforded a view of the inland hills. No sooner was the sun over the hills, most mornings, than my aunt had the laundry out on a rack. Many a time that laundry included my own, no matter how often I assured her that I could take care of it. She deserves the name Maddalena, as a woman who knew the streets; when it came to her son's criminal in-law, she had no illusions. By the time I got to know Maddalena, though, her essential gifts came out around the home. These included laundry and pasta, *si sicuro*, but what I appreciated most was her care and handling of my roughed-up, risk-taking heart. She accommodated my strange hours, and my quiet mornings over a notepad. Then suddenly she was gone, a brain hemorrhage. In '02 or '03, she collapsed in her kitchen. At that point I was in the States, and so afterwards I made time for the bereaved Gigi. I shared both the initial crisis of his liver cancer and its last ravages. I caught that farewell kindness about my father's choice, *'na donna ottima*.

Yet through all this I never saw the least improvement in the factory lot across wide Via Epomeo. An eyesore no one could overlook, if you were out on the seaside balcony: a rust-streaked hulk beside a weed-cracked lot. What sort of "factory" could it have been, anyway, hardly bigger than a hut? Had my uncle once mentioned a clothing shop, a sweatshop? It appeared to have shut down about the time my father taught me the facts of life. After that, throughout the 1970s as well as the '90s, the property sat abandoned, despite its prime location. Its industrial windows first lost a few slivers, then went wholly vacant, sprouting the same slum-weeds as the buckled pavement alongside. Only the fencing saw improvements. The lock got bigger, then a second was added, with its own heavy chain, and up top someone strung razor wire.

Then came Bassolino, sprucing up the downtown, and I imagined something similar for this lot. Via Epomeo could use a kinder touch. The boulevard offered Soccavo's only *passeggiata*, after all, and some nights clusters of teens on Vespas would force drivers into the oncoming traffic. The crowds would complicate even my midnight walk home to Gigi's from my stop. A bit of green, a vest-pocket park facing the sea—it might be just the thing.

My uncle took the suggestion seriously. Gigi had something of his father's commitment to grassroots action, and he too worked for the post office, a union man. His vote went to the Socialists one year, the Communists another. In his apartment *scrivania*, the steeply cubbyholed desk that functions as the business center in Italian homes, he kept some papers for the local citizens' committee. Their next meeting, my uncle pointed out, was indeed coming up while I was in town. Still, I needed to understand.

He leaned close; his wife, setting the nearby table, straightened her back.

I needed to understand, I was a *straniero*. For the committee the primary item on the agenda would be parking, it was always parking, and I would be a drop-in from the land of wide streets and seven-story garages. If I wanted more than lip service, out of that meeting, I'd best leave the New Business to my uncle.

Instead, he and my aunt had an idea that sounded, well, an American expression seems right. The idea seemed to come from out of left field. They arranged for an *aperitivo* in the building's largest apartment, the home of a widow in the landlord's family. For the get-together my aunt had my best shirt washed and ironed, and she did herself up in earrings and necklace. The widow greeted us in more of the same, full ornamentation, especially when it came to the coffee service. The cups and saucers, the ewer and sugarbowl, made plain at a glance that my relatives had taken me a few levels up the pecking order. No doubt this woman's family claimed some baroque chapel downtown. I recalled my visits with the hoity-toity remnants of my grandmother's clan. In Soccavo the family china might've been *Belle Epoque*, and I purred and cooed, following my aunt's lead. Such gilt, such roses! Light as a feather! Eventually it turned out that our hostess had fond memories of my father.

I saw my play. In those days Pop was still with us, and I could share a story or two without disappointing the old girl. She didn't have to know how the first heart attack had drained his face and blanched his hair. Rather I spoke of his cooking, his dancing, and the way he and Mom spoke Italian in the home. I softened her up, and then my uncle raised the question: the wreck of a lot, across Epomeo.

Yes, that was the play. As soon as the widow understood, she made a face.

Brutta, she agreed, *davvero brutta*. And come to think, she knew someone …

So we'd done it, we'd gotten leverage, but afterwards Gigi insisted we needed more. "In this city," he said, "there are always the types who don't *want* the kids to have a decent place. They'd rather keep the kids out looking for trouble, two to a bike."

But then, he continued, I was the *journalist from New York*. Wasn't I? I'd interviewed Bassolino and his ministers, and I could go back to those same suits and ties. Couldn't I? Gigi may even have used the expression, "the voice of the people." Truth be told, uncle, I was no more *the people* than I was on contract with the *Times*, but I gave it a flyer. I brought up the proposal in the corridors of power, and following one Bassolino press conference, I came away feeling real promise. The mayor announced a series of events around the *periferia*, concerts and performances intended to build community. The title alone brightened my day: *Non Solo Bronx*.

The presser featured young go-getters from the Neapolitan Bronx, and Soccavo's representative wore a mesh jersey for, of all things, the Mighty Ducks. Los Angeles hockey. The boy proved easy to approach and, better yet, he knew the Epomeo lot. Blighted, useless, choked: *davvero brutta*. A park, he agreed, was a great idea.

Actually, he added, he knew someone …

I came away feeling promise—but nothing. A couple of years later, during local elections, the posters for one candidate declared: *We too, out on the periphery, we deserve an island of green*. But nothing. A decade after *Non Solo Bronx*, out in Soccavo my uncle lay dying. His balcony still looked over the derelict shop-space, behind double-locks and razor wire. Gigi at least spent most of his time in the bedroom opposite, with the morning light and a view of the hills. He had that getaway.

* * *

Throughout all this, one of Gigi's sons never believed we'd see an Epomeo upgrade. This was my younger cousin, the one I'm calling Nando. Whenever he heard what I had in mind, he'd laugh, though not unkindly. We always got along. Rather, his laugh sounded shrewd, like his mom's. At times it sounded a lot like crying.

Nando, for years, was the family member I could count on for frank talk about the Camorra. I believe he was up-front about the *malavita* even back when we were teenagers, but in those days his dark asides went over my head. Certainly he pulled no punches once I started showing up as an adult. Circa 1990, Nando showed me some of the worst the city had to offer, and he spelled out the mob connection. He showed me the result of the monies misspent after the '80 quake, the millions of *lire* that went into Camorra pockets, especially those of Paolo Di Lauro. The bad news at last surfaced in the press: from Secondigliano to Soccavo, replacement housing had turned out to be crap. The buildings had begun falling apart, and Nando took me to see an example. At first glance, you'd think that the *terremotati*, the "earthquaked," had been stuck in a warehouse. A four-story hulk, Riot Architecture, the place had windows no more than slots, balconies no better than egg cartons. The monstrosity lay only a couple of winding blocks from the palazzo where my cousin had spent his childhood.

He made sure I didn't miss the exposed wiring, like filleted veins of red and yellow, looping out of a fissure at a corner three stories up.

"*Per carità*," I said. "There are lives at stake, the buildings next door too."

"Lives? What do they matter? What matters is, the crooks get the money."

"But, danger like that, even in Naples—the authorities have to act."

So I heard Nando's laugh, the one that contained a sob. As for "the authorities," what they'd done, he extended one wrist and gave it a slap.

That's the Nando I knew, a man who'd never pussyfoot, for a good twenty years. By the end of that time he'd become withdrawn; I couldn't even get him on the phone. As for email, years can go by. Yet throughout my Neapolitan Do-Over, he'd been the best for the deep backstory. We'd always got along. Back during my teenage sojourns, he'd been the brother with whom I'd had the most in common. He'd been *simpatico*, capable of hilarious faces, unambivalent laughter, and dazzling turns at the piano. Nodding at the keyboard, with a headful of curls, he looked like Dylan but played like Monk. After Nando quit playing, too, he remained up on the local scene. In the early '90s he treated me to a jazz concert on the waterfront, a multi-instrumentalist out of Naples who you'd swear was channeling Lee Morgan. Then there was the time Nando kept me in suspense for a long drive out of town to the north. Up on those panoramic bluffs, he'd made reservations at a legendary pizzeria. Built into a cliff, the place had its kitchen below its dining area, and down there was an odd window, peaked, pinched, Arab. Nando made sure I saw it, "the little window over the sea," immortalized in a Neapolitan song.

Before the meal was over, too, he taught me another stinger of a quip. The pizza proved underwhelming, alas; we agreed you could get better down off Spaccanapoli. At that, Nando declared *si mangia la vista*. You eat the view.

Cousin, I started using that one myself.

But more useful—more painful—was what Nando had to tell me about the Camorra M.O.

"You must hire these people," he told me. "*Malavita*."

This was an afternoon get-together, a break for coffee during the years of our parents' passing. My father had been the first, and the same years had robbed my cousin of his curls. Now he affected the same bullethead as his brother, and we'd hardly settled into the bar's outdoor seating before he'd drained his espresso.

"These types," Nando went on. "They walk in and say, 'You've got a good business here.'"

Across the bottom of his coffee cup, there sprawled a blue octopus. "They say, 'Now you'll have a new man on the payroll. Our man.'"

I drank in sips, all eyes.

"And you have to hire them, you have to pay. Whatever happens, you pay."

I tried for sympathy: "Every time they walk in, it's got to be terrifying."

"But you must never show your fear! You show fear and they put *two* of their people on the payroll."

Though I knew the answer, I asked about the police.

That gallows laugh. "You go to the police, eh. You have to pack your bags."

Which begs a question, of course. The same as reverberated across all my seminars in the Siren Lands: *But*, I asked, why *don't you leave?*

Before young Rikki raised the question, in fact, I'd heard it from a number of people. As for my father, I wouldn't be surprised if he offered the suggestion more than once. But the time that rang in my ears, as I lay half-submerged in the Paestum surf, came during lunch with his two Neapolitan nephews. His final meal with them, perhaps: his last trip back, exhausting for him. The brothers found a great spot on the *Lungomare*, where the view sets a high standard but the eating's no letdown. Still, *Zio Enz* sat at the table drained and blanched. Nando should've known better. He should never have let himself go, the way he did, tumbling into a rant. He brushed aside every attempt to change the subject.

The Mafia, that's what he wanted to talk about. The Camorra, the System, lying filthy bastard *crooks* by any name ... Only when his voice broke, or nearly, in mid-shout or nearly, did Nando catch himself. He sat up, squaring his shoulders over a plate of clams. With that my father slipped in his bleak question.

My younger cousin has a good heart, and I expect he regrets the scene. At the end of the meal he snatched up the check, his smile tight. Still, when he and I got together later—an increasingly rare occasion—he recalled the lunch very differently. He hadn't heard any shouting. Rather, he and *Enz* had talked like men of the world. As for the suggestion that Nando leave, eh. He'd it heard that before.

* * *

What can we live with? That's the question in a nutshell, and as I turned it over, *in pieno centro* and everywhere else, I came to see that in Nando's case, the way he gritted his teeth these days had a mirror image in an earlier choice he'd made, a hard choice. Decades ago, he'd abandoned his gift for music. Come the 1990s, he lived up in the Vomero, where his view took in a far wider stretch of the Gulf than his father's used to. Nando has a lot more space too. In one room, in a corner, he keeps an electronic keyboard on a folding mount. There's occasional Sunday noodling. No more than that, he tells me, frank as ever. Back during his years at university, he cast a cold eye over the sort of musical career he might expect. Around Italy, he asked himself, what avenues of advancement weren't blocked, either by long-established players or kids with connections? Once he had his answers, young Nando switched to engineering and computers. He gritted his teeth, determined to make the switch pay.

In Nando's chilly self-assessment, his settling for less, he was far from alone. If the streets of Naples were "teeming," at all, throughout my 20-year recovery, it was with young people out of work. Even my other, less candid cousin will open up about teens with no choice but the Camorra. As for the rest of the un- and underemployed, they've erupted a number of times into small riots. Garbage dumps were set on fire, shop windows smashed; the news got little play in the U.S.

More heartening stories come to light, now and again. One of the best concerns a few young people who turned lack of opportunity itself into an opportunity. In 2011, a twentysomething named Antonio Menna composed a witty Wordpress blog, *Se Steve Jobs fosse nato a Napoli*: "if Steve Jobs had been born in Naples." The post, prompted by the death of the Apple founder, sets out the hurdles that would've faced a high-tech start-up based in the Spanish Quarter. Menna of course was still living with his parents, and he imagines his *Stefano* Jobs under the same tight constraints. Financial constraints, too: just to scrounge up parts for his first computer, he's got to pay. That's cash, naturally, and no receipts, no guarantees. Next he's got to finesse a dozen regulations out of Rome and the *Regione*, then finagle underwriting out of the European Union and diddle the insurance forms. After all that, once he's got his initial rollout on the market, once the computers prove so user-friendly that the orders are flooding in, there arrive a couple of goons from the System. *You've got a good business here …*

Stefano's options sour miserably. Either he risks his profits or risks his neck—and if he goes to the police, he'd better head on to the train station afterwards.

Upshot: the man who gave us the laptop and the iPhone winds up doing auto repair. Antonio Menna, on the other hand, landed a book deal. His ideas appeared between covers the next year, and this success owed a lot to another group of young Neapolitans, media-savvy types who adapted the blog for YouTube. The video was, for Italy, a sensation; in no time it garnered more than 20,000 hits. The creators call themselves *Pata e Pisi*, a child's pronunciation of that humble staple pasta and peas (with none-too-faint echoes of "crazy" and "piss"), and like Menna they worked on a shoestring. The video features a single talking head in a plain white T. Still, the crew manipulates the software expertly, clever about jump cuts and changes in lighting. Better yet, after the Camorra has quashed Stefano's brainchild, the final seconds turn poignant. The actor calls for a better way; the screen fades to white-on-black script: *Napoli può cambiare* …, "Naples can change."

Pata e Pisi too have gotten some traction, I'm glad to say. These days their YouTube posts garner thousands of views, though I expect the budget hasn't grown much. I expect they're still beneath the interest of the clans. According to *Gomorrah* the bad guys look upon the arts solely as a means for laundering cash, and so you find their slime-trail only among the high rollers. Up in Venice, say, taking a bite from the *Biennale*. Generally the *malavita* sticks with the tried and true, like construction projects. The sort of work that requires Nando's knowhow.

His career choice proved a winner, anyone can see. That last lunch with *Zio Enz* was hardly the only time Nando picked up the bill. Five minutes in his Vomero apartment, and you realize he could've paid for a round of *prosecco* as well. As for his workplaces, I don't doubt they've had to carry a ghost employee or two; I don't doubt that, second-hand, against his will, he's participated in the System. Yet it's provided well for him. He's got a park within easy walk, Villa Floridiana, a camellia-dotted greenspace surrounding a museum of 18th-century ceramics. He's enjoyed a long marriage to a Siren of the old school, Lorenesque. Together with their son, the family has spent *Ferragosto* on Ischia. They too have an easy jaunt to the beach.

Who could've managed all that as a piano player? Or in the sort of mix'n'match that passes for my career? Nando knows he could leave—but he's reckoned the cost. As for his *Zio d'America*, at this point all the old man can offer is some memorable remark, a folk saying full of color.

* * *

Still, I'll never forget how this cousin came across back when he'd flirted with the arts. I doubt my father ever forgot. Looking like Dylan and playing like Monk, teenage Nando must've reminded Pop of the pre-War recitals in his grandfather's apartment, back when *Professore* Gioia was just another visitor, dropping by to play. Among the musicians in their circle, the most extraordinary landed a gig in Egypt. The story was one of Pop's favorites, a memory he never bothered to censor.

To describe the man, a relative, my father liked a piece of lingo you might hear on Turner Classic Movies. Pop would call him "a grand poobah," one of those scraps of B-grade Hollywood for which he had a fondness. He must've first picked up such palaver from the GIs who poured into Naples after October '43. It shows you how he was burning to get out: whenever the young man got the chance, he'd catch an American flick in the original. As for the real-life poobah, this was another *zio*—to me a *pro-zio*, like the priest with the plaque downtown. The musician, however, traced a wildly different career path, starting with the Rome Symphony Orchestra. His instrument was the piano, and his own diaspora took him over to Cairo. First he arrived for a concert, then he taught in the city's foremost *lycée* and then, talk about a lucky man, he moved into the Royal Palace. He became a favorite of King Farouk. After that, whenever this uncle returned to Italy, he traveled on the king's yacht. Even in the 1930's, when Naples was the busiest port between Suez and Gibraltar, the arrival created a stir. My father, decades later, would sound impressed all over again as he spoke of the boat's crescent-moon insignia, glittering against its smokestacks. The retinue included bodyguards who wore scimitars. The uncle handed out gold coins that bore the profile of his employer.

A terrific story, for my father it served as a tasty *aperitivo*, for newcomers at the family table. Also he liked the moral: the encouragement to quit the city. Pop might've had no idea what to do with a piano, but he too achieved a comfy emigrant sinecure. After he moved down to Florida, he got a boat of his own, if nothing like a yacht. Back on the Naples docks, meanwhile, the work that had provided a livelihood for hundreds of families kept dwindling. By the '90s, the bulk of the traffic was tourist business; commercial work had fallen largely under Camorra control.

So my father left. His brother stayed, though, and his sister too, and their sons my cousins. Then when I needed to escape the wreckage of my own former home—well, it's high time I put this in plain English. I investigated relocating.

To think I might become myself Neapolitan helped keep me up and moving. Among the prime movers, certainly, were friends like Nunzia. The afternoon I tracked down her studio, the evening she pointed out the sign *Niente Puttane*, couldn't these have been stops along the way to relocating? Learning layout and expenses and, let's say, population patterns? The same goes for my comparison between the Vomero, above the fray, and the Spanish Quarter, down and dirty. The *Quartiere* too has its congenial homes. A man who worked with local children at risk, also a writer, ushered me into a top-storey, split-level suite of rooms with as pretty a Gulf view as Nando's on the hilltop. Also—a father looks for these things—the layout allowed private space for my child. Plus it had a built-in aerobic workout, fifth floor, no elevator, and my friend volunteered that he and his wife got their home for a third of what they'd have paid up just a few blocks over, in the Chiaia. A third or less, I imagine, since I also did my due diligence regarding better neighborhoods. Up in the Vomero, there's more than one way to learn the facts of life, and I got to know a woman in the neighborhood. The encounter adds nothing to what I had to say in the previous chapter, another case of what the country songwriters call "livin' on the in-betweens." But she remained a friend and she's got a lot the ball, over time earning professor status at the *Orientale*. She put me in touch with colleagues there and at *Federico II*.

This other major Naples institution has the more impressive history. The founding came in 1224 under the Emperor for which it's named, a blue-eyed descendent of the Vikings known as "The Wonder." His pan-Mediterranean court welcomed Arabs, Africans, and Jews, and going on a thousand years later, maybe light from that long-dead star could yet reach a middle-aged American. Maybe I could swing some sort of position, an outcome that looked like a natural amalgam of what I'd come from and what I had in mind for the rest. Besides, *Federico II* lay hardly a block from the piazza formerly known as *della Borsa*—how'd that look? I came in for interviews. I shared my Vita and my updates thereafter, and these efforts, gathering strength, eventually spurred others. I stopped in at all the local institutions, never mind their age or prestige. I tried as well the overseas branches of American universities, sending queries as far as Rome. Closer by, out in the NATO complex, one of the better state U's had an extension program. But the initial contracts were semester by semester, I'd never teach anything but Comp I, and the big-box structures looked as ugly as *Le Vele*.

Over at *Federico II* or the *Orientale*, things turned out even less promising. When the interviewers and I got down to cases, I learned the Italian system for paying university adjuncts—or rather, not paying. The first check wouldn't arrive till long after the semester was over. So too, when I sat down with other expats, for instance getting coffee with the American Women's Club of Naples, the laughter always contained a sob. Every one of the women had spent a year or two, or three, living catch-as-catch-can. They'd known no better security than I had, for much of my life unattached. I began to think my best option was what Nando suggested, setting up private lessons with the women of the Chiaia, the goddesses …

Any radical change of life requires the opportunity. You need a nod from the Emperor, a contract co-signed by the University Provost. Everything else comes second, even the willingness to climb five flights. Just ask any of the bright youngsters doing time as a Camorra lookout: Eighty euro a day.

In my case, the ghost of growing old in Naples no longer drifts along the *decumani*. Ten years ago and more, I put it to rest. Still, I've no doubts about the seriousness, no less than mule-headed, of how I searched. My effort to relocate had nothing in common with that shoddy American daydream, a new life in the Old Country. Our best-known models are two women, and one I've mentioned already, Elizabeth Gilbert. For her, southern Italy offers a little more than that pizza; it bolsters her for prayer and love. As for the other, she's Frances Mayes, under the Tuscan sun, making repairs on the villa of her life. Her story too has its charms, but like Gilbert's, it emphasizes self over surroundings. The women's time in-country merely affords an exotic background for the graph of personal growth, not unlike when *Vanity Fair* goes to *Le Vele*. In Mayes and Gilbert, the recovery story omits the people falling down around them. When I mentioned their writing to W.S. DiPiero, the tough-minded poet and essayist, he sneered. "People like that, they don't even read the papers."

Myself, I read the papers. As best I can, I've inoculated myself against Stendhal Syndrome, the intoxication brought on by the Italian *abbondanza*. I know better than to claim any deep dive into Naples low-life. Gennaro Caldore and his accomplice move in different circles, and though I visited over the years, I could never risk more than half a day or part of a long evening. Nevertheless, I can't tell my story without theirs.

* * *

My father's circles, I've learned much better. In time I even learned what was in his pocket, in that photo from about '44. Wary and young, an urban blade, he keeps his stride short and one hand sunk out of sight. Much older and slower, a Florida duffer, he let me know what had him on high alert.

Our conversation must've come at the turn of the Millennium, just before or after his difficult final trip to Naples. My own mounting frenzy of visits was about halfway along. On either side of the Atlantic, anyway, I'd heard the worried talk about Pop. No one could overlook how he'd lost his spirit of play, instead sinking deeper into something a lot like archeology. On his return to St. Augustine, for instance, he'd swiftly put up a photograph out of the latest trip, one that showed him and my mother back in Sorrento. Together they'd found the estate that used to house their school, their camp, and there at the gate, more than half a century after their first meeting, they fell into an embrace. It's a touching shot, *davvero*. I have a copy on my own wall. Still, in my parents' place, lately more and more Naples material had gone up—such as the street portrait with one hand hidden. That black & white had at last come out where we could see it once more, out of its box in the closet. Whenever I found myself in St. Augustine, I couldn't help but take time with it. Then on this day not long before he died, Pop told me more. Gesturing at the shot, he made sure first that I understood this was after "the War." After he and his family were out of the worst, that is; the front had moved up the boot. In the wake of the hostilities, in Naples, the best jobs were with the British and Americans, and early in '44 he lined up a position in Allied intelligence. He hadn't yet turned 20, but he knew the territory and his English was solid. He pitched in on criminal investigations.

At this point, Pop hadn't told me anything I hadn't heard before. The work with Allied intelligence had come up over the years, even providing one of the very few war stories he allowed himself. A story never brought out for entertainment, like the one about the king's piano player, the anecdote was shared one on one and low-voiced. One evening in Naples '44, he'd been called in following an arrest. A serious offense in the eyes of Command, a local who'd tried to make off with a few tins of GI rations. Vicedomini was needed as translator and liaison, since the arresting officer was English. That man had a gun, plus plenty of latitude, and at first my father had little to contribute. The thief had been caught red-handed. When he spoke of his starving family, anyone could understand. But once the statement was taken and signed, all three men climbed into a lorry. Night had fallen and the perp wasn't going anywhere, but the Brit insisted they run him downtown somewhere. Some place like Central Booking. They drove the *periferia,* in other words, perhaps the very streets I walked a half-century later. But I was surrounded by new housing and double-parking; the three in the truck saw nothing but a few brokeback farmhouses. The road was such a challenge, the Brit had given the wheel to the Neapolitan. Then at some pockmarked void, my father was told to pull over. The prisoner was ordered out.

No one watching and a weapon handy.

"I knew what would happen if I let the Englishman out of the truck:" that's how Pop put it, avoiding terms like *summary execution.* As for what he'd said to the officer, his commanding officer, all he could remember was the obvious. Why bother, with such a "criminal?" Why, when the rations were back on the depot shelf and the arrest was on record? The sort of arguments anyone might make, but somehow they got the foreigner's attention. The thief, still hungry, took off into the night.

A good, somber story, and I'd found corroboration, by the time I stood with Pop in that hallway in St. Augustine. The officer would've been Field Security with British Intelligence, the same as Norman Lewis, author of *Naples '44.* The memoir, adapted from his diary, details the independence of an "FS man," and one scene feels all too familiar: "a British officer interrogating an Italian civilian." Once the questioning's over, "the officer called in a private ... and asked him, in a pleasant, conversational manner, 'Would you like to take this man away and shoot him?' The private's reply ..., 'I don't mind if I do, sir.'"

Lewis calls the episode "revolting," but at that point he still has more than a year to go in town. This civilian proves only the first the FS officer can't save, and his memoir never glosses over his worst days and nights. When it comes to the Camorra, Lewis works with the same cleansing acids as Saviano: "Every single item of Allied equipment … is openly displayed for sale in the Forcella market."

Among my earliest serious reading about the city, *Naples '44* may've been the first that didn't tell stories of gods and monsters (at least, no monsters of myth). The '76 text looks as well like my first attempt at investigating my father's War. It provided a vivid demonstration of how Pop could edit his memories—*puttane?* Never saw anything like that! The bulk of his redactions, as I say, were declassified years later, after I got back to the stony setting of his stories. The more I learned, the more he shared. But while I've got Norman Lewis down from the shelf, there are a couple of other books I should pull out as well. It wasn't as if, poking around the old city, I quit my reading. Just the opposite, as my trips grew more frequent, so did my library work. The late-'90s curriculum included two master-class fictions published just after the War. In Italian, there's a comedy black as the ink of a Tyrrhenian squid, *The Skin*, by Curzio Malaparte. In English, we have a kind of oratorio, a sequence of solo and choral pieces that, though often driven by satire, just as often choke us with tragedy. The title's another I mentioned before: *The Gallery*, by John Horne Burns. The author himself embodies tragedy. This 1947 novel was his first, and it appeared to usher in a brilliant career, but over the next few years Burns allowed his talents to rot in vats of whiskey.

The drinking may have been, besides an addiction, the novelist's attempt to drown his homosexuality. Gayness is central to David Margolick's revisionist biography, *Dreadful*, and I too, along with Gore Vidal and others, celebrate *The Gallery*'s "Momma" chapter. These 25 pages or so depict an evening in a Naples gay bar, in August, '44: bravura, kaleidoscopic, ear-perfect, heart-tipping. Burns places Momma's inside Galleria Umberto

I, the novel's main stage, "the tiniest yet the greatest city in the world," but his model for this fictional Stonewall more likely lay farther down towards the docks. Down on Calata San Marco, for instance, you find the cruising *trasvestiti*. Just which closet the author hid in, however, isn't the point. When he died, 36 years old and cadging drinks in Florence, his sexuality was only a part of what plagued him. After all, he was another émigré at loose ends in early middle age. Some of his suffering feels familiar even to a guy at the far end of the Kinsey scale. At risk of alienating my friends in gender studies, then, I'd argue that what makes *The Gallery* a great book is its compassion and far-sightedness. With sensitivity beyond anything in, say, *Catch-22* (set largely in Sicily), this novel portrays the callousness of a young superpower. American know-how is exposed as fumble-thumbs. "All we actually did," claims the recurring choral voice, "was knock the hell out of *their* system and give them nothing to put in its place." Naples sets the unhappy pattern for Saigon, for Baghdad and Kabul, as Burns dramatizes the wretchedness at street level, far removed from any noble purpose like stopping the Holocaust. A Jew figures in the novel, a heterosexual and a man of integrity, an exception amid this gallery. Yet this "Moe," even as he heads once more into combat, groans over the betrayal of the ideals that put him in harm's way: "we ... mouth democratic catchwords and yet give the Neapolitans a huge black market."

Burns himself never visited the front. The writer instead served in intelligence, and Curzio Malaparte, a man with more than a bit on the ball, milked the same cash cow. *The Skin* (just one of ten books) traces the scabrous and contorted picaresque of a U.S. Army colonel, a "Christian gentleman." American Manifest Destiny leaves a lot of wreckage in its wake, as in *The Gallery*, though the portrait has less nuance, less soul. Malaparte himself, I expect, wasn't so heartless as his creations. Working my father's beat, or roughly, I imagine the writer too intervened to save the life of some benighted Eye-talian. And while I'm imagining, I can't help but see all three young OSS men crossing paths, somewhere off Spaccanapoli.

If the author of *The Gallery* ever spotted the young Vincenzo Vicedomini, you can bet he got a good, long eyeful. My father, however, wouldn't have returned the favor, and not just because his proclivities ran the other way. More than that, he could've told at a glance that Burns was from the States. Even if the officer were in mufti, Pop would've swiftly spotted a tell or two, and he was more concerned—by far—about his fellow Neapolitans. He knew that they knew, via a social network far in advance of Facebook, a connectivity of whisper and gesture that could cross the city in no time. The Mob is nothing if not a flash-mob, and if there were any Camorra on those blocks, more than likely they'd have heard. This boy worked for the Man. One word from him could bring *i Mamma e Papà*, the MPs.

That day in St. Aug, he declared: "I've never been so frightened in my life."

I was later to learn this may have been an exaggeration.

"Never." I'd turned his way, but his eyes remained on the old black & white.

"I carried a knife in my pocket. Switchblade knife, German make. I always had it in my pocket, and I kept my eyes peeled."

Eyes peeled, toughneck patter.

"Every corner, there could be some gangster. Somebody Mafia."

Not long after the picture was taken, I remember, young Enzo switched to another line of work. He found a camp for children outside Sorrento.

"Any one of them, he'd have been happy to put me down."

In gun-crazy America we tend to forget the damage a knife can do. Even in the era of the Glock and Kalashnikov, though, the mob prefers at times to cut a target's throat. It makes a mess no one's likely to forget.

* * *

The *malavita*, in other words, had a lot to do with the difference between those two photos from the Forties. In the first, the outing with the family, he's grinning enormously, perched on a picnic table, and then in the second he's in shadow, back up and hips cocked, a weapon at the ready. The Camorra had a lot to do with that, though over the same brief period he suffered worse. And 50 years later, he was telling a favorite nephew to leave town. Nevertheless, whenever someone struck his Neapolitan flint, my father's hometown loyalty burst into flame. With me, he dismissed John Horne Burns as brusquely as he had Norman Lewis. My parents had a first edition of *The Gallery*, and it sits on my shelves now, one of my oldest volumes (though almost a century younger than my handmedown *Divina Commedia*). Yet when I asked Pop about the "Momma" chapter, it set him waving the book away.

What good was all this reading, he asked, if I didn't realize that people had been saying this sort of thing about Naples for a thousand years? Saying the place was nothing but perverts and thieves? Trying, I mentioned Boccaccio's *Decameron*, 14th century. One of the stories …

He gave half a nod, shrugging. "A thousand years, they've been talking that dirt. But don't forget, people used to say the same about Brooklyn. In Brooklyn it's nothing but gangsters, they used to say. Gimme a break! I was down on those docks every week."

Throughout the '70s, Pop's imports came in at the mouth of the East River.

"Every week, and the only time I ever had any trouble was when that one bastard wanted an extra hundred to unload a shipment."

I knew the story. He'd been in a hurry and some stevedore had taken advantage. Mom had been the one to tell the kids, grinning at the swagger with which her husband handled it. He'd smirked and whipped out a Benjamin. Come to think, it wasn't much different whenever I raised serious questions about Naples; Pop went for the smackdown. Really, long before I read *The Gallery, The Skin*, or even *Naples '44*, I'd understood that my father, for all his droll ease with food and music and women, had a lot of pride. Most of that pride was focused in the other direction— rather than honoring the Old World, it drove him to succeed in the New. Once he'd come down the gangplank in New York, 1948 C.E, few things mattered more than striding on into better. To do better, build a business, was why he'd first cut his name in half and then exposed his children to this red-white-&-blue cacophony. The noise and flutter might confuse him, but he had to make this work. He had to find the right product and, thereafter, achieve greater sway over the business than a, whaddyacallit? A "middle manager?" Forever fretting over how to please the boss? "Boss," gimme a break, the guy's only credentials were a piece of paper on the wall with a few words in Latin. In *Latin!*

I'm exaggerating here, highlighting the most acute angles in my father's thinking, but I'm hardly the only one to have noticed. His friends in greater New York tossed around expressions like "classic entrepreneur" or "self-made man." I heard the same from my own generation, years further on. Recently, out of the blue, I reconnected with a friend from middle school. African-American, the man was good for the heart, the way he'd surmounted the wear and tear. The guy who used to share my hall-locker had made it to Y2K and beyond. And he remembered my father, "larger than life."

After that, granted, my old friend said something about *"joie de vivre."* He didn't know the Italian, *leggerezza,* and more than that didn't understand how my father's light heart rode a special sur- face tension, that of an outsize ambition. He was one Neapolitan who'd never be satisfied with a mere *posto fisso.*

Even his jokes could reveal how he wanted to call the shots. A favorite punchline takes me back before I could drive. In those days Pop was often the taxi service, for games or lessons; he had the more flexible schedule. Then one evening out on the highway, a new muscle car came gunning past. Fastback, V-8.

Was that a glint I saw in my father's eye, as he watched the speedster roar away?

"These Americans," he declared. "These cars, with these names, Mustang, Bar-ra-cu-da." A glint, no question. "In the office they're *sheep*."

So, pride. That was his muscle car, roaring like a gangster in a gunfight even as the whole point was to escape the bad guys. I might question how Pop would've fared without a lucky break or two, like the lower costs of Eisenhower's America, but I've no doubts his ambitions would've burned regardless. He had a sense of self too large for the "Crater." Yet even as I acknowledge that the old place could never hold him, I can't ignore how Pop used his heritage to help get ahead in the States. It ranks among the richest paradoxes of his life—how his *Italianità* gave him leverage on this side of the Atlantic. Here his primary products were all out of the homeland.

Unfortunately, most of those were 25 or 30 years ahead of their time. Tri-color macaroni, for instance. Elbow-shaped or butterfly, this item made for eye-catching dishes over a couple of summers. Served either hot or cold, the results were a hit with the focus groups, namely, my parents' friends. One of these wrote free-lance for the local papers, and an article appeared. Was it in the Waterbury *Republican-American*? Carefully the piece explained that the colors of the macaroni, red, white, and green, were also those of the Italian flag. Promising PR, you'd think, and there could be no faulting the taste. Still, the product proved a dud, too weird for consumers accustomed to pasta à la Wonder Bread. Pop's tri-color experiment disappeared from the shelves, other than the one box in his office, his little museum of failed concepts. Only after I'd moved to the Pacific Northwest, to a city in which food stores sought the cutting edge, did I begin to spot the stuff again. The brand-name no longer ended in a vowel, but soon enough the

Portland hothouse wasn't its only venue. These days, I find tricolor butterflies and elbows (no, *farfalle* and *rigatoni*) in Iowa.

Pop's closest brush with the American zeitgeist came when he began importing mopeds, in the mid-'70s. For a while these did a brisk business between New York and Boston, where they made for a great campus runabout. Also the two-stroke engine proved sturdy, so that I was still riding mine a dozen years later out in Oregon. By my Portland days, though, the demand for such bikes hadn't kept up with the expense. American insurance, what else, was too heavy a burden. On my own moped, when some part wore out, the only replacements were over in Italy. Finally I let the bike go, only to hear, over the following decade, the rising roar of similar machines. As I began again to spend time on college campuses, I saw them zip across the quads.

Nor do mopeds and "Coloroni" exhaust the examples of how Pop foresaw the tastes of Italy catching on in the States. I'll never forget the conversation that followed my father's first sip of diet cola. Probably this was one of my Tabs; may God forgive me, I drank that misery by the jug. Pop tried a sip and made a face.

"This stuff tastes like gasoline."

A fair assessment.

Then he reminded me how they did it over in Naples: a thick slice of lime in a tall glass of Pellegrino.

"That's what somebody ought to sell here," my father told me, c. 1970. "Sparkling water and lime."

* * *

Okay, time to put *this* in plain English: every son has such a story. Every son with an ounce of family feeling claims he had a Dad Who Did It Better, who laughed at what he could whip up, in his kitchen or his garage, while the rest of America stood crying. But Pop was hardly the only businessman to notice the markup on a can of soda. My filial mash-notes matter, rather, for what they reveal about his thinking. My father's notion of Free Enterprise bore unmistakable traces of southern Italy.

Late in life he cast his lot with another Marcella Hazen staple, the eggplant. He developed a full product line, in a facility that was vest-pocket light industry, not unlike the hole-in-a-wall butchers and dressmakers of the *Quartiere Spagnoli*. A chittering beltway snaked the vegetable through peel and slice and the initial broil. After that it was layered with sauce and parmesan, the amounts and spices adjusted to order, and then each recipe was cooked again and flash-frozen ready-to-plate. *Beato lei*, blessed was he. This business at last delivered my father to success and autonomy, the twin Sirens that had sung him across the sea. As for the rest of the myth, the bit about shipwrecks and drowning— hey, this was America.

In order for Pop to put the happy ending on his immigrant saga, though, once more he needed to leave the country. He needed regular trips to the Dominican Republic, where eggplants grew year-round.

Pop worked out arrangements with an island farm family and, on the fly, on the verge of 60, he picked up Spanish. The language has much in common with Italian, *claro*, but that's not what brought him such pleasure. Every time he rolled the new verb endings around in his mouth, or corrected one of his own mispronunciations, there was no mistaking the pleasure. I didn't get to see him speak it often, but I knew the feeling, the same kick as I get out of trying out some new Italian expression. And whenever I caught Pop surprising someone with his Spanish, I broke into a grin myself. For a while, too, the cassettes in his car included a Caribbean mix, full of congas and ululation. The very soundtrack that, wouldn't you know it, often set me nodding in a Naples street market. Southern Italians who can afford the fare like to vacation in Cuba, and in a *mercato* like Sant'Antonio Abate, the music stalls crank up Tito Puente or the Buena Vista Social Club. The CDs are illegal to be sure, *lavoro nero*. Still—*arriba!*

Pop's delight shines through another photo, more recent but again a keeper. From the middle '90s, its color has the sort of saturation that's now an Instagram filter. The shot shows my father white-haired, stoop-shouldered, heavy-bodied, but nonetheless having a ball. His eyes alight, you'd think he was still thin as a rail and perched on a tabletop. Pop has just made a wisecrack, judging from the gesture, the spread fingers not quite touching across his belly. He's fun for the others, too, a pair of hefty *Criollos*. Tobacco-dark and clench-haired, they bookend my father beneath glistening palm fronds. Behind the trio, a stucco wall features a sectioned window, a checkerboard in island blue and white. It's the farmhouse in "the Dom Rep," and the men who flank my father are his partners. Brothers, as I recall. One keeps his smile restrained, his eyes low, while the other, darker, more athletic, hoists his chin with an Elvis leer.

A half-century beyond his scary moment in the *centro*, my father looks as if he couldn't have made it any farther. He's got both hands visible, empty, and at play. Yet he claimed that, down in the Caribbean, nothing helped so much as his native city.

"Completely Neapolitan," he told me. "I have to get back to that, *completely* Neapolitan. My Yankee training, the last thirty, forty years, I have to forget it."

A *Yanqui* was the last person they'd trust down on the islands. "They've had a hundred years of it, white men in suits. Talk like a preacher and pick your pocket."

Once I mentioned the Mafia, their grip on the Caribbean, pre-Castro.

"The Mafia? But excuse me, do you think they're out of business? There's always bad guys around. Drugs, girls, easy money—always. These days most of them come out of Columbia. But folks in the Dom Rep, they worry more about the Americans. The Americans, there's the real gangsters."

Didn't I hear the same over in Secondigliano? *There's your Mafia.*

"The real trouble's the *Yanquis*, their high-minded talk. They have the nerve to tell you it's nothing to do with money. *Worse than gangsters*."

Pop understood from the first that he needed to come across differently. "Down on the island," he said, "I couldn't finish my first cup of coffee before I got the picture. I knew I had to get back to what I was before New York."

In the photo, my father's shirt is a hard blue, *azzurra*, and the sleeves are rolled, the collar open. He's pale, but he must've just flown in; a couple more days and he'd turn brown as *espresso Napoletano*.

Well, me too, Pop. As I got to know Partenope, I tried out her wiles in the workplace. Results proved mixed, at best. I wasn't buying eggplant in the Caribbean, and the career path that trails my Neapolitan re-immersion bends and loops as wildly as the baroque filigree in some baronial doorway. Turbulence is only to be expected, I suppose, after you call for a do-over in how you make a living. In my case, I never quite reached cruising altitude. Even after I'd committed to my reinvention, to arts and academics, I remained a skipping stone on the American economic diaspora. One year I scrabbled along in Portland, among the bottom-feeders in Composition, and the next I was in Chicago, a visiting writer with a plush office—but almost 2000 miles from my child.

On bad nights, I felt as if my cousins had hammered out the better compromises, living with the *malavita*. Yet the old city also lent me fresh strengths. Spending time with Nunzia and Elmo and others, I came to trust more in the timeless art of *arrangiarsi*, "arranging oneself." Couldn't I arrange myself, month by month? Here was $400 for a piece in the *Oregonian*, here $500 for an Arts Commission grant, and if I picked up a pair of Comp classes, $5400 each—blessed is he. When I needed to bolster my Italian, the public library had tapes. A certain cool about my improvisations, a *sprezzatura*, came naturally. Even sporting an Italian tie, or starting an email with "ciao," helped me to feel at home, whether among writers or teachers. I realize how crazy this sounds. The tie might've been a gift from Marcaurelio, a hand-me-up. But were I to go back to my men's group and its facilitator, I'm sure he'd have the therapeutic terminology. Something about asserting an identity? A sense of self still in development?

What was good for my soul, however, could be dangerous for the Vita. Across academic America people dangle by their fingertips, on short-term contracts, and the administration can go whole semesters without offering a better hold. This tends to create a monoculture, with everyone keeping their heads down and their ass in the library. A flourish of *la bella figura*, as little a thing as that "ciao," can put off one of the decision-makers. A glass of wine at lunch and you're a wild man. And though to me the story of Diop and Caldore was almost *In Cold Blood*, with both killer and victim, white and black, snagged in the same web—who wanted to hear it? At one Midwestern institution I was warned that, whenever I was around the woman in charge, I should keep "the Italian thing" under wraps. What?

"You know, the Italian thing." This was the friend who'd got me the job. "Your New York Italian Man thing. Kind of, larger than life. She hates that."

Amico, I kept my head down.

Still, a time or two I was deemed one of that pariah tribe, the Bad Fit. I was again sent skipping across the economic diaspora, and whenever that happened, I don't mean to suggest I flew along in cape and boots. I'm no Superman, and I'm not offering some numbskull Nietzsche, claiming I was above the common herd. The negotiations of work and life, for me, weren't much different from those of others, thousands of others. Yes, never mind Nietzsche; think of Karl Marx, the rule of the market. It's harder to imagine a market so stingy as academics. In English and Creative Writing, what's the statistic, a hundred applicants for most positions? 150? Worse, I began my job search at an age well beyond that of the optimum hire, with crows' feet and streaks of gray. Then too, even against such steep odds, a couple of times the committee liked me. A couple of times, sailing along, I caught a lovely updraft.

Really, the insight that matters, when it comes to my *mezza-mezz'* of an employment record, is my discovery of this "Italian Man thing." I needed to understand: it wasn't just a journalist's cliché. It wasn't a pose, this *sprezzatura*, but rather something built in, traveling with me from Portland to Chicago and beyond. Its effect wasn't always toxic, to be sure. But I couldn't live oblivious to its potential for damage. I needed to remember, for instance, that some of the same distrust and suspicion had once afflicted an Italian woman I knew, my sister Amy. Her career trajectory was nothing so oopsie-daisy, but when she'd started out, she'd had to make her way in a field dominated by White Anglo Brahmins. To some of those guys, the Kennedys looked uppity.

The trait looks to me like learned behavior, an inheritance from the prideful Neapolitan at the head of the table. No question, the immigrant identity has all sorts of kinks, that's more or less what I'm writing about, but this particular kink has shaped my career. In some cases I was unfairly shunted aside, granted, but in one or two at least I was guilty of holding myself apart. When I came to town as Writer in Residence, the title rode my back like one of Liberace's stoles. So too, spending my life on a single campus, in a single office, never sat comfortably with me. In the back of my mind, throughout these makeshift semesters, I kept the Naples option open: *arrangiarsi*. If this were a book about Paris I'd say I was a *flâneur* (even as my knees began to creak and ache). I strutted around short-term and proud, even during a sweet gig like Northwestern or Grinnell. I was free of committee assignments, of a thousand bureaucratic emails, and this felt especially sweet whenever some older colleague waxed nostalgic. Perhaps I'd lured him into a glass of wine at lunch, and as we spoke he might even get a catch in his throat: *18 years now, in old Memorial Hall ...* Or was it 28? Meanwhile I'd sit thinking, gimme a break. You're crying with joy over having a job, and some towering mediocrity of a Dean sits laughing over how little you've settled for. Some mediocrity who can't even read his own diploma.

I too remained wary, one hand hidden. A grownup, and by no means independently wealthy, I knew enough to hide my sneer. Whether I was up at university level or down at a community college, I could always find something nice to say about my employer. I'd say it and my tongue wouldn't split in two, but all the same I bore a fundamental mistrust, thinking like an outsider. More than once, when a prof reached out to me, I'd assure them I wasn't lonely; I had plenty of friends off campus. And should that colleague start complaining, should he or she bad-mouth how the school had handled some request, some hire, I hope that my responses sounded sympathetic. Some part of me was always thinking, what did these guys expect?

One recent acquaintance has worked at two of the same universities as I, and even now, he can't let go of how the first jerked him around. Often I've heard him grumble that tenure was on the table and then snatched away.

But he has tenure now, I'll point out. He's Department Chair, no less.

Still he wants to vent about the other place, the disappointment. "And they promise the kids a quality education ..."

I'll keep up my smile, but down in one pocket, I'm making a fist. That's the System, I want to say. All they ever promise is an envelope of Euros.

* * *

Just lately, my cousin Marcaurelio has opened up a bit about the *malavita* in his life. A bit, and the news hardly came out of the blue. How could I fail to notice that he'd lost his boat? That the rehab center was taking less of his time, far less? Also I had his brother Nando, snarling and venting, plus the word from groups like *3 Febbraio*. Anyone talking about black-market labor had to talk, as well, about the Black Hand. How could I fail to hear it, the laughter and the crying, in bed together along Corso Secondigliano? Still, it's not as if I confronted Marcaurelio with some glaring piece of evidence. The prompt was simpler: the gathering solidity of our friendship, as the decades kept lopping over. By now we've both gone through difficult moves. We've seen parents into the ground and children out of the closet.

Five or six years following the Wars, he at last found a buyer for the apartment by Via Dante. He shifted much of his caseload to the city's hospital district, closer to the center. Yet my cousin never quit Secondigliano, keeping hours at both the office and the center. Occasionally we still meet out there. I'll never forget the evening when delinquents set fire to a heap of garbage alongside the Metro. Rot like that, laced with plastic, yields a stubborn, stinking flame.

Then came the summer Marcaurelio visited the States. *Miracolo*: with help from the American family, he made it all the way to the Heartland. In the home I share with my new wife, a long way from any Camorra spotter, he declared that Iowa's pork, corn, and heirlooms came together as beautifully as any Neapolitan combination. For the palate cleanser, I'd gone online; I'd found a worthy *limoncello*.

You'd think the dinner were a plot to get my informant talking.

The first secret to his staying in business, the first and last, was secrecy itself. Even under the influence of meat from Altoona and liqueur from Sorrento, Marcaurelio gave away nothing specific, like figures or dates of payment. Rather he taught me a new word, "*omertismo*." This derives from *omertà*, the silence on which the System depends, and my cousin declared he couldn't stand the term. Yet he observed its rule, and as he explained there was no mistaking his tone. His pride.

"It means I never ask, 'Where did you get such a wound?' Never."

Marcaurelio mimicked a doctor examining an injury, head down over softly spread fingers. I thought of my father over one of his eggplant contraptions.

"If there's something they wish me to know, it's up to them to tell me."

He was proud, too, of how he'd stood up to the mob's continued pressure. "Once they get your money, they try and see what else they might get. *Per carit*à, how they tested me! Beautiful women and bundles of cash!" He grinned, hoisting his *limoncello* to sketch an enormous heap. "A bundle nothing but 500s."

He started slapping his head: his impression of the stranger who'd left the bait. The guy would go into a whole song and dance when he returned to the doctor's. *Madonn'*, how could he have forgotten! And for so long, what, three days now! But my cousin had known better than to peel off a single bill. He'd likewise kept hands off when bad guys sent him some pretty young thing. The girl could strut all she liked, in her lipstick and décolletage; *il Dottore* wasn't interested.

Kà nisciun' è fesso: "Here, nobody's stupid." Another Neapolitan stiletto, it swiftly guts any deal too sweet to believe. If Marcaurelio had filched a couple 500s or sampled some young flesh, the *malavita* would've wasted little time. They'd have asked a favor in return, the first of many. Even at dinner in Des Moines, his listeners got it: the stakes had been serious.

"Bundles of cash," repeated Marcaurelio. "Beautiful women."

What do the goons care, if the neighborhood loses a resource? A good doctor, eh. To them he's nothing but a conduit for drugs, and after that a useful fall guy.

"I left them alone. If a person had a wound, I treated the wound."

He worked, in other words, towards his best option: a place of his own in the System. This took time, perhaps the entire twenty years of my Naples immersion, but by the evening of my cousin's dinner in Iowa, he'd earned a listing in the Directory.

"These days, they know me. They *respect* me, the doctor for a particular need, a particular case. I'm the doctor even for the wife."

The gangster's wife—well, just look at any *Sopranos* episode. A *capo* tends to lead a stunted life, day after day in the same rooms with the same bunch of lugs. The Di Lauros might've done business with Shanghai, but they stuck to Secondigliano, and most of the time the wives didn't get outside the compound either. In *Gomorrah*, Saviano transcribes the phone conversation, bizarrely moving, between a doomed mob lieutenant and his *fidanzata*. The man had gone to the mattresses, during the Wars, and actually he shouldn't have taken the call; even a lowly foot soldier knows about wiretapping. Still, he indulged his Best Girl, a day or so before the next round of gunplay cut him down. Miserable romance, stunted life. Among the few things the boyfriend could do for her would be arrange for a doctor.

My cousin's visits follow a strict protocol. If he ever lays eyes on a gun, it's at the first gate, the 21st-century moat and drawbridge. The frisk that follows gets into pockets and privates, shoes and bag. Then once he reaches the patient (at my Iowa table, my cousin paused to fix me with a stare) the two of them are never alone. There's always another woman, perhaps a relative, perhaps one of the new female Camorristi.

Once the examination's over, the doctor might write a prescription or make another appointment, but under no circumstances can he accept extra payment. The rate, the scrip, all adhere to guidelines set in Rome. Rather the healer's presence in the killer's lair allows for compensation less tangible but more significant. Not only does Marcaurelio himself continue to practice, in an office that never suffers a break-in, but also the clans keep hands off the group facility along the Corso. Both ventures no longer exist simply to be bled for everything they've got. No longer is the whole point of the relationship to leave another abandoned storefront.

"Respect": that's the word my cousin used, and I do wish it hadn't gotten so disfigured, over a century-plus of gangster stories. In Des Moines I couldn't mistake his tone, and over in Secondigliano, lately, I've heard how he'll assert his position.

"I'll speak to him *myself*," he'll say, in response to someone's plea.

The line never comes across, I should say, as if he's Mafia himself. No; he never implies a threat, and anyway on these occasions he's not talking with crooks. The truth is, I've never seen him with someone from the System, unless you count our visits with the in-law up above Paestum. Rather, I've heard Marcaurelio deliver the *pronuncimento* in his office, while I sat in the waiting room. The patient was old, frail, a woman, and I didn't quite catch what she'd asked. Not only did she speak dialect, but she kept things to a murmur. I caught the mood, though, the worry. Maybe she had a hoodlum in the family? Maybe her medication had wound up on the street? In any case, her concern disappeared at that single, forceful declaration from Marcaurelio. The Italian Man thing, unbothered by doctor-patient limits: "I'll speak to him *myself*."

At that her head came up, her smile closed-mouthed but satisfied.

Another time he spoke with a fellow therapist, in the rehab center. Taller than my fireplug relative, the man bent to gesture, agitated, and in this case too I've no idea what they were talking about. Still and again, a single line from Marcaurelio was all the other doc needed to hear. Whatever the problem, the solution was my cousin. What's more, both patient and colleague *wanted* him to go beyond the protocol. They wanted him to enter a no man's land and deploy a weapon he alone could wield. He alone had—respect.

Secondigliano supports more doctors than these two, naturally, and one of them is Roberto Saviano's father. In *Gomorrah* we learn little of the man; Papà's main role is as the victim in another grim story of fist, stick, knife, and gun. After that, he's forever "at war with someone," on one page waving a gun and on the next whispering, fascinated, about the Cammoristi in the pizza parlor. Father and son live estranged: a small but searing example of the mob's collateral damage. Their territory reveals such trauma everywhere. An obese *mammone*, a Mama's boy, cowers in his childhood room even as his hair goes white and sparse. A stump of a woman, a gargoyle at 35, rots in a *basso* doorway, over a saucer heaped with dead Winstons.

Marcaurelio, however, inhabits another narrative. When he whisked me and my fiancée off to the Secondigliano Sorbillo, I believe the crowd included a couple of clan honchos. A couple of big, tough types, you couldn't miss them, sitting with backs to the wall and legs extended far into the room. The waiters changed course around them, and the lone patron who approached kept his hands down and smile docile. Yet my cousin couldn't be bothered, concentrating first on our Margherita, then on the fried platter: cheese balls, rice balls, potato croquettes, battered sardines … Later, after most of the crowd had left, the cooks whipped up a dessert pizza. They spread Nutella on dough baked in honey, then sprinkled it with powdered sugar. To another visitor, it would've looked as if our table were the one with mob connections.

From that table out to the rest of the family, even down the coast, word traveled fast. Their Neapolitan American, rootless yet always with the questions about his roots, had found a *fidanzata*. Over in the States, he'd found a singer to replace the Sirens, and his cousins and in-laws needed to brush aside whatever they'd thought about him settling in Naples. Marcaurelio had understood this much five minutes after the woman walked into his office. Three, maybe. Down in Paestum, the next morning, my wife-to-be joined the others at the lido. She took part as best she could, mixing her broken Italian with their broken English. As for my in-law Carmela, honestly, who wouldn't enjoy a couple of hours with that woman, with her cooler well-stocked and her teenagers introducing a welcome note of youth? In summer Carmela's girls put in as much beach-time as work allows; one of them has taken over as the manager of a nearby shopping center. The father, up in the hills, holds the mortgage.

The family appears to be all over local real estate. This too has emerged, amid the *chiacchierà* under the umbrellas, and after twenty summers of such banter I've come to think Carmela's husband didn't achieve all his holdings by threat or swindle. Not necessarily: down the coast development's not so cheek-by-jowl as up around the *periferia*. Around here, if some other party contested title on some abandoned farmland or workplace, the deed might not have changed hands over that person's dead body. A dead dream, *senza dubbio*. Hopes and dreams went all to pieces. These however could be dispatched with, at the worst, a hammer blow to the knee. A thug can get his point across simply by breaking into a parked car and tearing out a child seat.

It could be I'm giving my people too much credit. I'm only making another educated guess, though I did at last raise the issue with Marcaurelio. After my cousin opened up, that night in the States, I figured I could ask about the capo in the hills. I found a private moment, but his greatest revelation was how much he sounded like my father. Brusquely he come to the point.

"But, excuse me. If a person simply keeps their *eyes* open ..."

Marcaurelio didn't get into details. Anyway he wouldn't have known the worst—but just like that, he was done with denial.

"All a person needs to do is keep his eyes open." He used a forefinger to tug down a lower eyelid. "A man with a fortune like that but no office, no staff?"

Gently, I shared what his mother had thought of the in-law.

"Eh, in this family, no one's stupid. But do you think Mama never spent a Sunday on the beach? With Carmela, with all of us?"

At that, I caught the counterpoint again, the crying and the laughing.

"We visit the same shops, that's all. In summer, we rent the same umbrella."

I glimpsed the advantage gained by Carmela and the daughters, in having a state-sanctioned professional they could call brother. The last thing they wanted from him was more *malavita* business; just the opposite, Marcaurelio and his family offered a life outside the compound. They kept the gears of community oiled, with errand-swapping, with all the friends'n'neighbors ordinary. If I thought like a lawyer, I'd say my cousin gave the gangster a certain "likeability." Out on the mozzarella ranches, the mongers smiled to see either family stop in.

Not long ago, in the years since the end of this memoir, Carmela's square-headed husband nearly died of by a heart attack. The first person the wife called was my cousin, and Marcaurelio took care of it himself.

* * *

So, what are we to say? "Compliments to the Mafia?" The bad guys got their hooks into the good doctor, but they allowed him to keep up his work and even help the community. Down around Paestum, where the daughters of the Camorrista run legitimate businesses, not one but two families enjoy new status. The *malavita* did more for my cousin, you could argue, than his *zio da l'America*. My father must've known it, too, even as he achieved his American Dream by way of the Caribbean. He must've heard all about his older nephew's hard times, though Marcaurelio probably did a lot less sharing after my father's first heart attack. That'd be like him, the doctor, looking to relieve an old man's stress. But then there was Nando, an angry bearer of bad news right through my father's final visit to Naples. Whichever brother raked up the muck, though, Pop gagged at the stench. I believe their struggles with the mob had a bearing, at the end of last century, on another of our significant talks.

My relationship with my father, as I've said, may come down to three conversations. If it does, then this second one took place between adults. My sister was a part of it too, though she wasn't in the room.

The subject was a piece of property, and by then Amy and I were on our own, well into the trial and error of marriage and career. By then we had homes in opposite corners of the country, NW and NE. My sister had started with a fixer-upper, seriously run down but in a solid neighborhood, and come the later '80s, she got lovely new neighbors, a nice elderly couple—my mother's parents. Concerning the American grandparents, of course there's plenty I could say. They deserve their own memoir as much as my mother. What matters for my father, however, and this second conversation between him and me, is that the grandparents grabbed the house next to my sister's as soon as it came available. Indeed, Amy wanted it that way as much as they did, because what I feel for the folks in Naples, she enjoys with my mother's people. That's the undertow, in her case. To this day my sister sets the holiday table with plates and silverware handed down by a Boston great-aunt. On her bookshelves, in the oldest volumes, jotted on the flyleaf, you'll find her American grandmother's name and a long-ago Manhattan address.

Not long after those grandparents moved in next door, their health began to break down. By the end of the '80s, about the time I began finding my way over to Naples, the old woman's dementia set in. The old man could no longer handle the stairs. Amy always made time, even if her schedule allowed no more than helping the frail duo around the yard. Really, as demands mounted, no one kept a steadier hand than my sister. Naturally my mother and her siblings pitched in, and as for me, every visit back East included its share of errands. Still, Amy was the one; she may not have attached the bathroom handrails herself, but she oversaw the installation. She arranged for the nurse and the Medicare. Her efforts extended through the final disbursements, loading up boxes and getting them to the right relations. Then in the midst of all this, my sister sat me down.

What she had to tell me, truth is, I could've told her. Everyone in the family figured my grandfather would give Amy the house. He'd transfer the title, and with that she'd have two properties, one already fixed up, in a solid neighborhood. Everyone figured as much, but she wanted me to hear it from her.

I fell back on an expression of our Granny's, a pet name. "Ambo-Rainbow," I said. "You deserve it."

If the place wasn't hers, I told her, it was nobody's.

"You deserve it, and I imagine it'll sell fast, too. A quick sale, a good price, wouldn't that be best for everyone?"

If our conversation was in a coffee shop, I imagine Amy picked up the check. Not that I'd just showed her my stigmata or something. Nobody's a saint, at that table, and especially not the guy who'd spent the past decade on the opposite coast—where I happened to be doing well, thanks. Not so well as my sister, never that well, but the grandparents' final decline coincided with my high-water mark as a moneymaker. Those fat contracts in advertising and PR, putting a temporary splint on the fractures in my marriage. I'd made compromises of my own, there at the opposite end of Ambo's rainbow. If now she and I handled this well, the question of Gran and Grampy's house, a lot of the credit belongs to her. My sister sat me down.

As for my father's part in the conversation, that came during the same visit East. In this case I remember the venue distinctly, a booth in an American restaurant. The salad was goopy, the BLT spongy, and my mother, sister, and wife were elsewhere. Maybe loading up a box, maybe treating the kids to *The Little Mermaid*. Pop wasn't himself, in any case. He was hesitant, even monosyllabic; I was halfway through my sandwich before I got that he wanted to talk about the grandparents' place.

I tried switching to Italian, though I was rusty then, at the outset of my Neapolitan reconnection. "Listen, friend"—*amico*, not *Papà*—"Amy and I have spoken of this. I know how things are with the … the house of the old folks."

He needed a moment, and he too kept it simple. "That's a good thing. Your sister, it's good she tells you."

A conversation with them both, yes: Amy and I on the level of banking and real estate, and Pop following through with philosophy and values. On its surface, granted, his contribution looks obvious: "With your family, you can't have secrets." On its surface this could've been a chat among the Corleones: *Mikey*, he's your *bruddah* … It could've been cited in another academic paper on clan fidelity in Southern Italy. Nonetheless, when I tune in this talk from twenty years ago, I hear something else. I hear an American ideal, straight out of Jefferson and Madison. My father was arguing, in Italian, against the baroque and for the square.

"It's better if everyone knows," he said. "The money especially."

An American restaurant, I'm sure of it. Pop got enough of Italian places on the job, nearly all of them old red-sauce joints, Gino's or Carmine's.

"Better the money is out where everyone can see it. Out in the sunshine."

In pieno sole: speaking Italian, my father and I mouthed principles that would've sounded right in an Arkansas accent. Bill Clinton was President in those days, and if he'd suddenly shown up on the TV over the bar, he could've begun his address by quoting my father and me. We believed in a place called Hope, in a conversation that remains one of my touchstones. It makes me dig in storage for the expression "cherished memory," careful not to snag its faded embroidery on my daughter's old xylophone. Seriously: across from me in that booth there sits a man past retirement age yet still busy with the polydactylic stuff we call growth. He's still learning when to select a vintage other than *Napoli D.O.C.*, just as he learned to do without the *case chiuse* and their notions of romance. So while we sat discussing Amy and his in-laws, the more profound exchange was between him and me. Pop was once more presenting me with his greatest single gift: trusting me to find my own career and livelihood. As a businessman, my father's best product might be Italian, but when it came to his son, he shrugged off the Italian thing. His oldest boy didn't need to take over the shop. If the *primogenito* had another calling—and for a few years there, the father could see that more clearly than the son—hey, this was the land of *The Little Mermaid*. His daughter could be the businessman.

So he came through with another good talk, one for which he had my sister along. Yet now as I replay it, as once again I smile at the recollection, I can't help but notice the dissonance in the background. Back in the city Pop came from, a city we both loved, nothing stopped the white noise of wicked dealing.

* * *

"My brother?"

Marcaurelio sighed, sitting up in his slatted lounger.

"Nando has never understood how to live in Naples. To have the good life, you understand. He's never grasped what that requires, in this city."

He wasn't complaining, my cousin, but rather kicking back. Inside the Paestum place, his wife had dinner on the way, and Marcaurelio had broken out the wine he saved for company, Fiano di Avellino. The unfolded chairs faced the sun, since catching the last of the long May afternoon was worth having to squint. We'd set up on the garden side, away from the dog run, and from time to time we caught the cluck of a neighbor's chicken or a croak from my cousin's frog-pond. A built-in, concrete, the pond's almost small enough to put your arms around, but it's bordered by healthy reeds and stocked with both goldfish and small amphibians. Myself, I've thought of the courtyards and atriums of Pompeii, though it's a stretch to call the place a villa.

Four or five gates down the street, there's an abandoned lot. The home within has pitted walls, lichen-stained, and the scrub in the yard stands so tall, you can barely see the broken windows. The only new touches are the double locks on the gate.

But my cousin too has a lock, and his fence is screened with flowering hedges. As we lounge amid the squawk and *ribbit*, the scent of bougainvillea and the satisfactions of the Fiano, it feels *fuori mondo*: beyond the world and its cares. It's just the occasion to wonder, where's the brother? The host's younger brother? Nando, however, had again sent his regrets.

This visit came at the end of my renewal-via-Naples. I'd arrived with my wife, and together we had city smarts enough, plus a budget enough, to meet the younger cousin wherever he liked. But this time too, I never laid eyes on the man. The relative with whom I had the most in common, the one whose *scrivania* of the Self included a drawer of musical scores, souvenirs from a life in the arts—Nando wouldn't so much as answer an email. Nor a text to the cell, nor an old-school phone call to the landline in the Vomero apartment. I tried them all, during the last years of my recovery.

Once I was lucky enough to get a month-long residency inland, between Naples and Rome. This was *agriturismo* country, where farmlands hung like hammocks between the hills and the hills were spiked with castle turrets and cathedral spires. Still, *Napoli Centrale* was less than two hours on the commuter line. I had no trouble connecting with other family, or surrogate family like Nunzia. I even got together with a teaching colleague, a Distinguished Professor who'd tried to find me a real job. Up another ziggurat of an urban hub, this man and I climbed basalt staircases to Sunday dinner. From his stoop we looked down Caligari alleyways to sweeping farm expanses, all wheat and green and ripple. I was lucky, oh yes, but not when I tried Nando. What little I knew came from Marcaurelio, eventually, and the news surprised him too. His brother had found work in the Middle East.

Then my mother received an email—even Nando had to respond, when the *capo della famiglia* weighed in. Word was, he had a project in Afghanistan.

The Afghan conflict has taken a few Italian lives, troops with the alliance, and every once in while there's been a news item. When I tried to pin down what Nando was up to, however, I felt like a Mafia investigator with a lead gone cold. I could confirm, at least, that my cousin hadn't gone into *lavoro nero*. The project concerned infrastructure and included a vacation package. Come August, Marcaurelio and I got another surprise: the brother had made it back to Ischia. He'd rejoined his wife and child, and once more I sent texts and left voicemail. Nary a peep in response.

Since then I've even less idea of what he's been up to. I've caught wind of work in Israel, or was it Iraq, but all I can say for sure is that he's not taking any jobs in Naples. Not since the Camorra snatched away his business.

This story I got from Nando himself. I heard it while the wound, the humiliation, still smarted and oozed. Indeed the night he told me, back before he began to take his talents elsewhere, can't have come long after the morning when he'd signed everything away. His rights to the property and all future proceeds—my cousin went down to the *Municipio* and signed it away. He did it again in pantomime, out in the cold that evening; he bent over a gloved hand and mimicked the signature. What sympathies I expressed felt likewise cold, out in the March night, the winds at the peak of the Vomero. We stood over the famous view, the city grid and sea crescent, and what heat we felt was outrage. You'd think Nando had caught fever, his glare showed such white.

A night nothing like summer, when even the boys on bikes kept their hands to themselves. Neither Nando nor I had a *mezza-mezz* to take the edge off the chill.

My cousin's withdrawal had begun before I hit town. Given the HD clarity of hindsight, and considering what he'd just come through, our getting together at all looks like an improbable long shot. My time in the city was brief, though the visit was another golden wallop. I've enjoyed so many over the years, you'd think I've been assigned a Naples angel and an endless supply of *ogetti votivi*. I'd had a prayer come true, you'd think, in every chapel and reliquary. On this occasion, this unseasonable March, I'd managed to swing a translation of one of my novels. Without an agent or anything you'd call clout, I'd found a publisher in town and he'd arranged a celebration at one of the prestigious stores of Port'Alba. So, a whirlwind visit, solo: just the kind of dumb luck that, in Nando, would stir up toxins. Poisonous thoughts were the least I could expect, weren't they, as the overseas relation with his head in the clouds? It occurs to me, as well, that my cousin may've hoped I'd write about his tragedy. He may have wanted an exposé, letting the world know how hard it is to live in Naples.

Nando, if you had that thought, if you believed I'd help repair the injustice done, I hope this feels like getting there. I hope it's a healing *Ragù*.

Back at the pizzeria, I'd made nothing of his joining me alone. I'd come up to his neighborhood, riding the *funicolare*, but I knew that at home he had a boy who could be a handful. At the table, though, Nando never got out of his overcoat. Granted, the restaurant had left the heat off, like most Naples places, right through winter. They got the ovens roaring and waited for the tables to fill. Nonetheless, my cousin's stone face, his coat buttoned to the collar, set our server fretting. Solicitous, a career waiter, the man offered to take our picture. The shot ended up one of those I emailed to my mother after I got back to the States, and her reply included a bulls-eye description: "Nando looks *very* dour." Bulls-eye, and Mom was too kind to mention, besides, his double chin. The slender boy with musician's curls had turned into a bald and heavy-faced lunk. And yet he barely touched his pie! Had Nando been packing it away earlier? Had he come here just to sulk? I finished my Margherita but, though I felt chilled, never asked for a second Aglianico. As for my good news, my book, soon I let the subject drop.

Still I didn't hear about the Camorra till we were up at the view that launched a thousand postcards. The climb had been my

suggestion, despite the dark and cold. I wouldn't get another opportunity, on such a short trip, and I had half a notion that the
view would cheer him up. Half a notion, wholly wrong.

"This city," he growled, "is sick."

Eyes showing a lot of white, grimace showing a lot of teeth,
he swung a gloved finger across the glowing scimitar of the
metropolis.

"Sick and dying and full of crooks." Turning to me, he gave a
shiver that had nothing to do with the cold. "And Bassolino is the
biggest crook of them all."

This last was a jab, deliberate; he knew about my interview.
The cousin with a touch of the artist, he'd made his way through
a couple of my Naples pieces.

"This city, it's still all Bassolino men." The former mayor had
moved up to the governor's office some years earlier, and after
that had come the charges of corruption. "There's not enough for
Berlusconi."

Another jab: of course I couldn't stand Berlusconi (and years
later, no doubt, Nando enjoyed a good laugh at Trump taking the
White House). But I knew lashing out when I heard it. I could see
how badly he needed to vent, and I held my peace while, between
vituperation and pantomime, my cousin's unhappy story emerged.
In midtown he'd found an abandoned factory, a vast warren, al-
ternating cubbyholes with high-ceiling atriums. He'd tracked
down the old mortgages and picked up the lion's share, seeing
the space as a medical facility. The renovation looked right up his
alley, given his engineering degree and work with infrastructure.
As for the special requirements of doctors and patients, he had
a consultant close at hand, his own brother. After all, wasn't the
younger cousin's concept the same as Marcaurelio's had been, back
when he'd put his money into a rehab center? And wasn't Nando's
venture a long way from a mob stronghold like Secondigliano? A
central property like this promised the city a major tax base. The
authorities would never allow it to fall into dirty hands.

"But you should've seen the man those bastards found," he went on. "The family, the connections, such a farce, just impeccable."

He was attempting to sneer, but under the good Vomero lamplight, he couldn't hide his pain. Downtown, the bad guys must've seen it too, once their straw man was on the contract. *You must never show your fear*, Nando had told me, but by then both of us were looking frail. Shivering, floundering, I asked if there had been threats.

"Eh, threats. They just start right in, robbing you blind."

For a moment this stumped me, the idea that someone would rob their own place. But then I thought of the man up front, the impeccable.

"It was never his money. That piece of shit, he never spent a Euro. And they stole everything, even the wiring. Put in an alarm? They steal the box *and* the wiring."

What did the goons care, if the facility never got up and running? What had they put into these renovations? The monies came from Rome, rather. The suits up there had often shared a *caffè e cornutto* with the suit down here, the one with the System at his back; if he assured the *politici* that his project was urban renewal, then the State was happy to open a purse or two. After that, should the venture fail, should local conditions prove impossible—what with break-ins, *microcriminalità*, punks ripping out both the box and the wiring—then the government waived any need for reimbursement. The U.S. laws offer the same potential for abuse; as Nando explained the scam, descending more and more into dialect, I recalled *The Sopranos*, a New Jersey variant. I got the picture even when I couldn't make sense of his growl. As the original investor, he'd had skin in the game, his own money. The others, silent partners to the corrupted honored name, only needed to wait him out. They only needed to keep the place closed, a drain on the wallet. They hit his car, too.

"Even my car," Nando groaned. "They tore out my son's *child seat.*"

The bad guys stood to lose nothing, while every day my cousin lost more. He ducked his head: "I went down to the *Municipio*."

Eyes feverish, with one gloved hand he mimicked the signature.

* * *

Ten minutes later, twenty, still reeling from the ugliest revelation a family member had ever made, I sat beside Nando thinking of Andy Warhol. The white-maned icon came to town a number of times. He had a local patron and a space for his fearsome productivity. The silkscreens out of Warhol's visits often do without his characteristic high key, the bubblegum colors; his best-known Naples piece mourns the '80 earthquake, and it's black on gray. When the artist paid the city a compliment, it felt distinctly backhanded: "I love Naples! It's so dirty, just like New York!"

Dissociation seems the word, again. Once more I was *Spacca*-psyche, so that whatever I said had an echo, hollow, across the console between the driver's seat and mine. Nando had insisted he would taxi me down to the B'n'B. When I turned to the window, perhaps trying to locate myself in the reflection, the city beyond my pale outlines had lost the promise it'd once held, 15 or 18 years previous. Back then, I'd watched its piazzas made beautiful; now they seemed nothing but stone and water. Antonio Bassolino, architect of the mid-'90s comeback, had revealed that his true gift lay in playing ball. He'd handed city contracts to the clans, kicking the metro into a heap of garbage. Even when the former mayor was hauled into court, about the time my cousin started to find his new property ransacked, every morning—even then the charges didn't stick. Bassolino's most startling defense was to demonstrate that, technically, he was homeless. The man held no property in his own name.

"No property?" Nando let go of the wheel, his hands flying up in disgust. "But, excuse me? Everybody's heard of his art collection, stuff from all over the world."

On the paperwork, the Bassolino whose signature turned up wasn't the mayor, but rather his daughter.

"Even Warhol," said Nando. "Andy Warhol!"

So there I sat, on the other side of an echo, thinking.

"Now, his daughter, where'd she get that kind of money?"

The car was winding through switchbacks, the conversation too, miles and miles of bad road. Maybe that's what got to me, or maybe it was Warhol, but at last I came out with something beyond *sorry* or *horrible*. Something radical, actually, for where we sat. I pointed out that Nando could turn state's witness.

Now he was the one silenced.

"Even in Naples," I said, "people do such things. Just look at *Gomorrah*, Saviano, everything he's got in there. It's all witness testimony."

My cousin, I went on, could go back down to the *Municipio*. The risks, yes, those were awful, risks to his whole way of life. His family would have to relocate.

"But," I went on, "if you move, it's not like you've got no alternatives. You've got alternatives and people to help. Myself, let me offer to put up your wife and son, over in the heart of America. This *malavita*, this omnipotent *malavita*, with tentacles everywhere. But, excuse me, Iowa? They can't even spell Iowa."

He didn't laugh, but he came as close as I'd heard all night.

"Nando, truly. Your wife, your son, they'd be welcome. Also I'm sure they could spend time with Amy and our Mamma."

Over the days that followed, a melancholy email or two confirmed that I hadn't promised too much. Nobody found it convenient, opening their home, but at that point Nando hadn't burned any bridges; we all thought fondly of him. Now too, on our midnight ride, my cousin showed family feeling. Often I've wondered about what I proposed—how quick I was to suggest a man uproot, jerking around his loved ones as well—but I've no doubt Nando softened. He undid a piece of armor or two.

"*Amico*," he asked, "can you understand?" He managed a smile. "Can you see, if my wife and son were to pack their bags ..."

"But it might do them good. For better or worse, I am a kind of artist, nowadays. I'm a writer, a professor, and for them it'd be like another planet."

He gave another almost-laugh, one in which you heard the hit he'd taken. The airless noise racked me with such a chill, a spasm, we might've still been out in the cold, up at the Vomero overlook. Or I might for a moment have suffered the whole city's affliction, the crooks who revved up and swooped in from everywhere, warping and crippling the man beside me and so many others, all these decent people with their own song of pride, with a vision of better, every one of them whacked to the street and ground to dust, and the worst was how the people blessed with comfort and security kept making excuses. The ones with connections, with a committee post or an official watermark, they kept making allowances. What was the point of *Gomorrah*, if not to knock the powerful out of their ruts, their collusion? Nor was Saviano the only one. My spasm, my inward freeze, also brought to mind Alexander Stille. For better or worse, I've become the kind of person who's always thinking of books, and Stille's got a great one on the mob, *Excellent Cadavers*. Also a documentary, *Cadavers* speaks primarily to Sicily, but that sickness of course infects the nation as a whole. In the documentary, the author does the voiceover, and his closing words rang through this shivering moment: "When the Italian State commits itself to fighting the Mafia, it wins easily."

All this seized me: the usury, apathy, and tragedy. Yet as the worst passed, as first I massaged my face and then discovered it again in the window's reflection, I came up with another idea. More of my own reconstructed slant on things, Midwestern by way of the southern Mediterranean:

"*Cugino*, listen, something else." I faced him. "I don't know of any successful person who hasn't at some point lost everything."

I meant this as an encouragement, but I had to wonder how it came across.

"Truly, Nando. I don't know of anyone who hasn't had to start over."

I used the musical notation *da capo*, a touch of the world's Italian, but once more I was talking like a Yankee. I could've been sitting over a BLT. But when Nando next caught my eye, he surprised me, looking a lot like my father. We'd found parking by then, downtown, and when he killed the lights he became Pop in black and white. Despite his 40-something flesh, he was the teenage Enzo, in either of those two photos. Starting over is hardly unheard of, on my cousin's side of the Atlantic, and now I saw the proof. He even got playful, asking if I thought he was Madonna—*La Signora Ciccione*, as she's known in the Italian press. That spring her career was in a down cycle, but my cousin knew as well as I, the woman would come back.

"Oh," I responded, trying to match his tone, "you know she'll be back. *La Signora Ciccione*, in no time she'll top the charts again."

"Next we hear from her," Nando said, "it'll be a whole new sound."

I could've mentioned my daughter, always a fan, now trying her musical gifts out in LA. But the man beside me had turned calculating.

"Madonna, eh. Nando, all right, think of Papà. Think of his mopeds."

He cocked his head. "I was there when the bikes came off the boat. Your father took me to Brooklyn."

"Exactly, but then the business fell apart. The whole thing with the mopeds collapsed. Fifty years old, and the man had to start *da capo*."

If we'd been talking music, Pop's was the melody my cousin could follow. My own example, starting over, would've sounded to him like so much noise. Just now my cousin might feel defeated and ashamed, but I'd never been his equal as a breadwinner. In the eyes of most fathers, most heads of household, I'd always looked like a freak. More than that, worse, whatever counsel I offered was only shouted in passing. Tonight I was headed to the B'n'B, and tomorrow to the airport. I had about as much stake in his life as the next pair of *scippatori* to whip past.

Still: "Your uncle Enz," I reiterated, "he lost everything, and then he went on to even better for the family."

To this day I wonder whether my Americana did him any good. Indeed this part of my book, all its sorry, bloody business, takes me to the limits of my connection with the old city. It leaves me with a deepening estrangement between two brothers I love.

"Also my sister, she might look rich and comfortable ..."

My cousin cut in: "But this is just what I'm thinking. I'm going to get it *back*."

His vitriol was rising again, his gloved fists getting busy. He'd never go to the cops, he insisted. Two could play this game, Take Away, and in the long run, he had the advantage. He knew how to run a business. The *Camorristi*, just give them time, they were bound to mess up. Give them time, and you'd see those idiots out hat in hand, looking for a new investor.

"That front they got, he's nothing. He can't run a *business*."

Nando had already started making calls. A friend up by Lake Garda had offered work with bridge repair, and he'd heard even better from Turin—defense work.

"*Defense* work," he repeated. "Think of the money."

With that glare, he could've been in a war zone in Afghanistan.

"The contracts they offer? These bastards in Naples have no idea."

At my lowest, I see all my efforts in Naples as a boy on a bike with his knife out, slashing through what's left of my father's family.

"These bastards," said Nando. "I'll show them *money*! I'll get it *back*!"

PART FOUR:

Natale cu i tuoie e Pasqua cu chi voie—
Christmas with yours and
Easter with whoever you want.

MARCAURELIO, I MUST SAY, DOES a lot more than minister to murderers. I wouldn't want my reminiscences—my speculations—to leave him looking like a bogeyman. That wouldn't do at all, especially since he's the one I can count on to correct and sharpen my speculations. Worse, if I flatten Marcaurelio, won't that pancake his hometown? The Neapolitan ragù is always in ferment, yielding briny intrigue.

So far, I believe I've got a couple elements of the recipe, first the romance and then the *malavita*. Now, however, I need to tackle something trickier, something I earlier termed "apocalypse put in its place"; a simpler way to put it might be "living with destruction." By any name, though, it's just the sort of thing to knock my Naples chip off my shoulder. For starters, it redraws my sketches of Marcaurelio, showing how he claims a more powerful ally than the Camorra. If you ask him, he'd say what matters most is his faith.

Over the years of his withdrawal from Secondigliano, as I've explained, Marcaurelio said next to nothing about the clans and their wars. He wouldn't duck a direct question, but when we spoke of life and death, generally it had nothing to do with the Camorra. Rather my cousin was concerned for aging parents, both his and his wife's, and for his wife herself. This woman deserves a name like Serena, she's so even-keeled, so quick to laugh. Like her husband she's built square, but she's got the expressive eyes and pout of classic *bellezza*. Even as the two of them worked out the move south, however, the wife often wound up in the hospital. Ovarian cancer: now there's a bogeyman. Some genetic predisposition kept triggering metastasis.

Successive operations took away tissue and organs and, finally, Serena's ability to reproduce. The swift adoption of young Rikki, even before the mother-to-be was finished with her cycles of medication, speaks volumes about the couple. Indeed, over the years I saw the same sense of promise ripen in their son; it made no difference that he turned out gay and brown. I saw as well that the family benefited from Italy's adoption process, with its more thorough, more humane consideration of parents and community. Rikki grew up knowing his birth sister, and he underwent testing that established he'd be somewhere near as smart as Marcaurelio and Serena, sharing some of their aptitudes. The Italian state, for all its flaws, proved a big help.

Even a callous adoption process, though, wouldn't have shaken the new parents' sense of the Spirit—their belief in the journey to grace. That too seems a genetic predisposition, especially when I think back to a fall weekend in the '90s. For me it was a difficult season, my father looking weaker each time I laid eyes on him, my reconstruction project still indiscernible under the dust and scaffolding. But for my cousins, these were weeks and months of worse. Serena, already stripped of her ovaries, faced yet another operation, the one she and Marcaurelio hoped would be the last. The new son was with them for a trial period, probationary. At the same time, too, they couldn't neglect the balancing act between the home up in Secondigliano and the old folks down in Paestum. The wife's parents in fact shared the duplex, the ostensible Paradise by the beach. Nonetheless, my cousins were more than happy to play host. *Niente problema*, they assured me, tossing an American and his bags into the mix.

My head wasn't that far up in the clouds. I asked: *davvero?*

But, the wife said, excuse me? Two nights under our roof, three? We'll have a great time. Yes, cousin, and in particular the Sunday drive. In two cars, we traveled with another small family, a father, mother, and tweener son. The route wound uphill, into the Cilento state park, now in mixed woods (stubby elm and fir, mostly), now alongside terraces denuded by harvest. Our first stop was an annual *sagra* of the figs. The outdoor ovens smelled of wood rather than charcoal, and the stalls of the orchard-growers filled the village. We hiked the whole length, up to the church, between *palazzi* often abandoned, the families away in Milan or Miami. The effort proved more than worth it of course, the village's tarts and *biscotti* never too buttery, all about the fruit. The boar was slow-cooked in burlap, so it retained its juices, and the wine had both earth and sparkle. Still, we kept that meal light. We were pushing on, up into the October clouds. We had to switch on the low-beams as we made for a pilgrimage site, a cathedral and monastery.

Our last ten or fifteen minutes were again on foot. The stairway to the sanctuary, hewn out of the basalt of the lower Apennines, is flecked with rough mosaics: crosses, wings, Greek letters. These add-ons are Franciscan colors, ocher and dandelion, and by then I'd learned that this was his saint's day. A murmur of blessing, *Francesco ti benedica*, passed among the pilgrims. Word came, too, that the buildings up top no longer housed any clergy. The brothers on hand had themselves only arrived that morning.

Still, by the dozens, the faithful gathered and climbed. One or two labored with canes or crutches, and from below, through the mist, I may have heard someone hauling a wheelchair. The creaking, the grunting, yes, maybe. In our own group, between gulps of moist air, the other family shared the story of their son.

As I say, the boy looked to be shy of his teens. When he gulped for air, you noticed the buckteeth, and for him the stairs were hard work. His gait, his balance, were off somehow. I noticed it down at the fig festival too, but then as now, he'd clambered along gamely. I tried taking his arm, but he shook me off. The parents began by saying that they'd soon correct the overbite, then opened up about the defects in his spine. Born with some kink in the vertebra, their son lacked full motor control. Most of his childhood he'd been confined to a wheelchair, and that included his lone previous trek up the mountain. Then a year ago, give or take, the boy had a dream. St. Francis appeared to him, alongside his dead grandfather. Both the deceased, even the one several centuries gone, looked healthy and well. They and the crook-backed youngster shared a vigorous handshake, a hearty laugh, and then together they'd climbed this same Cilento peak. All three made it up to the church, each on his own two feet. *Francesco ti benedica.*

Come morning the boy shared the news, seriously, reiterating key details. Before the week was out he'd taken on challenging new therapy.

And now look at him, the parents concluded. He doesn't want our help. He's got Francis and the grandfather.

It wasn't just my head in the clouds, that Sunday afternoon. All of us faded in and out, in the murk and cool, and the questions that came to mind had gaps as well. I wanted to ask, for instance, about the *sagra* below. All this morning the family had been looking ahead to a miracle, nothing less, and still, down the mountain, they'd stopped for—? Also I had in mind a more reasonable theory, about the way bodies change at age 11 or 12, and preteens assert their emerging identities. Still, I gave voice to no more than happy noises. Benedictions, I guess you'd say, which at the top blended into the murmur of the cathedral. Inside we found candles going and basins of holy water; I thought of the brothers that morning, shivering through their prayers, reconsecrating the space. Despite the cold most people wet their fingers before genuflecting. The boy skipped the knee-bend, but we all shuffled through the circuit past the altar. The priests had mounted a reliquary.

Back outside, at a corner of the compound wall, the clouds relented. I got a sense of the landscape, the woods and farms themselves seeming to stumble, crippled. Alone with my cousins, I spoke of the boy, the dream, and they of another damaged body. They'd been thinking about Serena's cancer.

"In any illness," they began, "there are three things that decide the outcome."

Honestly, I can't be sure just which of them said what. The memory's confused by having heard this twice more—the last time in a dream.

"Three," they continued. "The first is the will of God, and the second the will of the patient. The last, the least important, is the will of the doctors."

* * *

I made that mountain pilgrimage, I should add, with two medical professionals. My cousin's wife was in nursing, when they met. Now each time she or Marcaurelio make some demonstration of faith, perhaps touching the halo'd picture of a saint, I think of a surgeon in upstate New York. Richard Selzer, writer and surgeon, has essays that often turn theological. In *Notes on the Art of Surgery*, Selzer compares the body he's cutting first to a temple, then to an ark. Long ago, he memorized the names of these membranes and organs, the English and the Latin, but as he slices in deeper, he moves towards the Unknowable. What's on his table looks like dead meat, but after a few hours comes a resurrection. Myself, reading the essays, I think of Pompeii's baked corpses. What we see in the museums are plaster casts; the wet stuff was poured into hollows in the silt. But what of the hollow's inhabitant—the soul at prayer, under the gathering peristaltic cloud?

In short, I was receptive to what Serena and Marcaurelio had to tell me, there outside a chilled and fogbound church. Their suggestion lingered even after I heard the argument abused. I heard God invoked so a doctor could cover his ass.

This was the last man to treat my father, a couple of days following Pop's passing. He kept ducking questions, calling it "God's will." Granted, I sounded crabby, wracked with sleep-dep after rushing down to Florida. No sooner had I reached St. Augustine than I had to toss Pop's half-eaten *biscotto* and pour out his final glass of wine. No more than a day after that, I sat beside the phone with my shell-shocked Mom, the doctor on speaker. We had an obvious question, a simple one you'd think. We wanted to know what had killed him. Pop's general wear and tear was obvious, and just lately he'd opened up about a number of secrets. But this final crisis, what was it? An infarction, an aneurysm?

I could've dealt with textbook vocabulary more easily. Instead: "I can't say what killed him."

If I were crabby, the doctor was cringing: "It was God's will."

"Listen," I said, "we realize Pop had problems."

"He had a number of problems, and in the end he was in God's hands."

I waited, giving my mother a chance. She hadn't put in a word since "hello."

"What we're asking ourselves," I went on finally, "is whether there was something more we, we ought to've done."

"With your father, in his final hour, it was the same as with everyone. His time had come and God took him. Took him to his *reward*."

To judge from his accent, deep Dixie, he had a Baptist God. "We're asking if we, the family—if we could've done something."

"I can't tell you that."

"If we could've had him with us, still …"

But if my mother's silence wouldn't shame this guy into a straight answer, what chance did I have? It took me a few weeks, and a return north, before I learned better. By then I'd landed a solid position in Chicago, and I had a doctor out of the old Jewish South Side, the lost neighborhoods of Augie March. Not ten minutes after I brought up my father's passing, I had my answer.

"Your father died of an infarction," he told me. "First there was an embolism, then the whole *kurbim*."

His Yiddish usually conveyed warmth, but not this time. Wizened, unsmiling, the man went on to say that, during Pop's final day or so, there was nothing anyone could've done other than shuttle him into Intensive Care.

"And let me tell you, that wouldn't have been any picnic either."

Cocooned in tubing and plastic curtains—that had never been what Pop wanted. Years before, he and my mother had drawn up the documents.

So I thanked my Chicago doctor and left his office with, what would you call it? Diagnosis? Absolution? A bit of both, I guess, though once I was back in my car I suffered a fresh bout of tears. Often these squalls hit me like that, either as I settled in or after I'd finished parking. It became almost the norm, a breakdown behind the wheel, and years later I saw the same in my new wife. A few days after her own father passed, I saw her fall to pieces in the car.

The grief seized her ten years after mine did, and in the middle of Iowa—but again at the wheel. I offered what I could, a hug, a kind word, but meanwhile some part of me, some essayist-surgeon, was trying to make sense. Our helplessness looked to be all about the machine. A car is central to American comfort and power; we own the road. But when the rotors go quiet and the dials dark, the world outside rolls over us like fog over a sanctuary. For a moment we're aware that the works behind the dashboard aren't nearly so well calibrated as our own hands, feet, and eyes, and yet neither construct can keep us safe forever. We sense our fragility, even encased in steel, and whether we strap or unstrap, we come undone.

* * *

Getting waylaid by grief, or by a ghost, seems a better fit for an older civilization. When I explored Spaccanapoli, I was never in a car, but everywhere I came across souls turned to vapor. Here was a baked corpse, there another spray of bullet holes, and a half-hour across the Gulf, out on the islands, I stepped back into the

Kasbah of the Saracens. The buccaneer jihadists gave Capri its distinctive look, with domed cottages and cubbyhole windows, but you see the impact over in the city as well; look at the Moorish Quarter.

Oops, no, the *Spanish* Quarter. In this city you're back in *Europe*.

In the Quarter these days, actually, you'll find some of the new Muslim Neapolitans. These Africans are the lucky ones, with stable housing. As for the earlier blacks, the Moors and their sea-cavalry, they were quelled by Crusader Normans. *I Normani* put up Castel dell'Ovo. To an 11th-century pirate out of Barbary, or for that matter a 21st-century sheik on his yacht, dell'Ovo might be the most striking landmark around the entire Italian boot. Even Venice has nothing so dominant from so far out at sea. The hulking keep sits atop a tufa beehive, and somewhere within, legend has it, there hides a talisman. The first of the *ogetti votivi*, it's a supernatural egg, in eternal balance, put in place by the poet Vergil. So long as the egg doesn't break, the city will stand. Castle of the Egg.

A tall tale, *si sicuro*, but it has some basis in archeology. Researchers have scratched out traces of settlement, perhaps the original *Paleopolis*, on this big, port-protective rock. To me, though, it matters little to pinpoint the location of Naples Prime. Rather, I'm once more caught in the loops of that mental game, the one I played at the eastern end of Spaccanapoli. The hole in the street, there, seems a pot in which time itself simmers (not my metaphor; it's Dubravka Ugrešić again): where I glimpse the collapse of one urban framework after another, each of them known for a while as "home."

With each successive cataclysm, too, leftovers mount up. A few are solid as the Greek cornerstones, but others amount to no more than some fresh tang to the sauce, some spice previously neglected. These days the ruling acronym has changed from SPQR to NATO, and no doubt the Americans too will sprinkle a few morsels across the long-simmering downtown. No doubt Neapolitans will continue to employ the word (is it a word?) *O.K.* Vowel-in, glottal-out, it's a keeper, O.K.? Locals render it in a full spectrum of ironies. I found it handy myself, struck by the irony of my own position in town, c. 1990 CE. A white American in midlife, I might've ranked as one of the world's Top Dogs, but I felt quite the opposite, especially when it came to calling myself a "writer." I didn't need a Ford to feel flimsy. More than that, all over the city I saw proof that, if humanity had a future, it would reduce my growling superpower to just another mosaic in the House of the Tragic Poet: *Cave Canum.*

So, feeling my way along the loops of both a civilization and a life, I come to another aphorism, a quip slow-forged in Catholic heat: *Natale cu 'e tuoie e Pasqua cu' chi vuoie,* nah-TAH-lay koo ee TWOIY ey PAH-skwah koo kee VWOIY.

A simple rhyme, it has a simple translation: "Christmas with your folks," meaning the family, the community to which you're born, "and Easter with whoever you want." As ever, though, there's a *dietrologia*: a logic behind. There's more to it than a pair of parties. The two holidays bracket the most evocative interval in the sacred year, between winter solstice and vernal equinox. In every culture, divinity guides that journey across the seasons. It begins in humility, not to say helplessness, in shadow and cold, and ends in sunshine, redolent with herbs and noisy with the newborn. In that transformation, every culture sees the hand of some god. Few landscapes, however, offer a ripening to match Campania's. Around here the springtime celebration often extends into Monday, the *Pasquetta*, when folks head out for a picnic in the country (up the heights of the Cilento, perhaps). They seek a more generous setting for transcendence. The Gospel, after all, concerned a prophet without honor in the place of his nativity. He had to find another home and his own Elect.

Or put it in the language of American business. He's executive material, this Nazarene. He'll never be satisfied at Joseph &

Sons, not so long as he's the one after the ampersand. That's the way the line would work for Pop, a born entrepreneur, and a man who preferred to take his gospel with a grin. What good was a proverb if it didn't offer a pick-me-up? As such, the saying suits the worst of what I uncovered, secrets Pop hid somewhere in his own castle for almost his entire life overseas, out of a time when everyone kept calling on God as their world fell to pieces.

* * *

That generation, the War generation, is about gone now. Among the Naples family my father was the first to die, in his second crisis of the half-decade, despite the comforts he'd achieved in the US. Then too, on either side of the Atlantic, he'd been encouraged to better habits. Pop had quit smoking; he was keeping the weight down and enjoying a social life. Still, two heart failures by age 75—it can make you wonder. Sins of the father? The wear and tear of the War? It can set you poking around the open dig of an ancient city, poking sometimes in two places at once, since you're already investigating the collapse of your own old order. That recent detritus, the shed skins of my past selves, never stopped turning up. Still, the deeper I looked into the worst of Pop's time in Naples, the greater became the differences between us. No other part of this *Archaeology* sets us so far apart. The distance was one the old man couldn't bridge, either, though he did what he could during his last few months. Also, like any father, he raised occasional complaints about how the world had changed: *kids these days*. Harangues like that, however, tended to the light-hearted, the speculations of a prof rather than the howl of a Jeremiah. I recall a dinner during the mid-'90s, with all three grown children at the table.

"You make your living talking," Pop declared.

Amy, Tim, and I shared a glance. The Sermon at the Head of the Table.

"I made a *product*," he said. "I came up with my own recipe and I designed the machinery."

This was the purpose in a life's work, for the men of his era. "We *made* something. We tried to make it the one you'd buy." But his children had a different concept entirely. "Amy, she makes her living talking. Just showing slides and talking. And you, and Tim too. You all just …"

I figured the takedown was up to me. "C'mon, Pop, look on the bright side. I don't make a living anyway."

My sibs were there for me, they cracked up, but my father was no longer so quick to laugh. How could I treat this like a joke, he wanted to know? For God's sake, I was a father myself. And didn't I owe that child something? The way he barked was hard on us, my mother as well; none of us could fail to hear the toll these last years had taken. As for what he asked, though I could shrug and move on, I spent plenty of nights wrestling with the same question. The nights half a world away from my daughter, in particular. Was she losing her Pop, at the same time as I was losing mine?

In *Hamlet* we hear of fathers passing through Nature into Eternity, and the play was first mounted just as Naples was putting up some of its most formidable Baroque church work. These render Eternity with such marble heft that, centuries later, even the deconsecrated spaces could quiet an American past middle age, a man who'd lain awake till the wee hours. I'm no Hamlet, I never saw my father's ghost—though I do believe I heard it speak—but his hometown held actual monuments, reliquaries, bones. They brought home how little my daughter had, out by the Pacific. What could I show her, a couple of photos? A drawing she'd done in 3rd grade, one corner torn by the refrigerator magnet? These days a father was more likely to pass on into the Internet. A crypt seems a poor use of space, a sarcophagus downright ghoulish, and both put a strain on the pocketbook. Instead, our ancestors have moved online, tucked into a file on Dropbox or Instagram. Yet some of us can't shake our respect for the marmoreal, the palpable.

Myself, when I tasted hashish, I needed to put my finger on more, like the slang and the history. The earliest record, I discovered, dated back to the Saracens.

So too, in the New World, in its "oldest city," St. Augustine, I couldn't resist a whiff of my old man's last splash of red. The same impulse had me thumbing away the spittle at the rim of the glass. It's Catholic, isn't it, this attachment to a token? Doesn't it prove I've got a genetic predisposition? Yet I wasn't raised in the Church, and it took a long time to discover why not. Nonetheless, from my first midlife returns to Naples, I was fascinated by its ecclesiastical trappings, in particular the miracle of *San Gennaro*. This "Januarius" lost his head at the beginning of the fourth century, but an acolyte scooped up vials of his blood. The relics, kept in the Duomo, turn liquid again twice a year, and the transubstantiations, according to believers, have the power to still the cantankerous Vesuvius. They claim the worst recent eruptions, the latest in 1944, were checked by the liquefaction. Myself, I've never gotten that close, the crowds are too much, but I imagine the blood swirls in its vial like the last swallow of red at the bottom of a wineglass.

The totem that matters most to my Naples family is of recent vintage. He's Padre Pio, the closest thing to Elvis, for a 20th-century Catholic. By the 1960s Pio was showing stigmata, and beyond the miracles confirmed by the Church, you heard a rich apocrypha. One story had the friar visiting Fellini's producer in a dream, after which the man wrote the check for *La Dolce Vita*. Pio's church on the lower Adriatic became a pilgrimage site, and after his death in '68, the Holy See waived the standard waiting period for beatification. More recently, in 2008, the saint's corpse was exhumed and his embalming retouched. The sanctified remains, the *salmò*, were laid out for viewing. My cousin Marcaurelio talked about taking the family. The trip proved impossible, in the end, but the Paestum home picked up another statuette. Also Nando, in his Vomero apartment, keeps a photo on one wall, in a gold-leaf frame. The younger brother's estrangement doesn't prevent him from giving Pio the benefit of the doubt. Their father, my uncle Gigi, made a pilgrimage to the Padre's church in the early '60s.

The way I heard the story, during one of my last dinners in Soccavo, the little Capuchin broke off his homily to go into ecstasy. Head back, mouth open, arms outstretched, he seemed to float behind the pulpit.

Pio ti benedica: my uncle tried to show me, extending his unsteady hands, spotted all over.

* * *

All gone now, Gigi as well as Pop, and their sister too. Whatever remains is going dark, like the skin of beloved hands, and as for the darkest times they came through, my father shut it up in the closet for decades. "The War": a box in a closet, for nearly his entire American life. Granted, over his final years he composed a couple of brief letters for his grandchildren, sharing a handful of details with the young Millennials. Naturally I've kept copies, a slender blue folder, and those few pages never fail to move me. From the first, however, I couldn't help but notice all that Pop left out, disturbing business I'd already started to turn up over in Naples. The letters spoke of the family getting banished to the hinterlands, back in the '30s, but made no mention of later terrors. As for the musician to whom the Carro grandparents gave sanctuary, the Jewish *Professore* Gioia, the letters say only that he was "kept safe till the end of the war." Claims like that might satisfy the grandchildren, but a son pushing 40 wanted more.

I thought again of Pop's small selection of War stories: the British officer gunning for a hungry Neapolitan, or the Austrian nuns feeding him mushroom soup. In doling out such anecdotes, wasn't he like the legendary New Yorker who keeps a twenty-dollar bill handy? A sop to that city's *scippatori*? A kind of defense mechanism, those stories seem—not that Pop cared what anyone called it. If anyone wanted to play psychiatrist, concerning his war experience, why didn't they look at the Americans? Just look at them, practically Sterling and Draper from *Mad Men*, the most fortunate people on the planet. Out on the patio, over their whiskey, all they want is a little entertainment. Hey, *ami-go*, tell us about the war.

Those were the guys who needed counseling, if you asked Enzo Domini. They didn't want the war, they wanted a fairy tale, *The Greatest Generation*. I think of an evening when my father and I watched a war documentary, probably *Victory at Sea*. Pop was younger then, his heart still strong, but before long he became irritated.

The soundtrack for the battle scenes, he grumbled, the horns and the drums ... you'd think it was a football game.

Good ear, Pop. That's putting it mildly, come to think. The hostilities couldn't have felt less rah-rah, to my father. "Victory," *per carità*. Tell it to the rubble. And as for standing up to Fascism, or simply pleading for peace, by the early '40s anyone who raised a complaint suffered worse than "internal exile." Even Benedetto Croce went on the list: deportation north. The philosopher escaped, but many others wound up on a train, manpower for the Reich. Up north, they had ... facilities. Factories, farms, something. Then the year my father turned 15, overhead appeared the first of the bombers. On his crowded blocks, families were obliterated while they slept. The city's casualties would eventually reach the thousands, and this included many who took shelter in the *Sotterraneo*. A faulty electrical hookup might kill you quickly, a cracked water main more slowly.

Breakdowns came one on top of the other, right through '42 and '43, and they must've shattered the promises of an Italian childhood. Even a family that languished a while on Mussolini's blacklist saw an improving city and region, with a range of public investment. Schools got gymnasiums, highways better grading and guardrails, and down on Via Monteoliveto there rose a spanking new Post Office. The building's massive clock, olive on gray, must've seemed a portal to a better future. Such confidence shines through the earlier of the two Vicedomini black-and-whites, the photo of the young folks around a picnic table.

As I say, I first saw the picture when I was 19 or 20. Nonno kept it in the album he'd labeled with the War years, and there's no forgetting the old man's delicate cursive, "that fine Italian hand." Myself, I've got a writer's beaten scrawl, but now that the photo's crossed the ocean, I'd label it "Easter." Signs of spring are showing, greenery that sets off the trim teen jawlines, and my father's cardigan appears to be a bother; he's left the sweater half-unbuttoned, and with his hair coming undone, his saddle-shoes perched on the bench—yes, he's almost a surfer on his board. Not that the gang's at the shore, of course. They've found a park, that's all. But doesn't that too suggest the *pasquetta*? A getaway, the day following the year's longest Mass? Then too, if my father's a heartthrob, it's not just because he played all that soccer. Also his diet, even Easter dinner, must've been slim pickings. Most families didn't even have much olive oil. But this is a party, and everyone at the table appears lit up with trust in their world.

Then hardly a year later comes the photo on my desk: the downtown shadows, the hand in its pocket. My father has a bit more meat on his bones, but the significant weight is in his cagey look.

What happened? Where's the boy who looked ready to bounce? I've already offered a couple of answers, namely, his deepening seriousness of heart and growing awareness of the odds against him. Both those elements of hometown life went back centuries, however. Now I've got to look closely at a moment more confined and more devastating. In July '43, Mussolini hightails it up to Germany, and the following month, Sicily falls to the Allies. Bomber bases like Yossarian's get busy, and over on the mainland, those who survive the air raids live under martial law. No region looks more likely for the assault than greater Naples. The metro crescent gets a Wehrmacht scouring, as the troops carry away whatever they can use: the lamp, the icebox ... For locals, getting by day-to-day collapses almost to the level of the ghettos in Warsaw and Lodz.

The first week of September, the British and Americans come ashore at Salerno. That's only an hour's drive south, but German preparations keep the beachhead pinned down, in a long and bloody rehearsal for Omaha Beach and the hedgerows of Normandy. Up in Naples, meantime, conscription orders went out. Civilians were set to work breaking up the blocks left untouched by the Flying Fortresses. As Neapolitans pried out stones and strung barbed wire, *Tedeschi* sited machine guns and planted land mines. It didn't take a Clausewitz to figure out the strategy— a meat-grinder.

Other Italian cities fell prey to such catastrophe. The worst came a few months later in Ortona, over on the Adriatic, a port smaller than Naples but likewise impossible to bypass. The Canadians who took Ortona called the place "little Stalingrad." As for Salerno, even a day-visitor can see how little remains of the prewar city. As it happened, rebuilding from scratch helped that port replace Naples as a shipping capital, over the '60s and '70s. But in 1943, the blasted roads and *palazzi* were nothing but trouble. The Allied advance was reduced to a creep.

Come the first week of October, however, Mark Clark's 5th Army found an open city. A welcome surprise for the troops, for the Neapolitans this hardly amounted to a fairy-tale ending. Starvation and disease continued to threaten, and there remained the Nazi land mines. Norman Lewis witnessed such a late explosion, downtown. The blast leaves a couple of corpses, white beneath the tufa rain, recalling the plaster figures of Pompeii. Ugly incidents like that also turn up in Malaparte's *Skin* and Burn's *Gallery*. Burns cries out like a latter-day Isaiah: "we are all of us bugs, writhing under the eye of God."

Granted, both the American and the "FS man" finished their tours under the spell of Parthenope. Both books join her city-song. Still, my father heard little happy music, during that period between one photo and the next. As for what he did hear and see, by now I've pieced it together. By now I'd say he was 17 in the first picture, 19 in the second, a critical interval for any young man, and considering what it held for him, I don't wonder that he spent the next half-century deflecting the subject. Till his final months alive, my father denied his participation in one of the most heroic guerilla actions of the European conflict.

* * *

The battle, well-nigh unheard of in the U.S., is known as "the Four Days of Naples." Between the 26th and 30th of September, a spontaneous city-wide uprising accomplished what no other community on the Continent could manage—they threw out an occupying German force. Often the fighting was close-quarter, face to face. Often the citizens, many of them teenage or younger, took to the streets with little more than kitchen implements, and with only one way to get their hands on real weapons: close-quarter, face to face. It was as if the Wehrmacht got the Stalingrad they wanted, erupting under their feet and out of their closets. On the 30th, Colonel Walter Scholl sued for peace, meeting with an ad-hoc civilian leadership to arrange a safe withdrawal.

This capitulation doesn't amount to a rout. The Nazis had a natural next line of defense up at the Volturno, the Crater's northern border. To cross that small river cost thousands of Allied lives, and farther north other meat-grinders awaited, not just Ortona but also Cassino. Still, the Naples resistance helped create this shift in strategy; it changed the campaign.

Not that such big-picture stuff mattered to the guerillas. To them, hatching plans down in the *Sotterreneo* or up in the woods of Capodimonte, the Four Days came only as a last straw, following a hundred more civilized efforts. Among these was a stiff-backed gesture by my troublemaking grandfather. Nonno Giovanni refused to report for his local "labor battalion" and, what's more, refused to go into hiding. The latter move, the second protest, that's what set him apart. Around town, fugitives far outnumbered the people on the crews. Nonno always insisted that, around the Piazza della Borsa, the call for workers turned out just eight able-bodied men. Eight. The number does seem in line with what I've come across in the library—but my best source remains those teenage conversations with my aging namesake. My grandfather's war was part of our Laurel and Hardy meanderings, and in time the other Vicedominis confirmed what Nonno told me. His experience became a family legend, a miracle play in two acts.

By late summer of '43, when the *überfuhren* issued a work order, a shirker needed to disappear. Yet my grandfather kept his usual rounds, and besides that, the troops who came to the P.O. knew about his Communist sympathies. Nonno figured the men with the guns must've heard this from one of his colleagues, *farsi arrangiarsi*, "arranging oneself." During our walks, c. 1970, he kept the explanation matter-of-fact: someone in the office must've ratted out Vicedomini in exchange for avoiding the roundup himself. Going on 30 years later, the old man shared this with a withered smile, nothing worse, and for my own part, still more years later, I've got a sense of how he'd come to terms. Older now than he was then, I realize Nonno must've known the hard choices that faced his betrayer. More than that, look what the "victim" had come to! Look at the happy grandfather, idling away his *riposo* in a breezy and well-kept neighborhood, alongside a young relation whose biggest challenge seemed to be finding a presentable set of clothes. Why not share a scary story out of that corpse-ridden late summer?

Vicedomini was made an example of. The *Tedeschi* yanked off his shoes and roughhoused him into a truck packed with others. All my grandfather could recall of the ride was that the men with him were office types, many still wearing a tie, though no one appeared to have shoes. The lorry pulled up near the train station, some lot knocked open by the bombing. Here other trucks were unloading. Here the soldiers carried machine guns. You saw onlookers too, a crowd beyond the guns, though the lot's only feature was a single standing wall.

I've seen such a wall, preserved as a memorial up in the Vomero. It's all that's left of another Mussolini project, a neighborhood stadium. Across one stretch, at stomach height for this American, there ran a black and green roughage, the back of a toad. The stone has weathered so much, I couldn't make out individual holes.

Nonno's downtown lot was hell on the feet, filthy and littered. The men couldn't keep still, forever finding something to touch: a crucifix, a locket, that workday tie. One or two checked the knot of the tie, and one or two took the hand of the next man over. Nonno didn't recall anyone approaching the guards or raising a complaint—"everything happened so fast"—but he was sure he'd heard snatches of prayer. A song too, one of the city's love songs, though he couldn't say where it came from, the crowd off the truck or the crowd beyond the guns. Myself, spellbound, I wondered if it wasn't himself he heard. His own vapor, brimming at the mouth.

Along the wall, each group was hauled away as soon as it went down.

My grandfather recalled getting busy with his wedding ring. A simple band, this was passed on to me, and for my second wife the gold bears a fresh inscription, but on that day the original owner kept working it, twisting it, either singing or praying or silent, and then out of nowhere came a change of orders. Was it business as usual, *arrangiarsi*? The doctor, the patient, our generous God? A miracle, in any case, like the one that turned up later in my reading, when Pierre Bezukhov finds himself in line for execution in Moscow. Abruptly and without explanation, the

French call off the firing squad. In *War & Peace*, it's one of the defining twists of fate; for my grandfather it was his first, that otherworldly September.

He and the others still standing were shuttled over to the *Stazione*, a loading dock. Word was, north. Some sort of farm or factory.

The reminiscence hardly took up all my time with Nonno, back during my own interval between 17 and 19. He wouldn't have gone through it more than once, and I was too stunned for follow-up. Still, I don't doubt I've got the details right. It's not as if they're easy to forget, and I've found corroboration. Among my earliest Naples reading was *I Mammà e Papà*, a war novel by Hans Ruesch. Yet another writer who developed an attachment, Ruesch spent much of his later life in Naples, even after he found success in Hollywood. In his novel, *Mammà e Papà* is street code for Military Police, and there's a likely explanation for why the firing squad quit when it did. MPs of the Reich followed a strict formula, when it came to summary execution. If one of the Wehrmacht suffered a suspicious death, they'd take ten civilians. From the English Channel to the Ural Mountains, it was ten for one, and no more.

Likewise convincing was the old man's ease with his recollections. He even threw in pantomime, cocking his arms as if to cradle a machine gun, pointing it my way. The act gave me a shiver, but not Nonno. He'd had too much practice for that, just as my father had, with his small selection of war stories. As I compare what the two men told me, in fact, I can spot the critical difference. My grandfather got repeated tours of his former inferno, whereas my father severed himself from those hardships irreparably, and at a young age. Granted, he got his visits, but none so long and meditative as to close the wounds. Nonno however had thirty years to reconcile with the horror, fingering its tokens: a desk in the Post Office, a bullet-scabbed wall downtown. As the decades lopped over, he saw the furniture replaced and the ruins bulldozed. And he got to talk, to go on talking, until he heard his story likewise transformed.

By the end of the 1960s, when one of the other relatives spoke of Nonno's hard times in September '43, they didn't end with him locked in a cattle car and headed north. They went on to the man's second miracle. This followed soon after the first, a matter of days, before the train left occupied Italy. Some Allied bomber found its target, hitting the Brenner Pass supply lines; at the base of the Alps, the transport was thrown off the rails. The prisoners broke free, and Nonno got the boots he needed off the body of a dead soldier.

"And now look at your *jacket*," he told me, one afternoon in the Vomero.

In another bit of street theater, he tugged on one weathered lapel. Second- or third-hand, big enough to hide a sawed-off shotgun, my coat had leather so distressed you thought of drift-wood. All wrong for summer, to boot. But I'd picked it up in a shop off the Brooklyn docks. While my father was checking a shipment, I'd paid for it like a young tough who earned his own folding money. Slipping the thing on, I entered my Dream Self.

"A piece of junk like this," my grandfather went on, "you *must've* got it from a dead soldier."

He was spry, light at heart, a lucky man. Christmas '43 had been the worst of his life, but he'd made it to Easter with the ones he wanted. After that he'd returned so often to the nightmare, he'd worn it smooth as an old saint's medallion. Come the end of the '60s, well, what good was his long-ago *terribilità* if it didn't help him connect with this Grandson From Another Planet? For all I know, the afternoon he told me how he'd twice cheated death, he also trotted out the line he used whenever we passed a pretty girl.

Come si soffre …

* * *

There's a movie of the Four Days, a late stab at *neo-realismo* by Nanni Loy. Wouldn't you know it, the film premiered while my family lived in town: the same year as Pop sat me down, teaching me the facts of life and when to deny them. *Le Quattro Giornate di Napoli* must've been that winter's Cinema Event, though unfortunately the movie doesn't rise to its occasion; *Battle of Algiers* delivers a more fitting dread. But that's the critic talking, the grownup; at the time, I couldn't tear my eyes away. In the movie the turning point comes after a couple of German tanks smash through a makeshift barricade. Whoever set the scene must've studied photos from the conflict, and they put together a convincing barricade, with an overturned bus, a taxi stripped of its doors, and mattresses, sticks of furniture, chunks of fallen concrete. Less plausible is the boy who takes it upon himself to turn back the Panzers. His eyelashes flutter, silky, and his pout's camera-ready. Still, the kid's case sticks close to that of Gennarino Capuozzo, 11 years old. The child was cut down by a tank gunner on September 29th, when there was still no telling whether the uprising might succeed. To see the boy fall incensed the other guerillas, and they took out the tanks with Molotov cocktails.

Myself, watching, I had an obvious question. Afterwards, I believe there was a family dinner, so I had to wait till it was just the Italian-Americans.

Pop answered in plain English: "I had nothing to do with that."

My mother, I remember, nodded. Could we have been in the car, at this point?

"My brother and I," Pop said, "we hid out in the hills."

"Out in the country," Mom said. "Not that it was any easier out there."

"It wasn't easy anywhere."

And for 40 years, that was Pop's Four Days. Times were terrible and he'd made himself scarce. Beyond that, what did a comfy young American need to know? *The war,* eh. The way he growled came back to me when I first encountered "the horror" of Conrad's Kurtz. Granted, during my teens I heard a bit more, the YA version, *Vicedomini & the Ghostly Hallows*. Enzo and Gigi had help from some nuns, went the story. The sisters fed them and hid them down in the crypt.

To get the whole truth had to wait till I got back to Naples. Only in my 40s, for starters, did I grasp what my parents meant by "out in the country." I think I got it the first night I spent on the *periferia*, off the commuter line in Soccavo. Call it freshman re-orientation: I saw how my uncle's neighborhood, half a century earlier, could've been the setting for the story of the rations thief and the gun-toting Brit.

It took a good deal more rattling around to discover the scrublands where Pop and Gigi found their Sisters of Mercy. Out in the area known as Camaldoli, so much of the land remained undeveloped, I'd never have seen it if the '90s renewal hadn't included extending the Metro. Bassolino, with or without Camorra collusion, made sure the subway system reached all the outer boroughs. Even so, the heights of Camaldoli still contain wide swatches of former orchard and garden. Its clusters of housing, often converted farm buildings, run as cheap as any in the greater metro—which is what attracted my aunt, during those same 1990s. The oldest of my father's generation, she'd lasted too long for her schoolteacher's pension. Another teacher in the family, yes: our knack for churchwork has found expression, lately, in the schoolroom. My aunt, in her final decade, found a Camaldoli cottage.

My first Sunday out that way, I discovered that to sit through a handful of stops on the Metro was just the beginning. The real workout came after I emerged from the station. Not that my guide was any sort of athlete. At the stop I was met by my aunt's son, a man not much younger than I but, into his 30s, his 40s, living like a teenager between summer jobs. He was the *mammone* among the Vicedominis, a textbook case. If he left the house, it was generally for a coffee with another aging school-chum. As for the job search, eh … Anyway, this was Sunday, and outside the Metro, the two of us had to climb one of those long *periferia* doglegs. Whenever someone drove past, we were squeezed against the parked cars. Someone might've paved the old sheep-path, but they hadn't bothered with a sidewalk.

Yet one side of the road could've easily handled a sidewalk. Beyond the parked cars spread an enormous green space, largely unmaintained. It could've been a farm property gone to seed, but what farm would have such thick stucco walls? Spiked up top? The spikes had rusted some time ago, and the stone itself was sketched with lichen. Also my cousin and I passed two or three gates along the way, their bars likewise rusted but their chains and padlocks new and clean enough to catch the sun. Beyond, within, I caught glimpses of orchard and berry patch, thick with bramble and deadfall. They might've gone untended since 1943. Yet though the landscaping would require an army, the hilltop had sweet potential. Camaldoli could offer one of the loveliest parks of southern Italy, not even an hour outside city center. Yet when I raised the question, my cousin barely summoned the energy to swat it away. *Tutta privata*, he said.

Exhaling a cloud of Marlboro smoke (Mama didn't allow it in the house), he pointed to the crest on one gate. A nuns' order.

The convent wasn't the only one I heard of, during those visits to my aunt. Two or three of the communities remain active, the most spectacular a monastery, with a chapel and gardens occasionally open to the public. But on those heights, even the unstaffed compounds remain under lock and key. Whatever holy order claims the property maintains control, somehow, and naturally the site's founders, whether men or women, tended to set up near others. A cluster of such places could share resources, at a safe distance from the Cities of the Plain.

Then came the days of the Wehrmacht MPs and, among the locals, vengeful rumblings in gutter dialect. Enzo and Gigi headed for the hills.

* * *

This could only mean Camaldoli. When my aunt first moved, she and her son had chickens and rabbits for neighbors, across a cracked alleyway. One of those summers I was able to slip my daughter over for a visit, and I remember how she enjoyed the chickens. Also Vera was fascinated by the apiary, nothing like the white boxes back in Oregon, rather conical and gray, a bird's nest. As it happened, unfortunately, the beekeepers didn't stay for long. An investor spread some money around and, in direct violation of local zoning, a Fiat lot went up. Still, to my aunt's dying day she had camellias and a miniature lemon tree. *Abbondanza* like that, everywhere across these hills, must've entranced the teenage refugees of '43. Even in wartime, late September is harvest season. Those walls couldn't keep out a pair of hungry boys, one of them a supple surfer boy.

My father, for all his evasions, always admitted that he and Gigi had to scrounge. "Half an apple," he'd say, "that was it for a whole day."

He never got into how he and his brother made it so far, but I've noticed that the area remains a place to lay low. Often the police have to clear out squats of *clandestini*. The news reports usually include a photo, a cluster of scrawny souls, their ragged clothes unchanged in days, and when I see such a shot now I think back to the *Ebrei* like Flavio Gioia. Naples still has its synagogue, from the mid-19th-century. At the end the Holocaust, somehow, it claimed a congregation in the hundreds. Often, as with Pop and Gigi, it was clergy who'd provided protection.

During the Four Days, the countryside also served as marshalling grounds for the Resistance. Closer in than Camaldoli lies the park at Capodimonte, the former Borbon playground, and its lush growth is riddled with caves. Legend has it that a couple of these lead to tunnels that can take a person down under the city's streets. Spelunkers can't confirm the claim, not yet at least, but during the uprising a number of ambushes did erupt from underground. Half a century later, as I first picked my way through *Napoli Sotterraneo*, I spotted further mole-runs, veering off into the blackness.

Meantime, even the pretty young Anna couldn't much improve the broken remnants of the bomb shelters. Looters had long since made off with the gold-plate. The prayerful graffiti, the Madonna and her radiant cowl, was hashed by water stains and the leavings of insects. Yet half a century earlier, the folks on their knees before the image could've included young Enzo and Gigi. It bears repeating that, after the *Sotterraneo* reopened in the '90s, Pop's younger brother wanted no part of the tours. To Enzo, I'd guess, the sub-cellars must've felt even worse. At 18, he'd all at once become the man of the house; their father had been hauled off. Now was he taking his loved ones back to living in caves?

Maybe not, but they did lose their house. The Vicedominis endured something of a wartime odyssey, living out of satchels and sleeping in corners. In this they had plenty of company, yet the story was another that came to light only after years of poking around. Before I learned even the outlines, Pop had succumbed to his heart attacks and Gigi to his liver cancer. Only their sister remained, and she was doing poorly, in the hospital. After she shared the recollection, I never again saw her alive. I never got back to Camaldoli. What felled the woman was the same bad circulation as hobbled Pop; her legs went first. Her burdens, however, weren't the same. She hadn't suffered the Four Days the way her brothers did, a difference I'd understood since my first few visits as a grownup.

I'll call this woman Bianca. She was the whitest of the siblings, certainly, with faded-carrot hair and robin's-egg eyes, and for her the worst of the family's experience got a whitewash. A *donna d'antica*, a woman of the old ways—which isn't to say Bianca lacked a spine. She taught public school for 30 years. In retirement, after the Fiat dealership sprang up, she scoffed at the notion of going to the authorities. If anyone went to the *law*, she told me, she and her son would have to pack their bags. Still, I'm sure she knew nothing of how the *malavita* had muscled in on her nephews. Years earlier, she hadn't been consulted before her husband took a certain horny young American downtown, steering the kid to a girl in a doorway. By the time I sat down beside Bianca's hospital bed, the last thing I expected was to close another gap in my father's story.

She'd spoken previously of the war. Voice quavering, sentences half-finished, Bianca traced the same family fractures as Pop and Nonno had sketched:

"*Papà*, they took him, a train north …

"Enzo and Gigi, they ran off … in the country, there were nuns …"

The hospital chairs might be plastic and stackable, but mine triggered long thoughts. Bianca would soon die in a bed like this. If someone neglected to draw her curtains, she could go into the final crisis in front of strangers. A doctor did stop in, but only briefly, and the orderly was likewise perfunctory. The man was African, I noticed, a rare case. Otherwise, the place could've been a wartime infirmary. The crucifix on one wall was nothing special, and the room had an earthy pungency, terracotta and wood. Bianca too made the connection, murmuring that the setup reminded her of the bomb shelters.

Mellowed by blood-thinner and pain meds, her tone had almost a playfulness, something like her father's, my grandfather's. Sitting so close, gauging her smile, I had half a notion that, like Pop, my aunt had been holding back. She was sharing another kind of old trouble, something else I'd never heard of. She and her brothers had fled the house in which they'd grown up. Their mother had again proven herself the true *donna di antica*, appealing to a relative up the city slopes. As the streets around their home began to erupt with gunfire, the Vicedominis found what seemed like sanctuary. "They had room for us …"

But, excuse me. Did she mean just the immediate family? Her mother and herself, plus the two boys?

"*Si, Giova'*: my mother and I shared a bed…"

But not the grandparents, the Carro family. They're still on the Piazza della Borsa, and in the closet they're hiding the old violin player …

"*Professore* Gioia was kept safe till the end of the war."

The old woman lost her smile, her sallow face shrinking. By this time I was taking notes, but I didn't want to press, to disrupt her recollection. She'd left the downtown behind, but she'd begun to frown.

"The evening the planes came," Bianca told me. "everyone looked to Enzo."

I never did pin down just what sort of "cover" my father found for the family. After all, they'd moved up here to get out of the bombing lanes. Where could they take shelter, then? A funicolare overpass, the vaulted portico of a church? I never got it—nor just what Enzo's sister discovered she'd left behind.

A token, a totem, a keepsake: Bianca kept returning to the expression '*na cosa*, a thing, and I don't have a better word. I do know that, 60 years after the air raid, while she shuttled between Camaldoli and the hospital district, she always brought along some brooch or necklace. The jewels weren't much, nothing to interest some quick-fingered type trolling the wards. Bianca never strayed far from the usual icons, Church stuff or older; one cameo bore Hera and the pomegranate. Could it have been something so ordinary as that, back when she was a homeless teenager, another Displaced Person? Could such a bauble have seemed essential, under the rumble of the B-17s? "A thing:" she'd started wailing for it, alongside the new man of the family.

Not many photos remain, from those days, but in all of them it's obvious that Pop was a whippet.

"Enzo, he ran back inside …," Bianca said. "But then, the bombs …"

As for what she saw as the dust cleared, I've some idea. I've seen pictures, though of course not in family scrapbooks. In the history books, rather, whether I was reading about Richmond, 1865, or Fallujah, 2003, I never lacked for photos of the rubble. For homes cracked open and ruined.

"It was brutal ... bits and pieces ... then we heard. *Siamo vivi!*"

We're alive: "we," plural. I double-checked, there at my aunt's deathbed. She believed her brother meant someone else in the building, in some other remaining fraction of a room, and no doubt there was another survivor. The histories all mention similar miracles. Still, I hear more in my father's cry. The way I got the story, I got the feeling, or as close to it as I could come, as one of those who Enzo spent half a century protecting. I experienced first the terror and prayer, and then the utter opposite, joy just for starters, at that voice from above. In Bianca the memory triggered an amazing smile, girlish, as if for moment she was a teenager again, out for Easter: *We're alive*.

* * *

For Bianca's older brother, however, the transcendent moment swiftly collapsed. An understudy for the Paterfamilias, he found the role overwhelming. That's the feeling, or the vacuum, to which I drew closer with every visit. A coddled American who'd never seen real violence, with every visit I experienced more of the damage done a child of war, in a country far less powerful. As I spiraled through investigation, meditation, and best guess, the inferno of late '43 came to demand more and more effort. To know young Enzo's war came to seem the catalytic agent in knowing myself.

My discoveries also kicked up a paradox. Despite his many coverups, my father proved in fact an able *assistente*. The few difficult memories he'd shared revealed telling details once I was back in his hometown. The family he'd left behind were my most useful informants, whether as a teenager strolling the Vomero or a man of middle age hiking up *Corso Camaldoli*. Then too, I'd been raised with a sense of how their minds worked. Really, if I were on a dig, could I have asked for better tools? What's the *problem*, really? One answer, one element that drove my digging, that lent it something like frenzy, was that the work didn't just concern my father, but also the father business generally. For instance there's the primary obligation, for a Pop: to be there for the family. Yet as my daughter reached middle school, and her own home took a bomb hit, I began—let's put this harshly—to gallivant off for weeks at a time.

As I say, insofar as this book has a plot, it ends ten years back. At that point I'd been shepherded safely from Christmas to Easter, or the midlife equivalent. Yet just as my father had his brother along, throughout his few most difficult days alive, my own far more leisurely transition had a constant companion: my growing child. By the time "V" reached her 20s, she'd shared in all my Neapolitan challenges, one way or another. Whether I stretched out on the burning Paestum sands or stood up on the bone-chilling viewpoint in the Vomero, I could never define my own best outcome without considering its impact on this young person overseas. In other words, assailed by the worries of a father, as a son I put still more elbow grease into my digging for answers.

My need to know surged through me so desperately that, from where I sit now, it appears to have prompted my father to open up. During his last months alive, when I told him I'd been out to the Naples cemetery, he told me about his visit to the place—carrying a baby's corpse. Not his worst chore as a teenage head-of-household, but a grim balancing act. The poor thing was so small it fit in a box under young Enzo's arm, all the way to the end of the line on one of the only trolleys still in service. To hear Pop talk, the necropolis and its lone clergyman-caretaker had a greater impact on him than his miserable cargo. The child was only another statistic, what with malnourishment and disease on top of the heavy ordnance. Most likely it came from the mother's side of the family, the side with rank. My father recalled he had to wear a tie and deliver the shoebox, by then faintly stinking, into the hands of the priest. Just to find a *Frate* on duty, too, struck him as a miracle. I must say, I didn't have any such luck when I got out there. The cemetery lies to the airport side of Secondigliano, the back of beyond in Pop's day. It suggests a rolling plain of ritual objects, outsize and freestanding, and amid the bas-relief and chiseled names, visitors have no trouble getting their tactile connection. I bought a flower and on the card wrote my name and my child's, intending a kind of connection. But though a number of the Vicedominis lie there, I never could locate them. Densely populated city, densely populated cemetery, and I never found some sort of caretaker, either with or without a collar. Come the 21st century, they took days off.

For my father, the encounter still astonished him, decades later: *A priest, imagine. He can hardly keep body and soul together but he's there with a rosary ...*

The closer Pop came to combat, the more it stripped him of what he'd counted on. If he were a "temple," if Richard Selzer was right, he was picked clean of *ogetti*. Few scraps remained by the time he took off with Gigi, splitting up the family in order to save it. And in Camaldoli, as in the cemetery, he must've been the one to find the church people. Out there on the farther curve of the Naples crescent, he and his brother could've gone on sleeping rough and splitting an apple a day, right on into October. Yet before long they sat in a convent kitchen, enjoying hot mushroom soup. Regarding the food, from the first he shared the story, Pop was specific: a soup meaty with fungus and tangy with local garlic and parsley. He recalled a sort of seed-bread, something he wouldn't have believed possible if it weren't so chewy. Yet only he could've made this happen, the older brother. No doubt they'd both gone a long time without a bath, let alone a change of clothes, and it must've been the boys who'd spotted the sisters, not the other way around. Another of Pop's favorite Americanisms comes to mind: spotted them a mile off.

Then too, these women could've posed a threat. Churches everywhere were reduced to skeleton crews, and you never knew what arrangements the keepers of the faith had struck with the Occupiers. Also Enzo and Gigi would've noticed their accent. Any Neapolitan with half a brain had picked up some German, and the boys would've overheard something, a conversation, a prayer. The nuns' order, it turned out, was based in Vienna. An odd detail—what difference did it make?—but my father always insisted on it, part of the story. They came from Austria and only a stubborn half-dozen remained.

Considering what I've learned of the episode since, it's clear that Pop and Gigi weren't the first to approach. There must've been rumors of handouts, and my father must've had his crucifix. One way or another he won the sisters' trust, just as earlier, from a distance, they'd won his. The slash-&-burn of every war yields a few small glimmers of humanity, and this one, I wouldn't be a bit surprised, may have received a boost from my father's looks. What a hottie, as my daughter said. Still, what mattered more to the nuns, I imagine, were the college boy's turns of phrase, and beyond that they must've sensed his receptiveness to the Spirit, the Divine, so resonant in the Vicedominis. We'd spent generations as helpers of the Lord, and what took place that evening out in the hills was Gospel chapter and verse. If to say so smacks of the sentimental, *The Sound of Music*, well, why not? Broadway, I mean, that's *my* hometown. Not to mention that the Von Trapps were Austrian. But of course there's a more pertinent connection to the best of Christianity; the younger brother, it bears repeating, grew up to tell me that his entire life's journey had been blessed. Sixty years after the nights and days in Camaldoli, Gigi assured me that Padre Pio had revealed Heaven's goodwill.

With or without singing nuns, at this point the story's upbeat. The boys got their soup, bread, and bath. The nuns most likely set them some task, some men's work, and the guests would've recited, at least, the Our Father. The comfort the brothers took in this, the relief—truly, my life has no equivalent. I did experience a cross-generational synchronicity, though, an overlap in which Gigi or Marcaurelio might see God's hand. I did learn of the 9/11 attacks in a Naples convent.

* * *

September, again. One of the sisters pulled me into her office. On a pint-sized black-&-white, the antenna began to suggest the Twin Towers. Didn't they look likewise easy to snap, those Towers? The devastation unfolded before us, gathering in the small room, now three, now eight. Often the only sound, with the TV on mute during work hours, was a woman praying the rosary.

This was in Santa Chiara, Clarisse, still staffed by members of the order if no longer a convent. The church stands along Spaccanapoli, a landmark really, in its way as prominent as the Towers. Out back, you might almost be in Camaldoli. The garden cloister, bordered by cooling galleries, startles a newcomer with how it subdues the roar and hustle of downtown. All at once you're in the Peaceable Kingdom, the greenery almost bonsai, the majolica everywhere and painted with bucolic 18th-century scenes. I never tire of playing the tour guide, and on that afternoon in '01, I was speaking American English with some visitor. The nun who took my arm may even have heard me say "New York." Together we spent, I don't know, almost an hour with the news. When I had to back away, I did manage to thank the Chiara sister, but only the power of her look, commiserating, penetrating, brought me out of my shock enough to notice she was dark, perhaps Egyptian, perhaps Syrian. She might have been a refugee. And my friends in lower Manhattan, friends and relatives and, for that matter, the whole city? I wound up in the sanctuary, in a pew. Between prayers, I'd lift my eyes to the 14th-century vaults, barren and gray. At one time the church's tall interior had been a show-case, smothered with painted majolica of its own, here Gothic and there Baroque. The ornamentation couldn't survive summer '43, when a blockbuster hit left fires burning out of control for days. Many died, including clergy.

Myself, in '01, I remained lucky. Lucky or blessed, I lost no one in Bin Laden's attacks. Still, that afternoon in a Naples church, in shocked communion with other, older killing rains—it takes me to rest of my father's story.

The nuns might've been Austrian, but they were nothing like on Broadway. They knew about the roundups, the reprisals ten-for-one. They must've had visitors before these two, and they were smart enough to consider the neighbors. You never knew who might need a touch of *arrangiarsi*, wrangling some advantage in exchange for what they'd seen. The only way to be safe was to make the boys disappear, and if that sounds like a horror story, what these women came up with was worthy of Poe. Beneath the altar lay the crypt for former colleagues.

Over in the US, as it happens, I found the same on a Trappist acreage. This was during the divorce, of course; I never got that cabin in the woods, but I did spend a long weekend on retreat in Willamette Valley wine country. My evenings ended in medita-tion, on a rise above the Trappists' graveyard. There, the flesh turns to mulch, to fresh seedbeds, but in Naples, as I say, the afterlife tends to the Baroque. My great-uncle in San Pietro ad Aram, had he served another parish, would have his bones on display. Skulls, in particular, are on display, the most famous array up in the Vomero, keeping watch over downtown. A few convents still have their gallery of the dead, in which the deceased used to perch in their church finery. The corpse-stalls sit empty now, but each has a hole at the center of the seat, and the sisters' graveclothes were tailored with a hole to match. Over time, the bodies drained away; the spectacle was felt to be instructive. More than likely the young Vicedominis got a viewing, too. My father had a recurrent nightmare, in which he was run over by black funeral horses drawing a hearse.

The bad dream struck him, somehow, as something he could share. At breakfast once or twice, he told us, and I recall loving him for that. What a neat thing, a Pop who shared his terrors! And the stuff was so old-school!

Likewise, whenever he told the convent story, he didn't gloss over the way the sisters prepared his and Gigi's beds.

"They cleared out what was in there," he would say, "and put us in instead."

The accommodations alone could've brought on my father's funeral horses, but then came the night's foot-traffic. The Germans arrived, a squad, more soldiers perhaps than nuns. Their search didn't stop at sundown; in the city the fight had gotten serious.

My father never forgot the heavy tread above, boot-steps. He believed he heard the officer in charge, pacing, nervous. "Holy ground," he would say, "It made the *Kommandant* nervous."

I risked a joke: *You and Gigi were turning over in your graves.*

If anyone laughed, it would've been my mother. My father had done some heavy lifting just to reveal this much, and the best I recall, he only reiterated that everyone in Naples knew the consequences. His shrug seemed to add: look at me now, smart guy. If I wanted, I could have mushroom soup every night. And with that his story ended, or seemed to. The *Tedeschi* withdrew, their tread receding down the nave. The sisters, I imagine, redoubled their prayers, and nobody got much sleep. Come morning, the only choice for Enzo and Gigi would've been to head back out into "the country." Their benefactors of course had chores, harvest season, and the brothers knew better than to hang around. They ran off, disappearing into the same story I'd heard since I first saw the movie.

The whole truth perhaps would never have emerged if Enzo's son hadn't become, himself, such a shook-up father. My lurching between Old World and New appears to have jarred the lid off long-ago hardships for both Pop and his siblings. Every year, after all, my Italian grew a bit better and my questions more pointed. Besides, not long after I began to dig in his past, to dig and sift, Pop suffered his first heart attack. Few things will prompt confession like a visit from the Reaper.

After his heart first failed him, as I say, I was the child who could rush to St. Augustine. I could spend an evening alone with Mom, and hear about a night in a Naples hotel, sometime, maybe. The ambulance arrived the following day, and Pop came out wearing a catheter and a face like trash. Like the brown bag you've used too often for lunch. Whatever Paradise the man had enjoyed in America, in the Apple or St. Aug, it'd crumpled, grown greasy, and started to reek.

Soon enough there came another evening. This could've been my next visit, and once more I found him sagging before the TV. He'd been spending a lot of time with *RAI Internazionale*, the soccer especially, but now the set was off. It shook me just to look at him, really. The cushions, molded to his shrunken frame, called to mind a shroud. The head of hair I've inherited, the lush moil we owe to some African or Arabian in the bloodline, lay in limp shreds. As for Naples, at that point he had one trip left.

Then his eyes rose. He asked if I remembered his story about the nuns.

At least I kept it serious: *Must've been a terrible night …*

"But the worst," he cut in, "was the next night."

After dark, returning to the convent church seemed harmless. The countryside was quiet, at this turning point in Pop's war.

But older brother found the church door ajar. "And in there—the worst."

All over the Camaldoli hills, folks could use a favor. As for the *Kommandant*, the night before he'd shown a certain weakness. Now he left all six of the sisters strung up in the rafters.

* * *

The Four Days demanded so much of my father, any comparison with my midlife ups and down seems a travesty. I faced no enemy worse than jet lag, loneliness, or the occasional shortfall at the end of the month. But, again, I'm not just writing about myself; I'm looking over the whole city. Naples as I came to know it, over a double decade, had something in common with young Enzo's. Both were places under siege.

Throughout the '90s and the Aughts, an actual shooting war was never far off. Back during Iraq I, the George Herbert Bush Iraq, some Neapolitan friends and relatives began stocking up on non-perishables. Even Bianca's boy, the *mammone*, filled the shelves with canned goods. I heard gallows humor: *maybe over in America, we'd be laying in boxes of bullets.*

The hostilities never crossed over, no more than did the Libyan upheavals, Khaddafi's fall and the clan wars, twenty years later. But nowadays looms the shadow of fundamentalist jihad, linked to tragedies in Syria and elsewhere. And even with all these threats from abroad, the more serious danger may be gestating within. Up and down the Neapolitan crescent, local ecosystems are strained to the breaking point. The toxic Camorra dumps are just one smear in a far larger mess—though this at least has prompted efforts at cleanup. The waterfront sweep west of Dell'Ovo, the castle that holds the city's egg, was first made swimmable and then pedestrian-only. The whole stretch became a park, in one of the loveliest changes since the end of my own changes; known as the *Lungomare*, the walkway has a view that takes you from Inferno-Vesuvius to Paradiso-Capri. Between the stone breakwaters, maybe ten minutes from a mob brothel, you can forget your troubles with a dip in the *mare morbido*. You can float mindless.

The environmental challenges that face Southern Italy, to be sure, are the same as around the rest of our wounded planet. The summer headlines in *Il Mattino* reflect the global nature of the crisis, lamenting the *calde Africane*, African heat. For contemporary Neapolitans, however, it's not climate change that poses the most visible threat to their way of life, no more than it's another invading army. Rather, throughout my decades of Do-Over, it appeared that the social fabric might come apart. The crowds in the piazzas and *decumani* contended more and more with a new demographic, difficult to know. Everywhere were new *immigrati*.

Some lighter and some darker, all heard themselves dismissed, pejoratively, as the *neri*. The blacks. Some came from the East, as close as Gaza or as far as Bangladesh, but the type uppermost in native Italians' minds, the poster boy, was an African out of "the South."

My first extensive exposure to these new Neapolitans came thanks to an older technology. Back when I was beginning re-entry, wi-fi didn't exist and cellphones were the size of a brick, and so just about every piazza had its International Call Center. Often you found an Internet Café as well. In those, in a city off the tourist circuit, it was rare to come across another American. Rather, as I waited for a hookup, I'd be surrounded by *immigrati*—perhaps, in those days, the older brother of Ibrahim Diop. Space would be tight, and the booth walls cardboard. It required no snooping to ascertain that nine out of ten of my darker fellow-clients came from across the Mediterranean. From Morocco, in particular, the base for the first big wave out of Africa. In the '90s arrivals out of Marrakesh or Rabat filled the Call Centers and helped to found *3 Febbraio* and *'O Pappacé*. According to their spokespeople, *pro bono*, in Naples the Moroccans functioned like village elders.

By the later '90s, though, the US media had quit using "Boat People" to refer to Cubans or Vietnamese. Rather it meant the passengers crammed into some unregulated transport out of Africa's Mediterranean coast, headed for some unwatched cove on Sicily or the boot. By this time, the travelers came from all over the southern continent. My father's home ground might've soaked up a lot of blood in the 1940s, but by century's end, worse stains spread across Africa. Down in the sub-Sahara, the most hopeless case might be Somalia—and for decades, any Somali with a bit of education spoke Italian. Well before Mussolini, entrepreneurs out of Rome or Turin set up businesses around the Horn. Come the early 2000s, in the Mogadishu novels of Nuruddin Farah, a political prisoner trying to sleep off his torture might dream of linguine and *vongole*.

And that's just over by the Indian Ocean. Along the Atlantic, the depredations have ranged from Lord John's Army to the Ebola virus. In Liberia, in Burkina Faso, many a family has some-one wiring money from "the North." The Diops had contracts and housing, while others scrambled month to month, but there's al-ways plenty of work, making life easier for white folks. So vast a cultural shift has generated a considerable library by now, books about immigrants, written by Europeans. These include the chil-dren of immigrants, like the Goncourt prizewinner Marie Ndiaye. Italy has a handful as well, notably Amara Lakhous, an Algerian who's brought off a successful transition. He's a novelist, but what-ever their genre, literary types all over the Continent have been drawn to the struggle of disparate peoples to sit at the same table. A few have even taken on the true outlaws, the *clandestini*, men and women without papers. Such bottom-rung refugees are the central players of Erpenbeck's *Go, Went, Gone*.

The point is, I can't ignore the subject either. Regardless which text I pick up or whether its *immigrati* have their papers in order, it's part of my *Archeology*—as much, surely, as the rules of romance or the burdens of the Camorra.

By the same token, I can't ignore the mortal stakes that un-derlie the literary prizes and academic papers. It's life and death, for many of the *immigrati* in Naples. They've made their cross-ing as part of a slave trade, putting a grim new spin on the term *lavoro nero*, selling their arms, their backs, and the rest of their bodies. Prostitution keeps up its grind, as ever, and the whore-house *bassi* near Nunzia's must be staffed by Ibo and Tuareg girls. A few of them, I realize now, must've guessed they'd fall so low. A few may even have turned their first trick just to get on the boat, and all of them knew it would be hard, making a living up North. Nonetheless they came to the pirates. They risked dysentery, dying of thirst, or getting dumped overboard. What was the choice? A drought-blasted farmland or the lawlessness that follows a dictator's fall? What, except run or die?

* * *

It's the Africans I've known best. The street salesmen lay out mats along all the major thoroughfares. As for the stalls, across the *mercati*, most are still run by whites (in the Forcello, the Camorra maintains its grip), but it never takes long to find a proprietor out of Eritrea or Mauritania. Then come nightfall, you'll see them cruising on foot, pushing cigarette lighters in plastic pastel or key-rings with LEDs. The most successful create the impression they've only dropped by for the party. They grin and chatter, and their get-up strives for color, a *djellaba* in jungle greens or a head-wrap in glittering purple. It's the same trick as sells the *presepe* figures over on San Gregorio Armeno, the bright livery of the Moors. Occasionally, one of these night-trawlers will single me out: *Hey, America, Obama.*

A few others, with more solid legal standing, have joined me for a bite of octopus. Or a *mezza-mezz*, a toke or two, sure. There's one African I'd call a friend, a man with a salaried position at a hotel. To hear him tell it, he's a supervisor, and besides that co-owner of a leather goods stall over by Castel Capuano. A Moroccan, what else? He taught me a thing or two about the city's gathering dark trace—but I can't yet leave behind the rawest among the *immigrati*, the ones without legal standing. I need to talk about my day at a camp.

The site lies outside the Crater, off in the countryside. The facility went up during the last years of my Neapolitan recovery, one of two on the mainland, absorbing the overflow from the island of Lampedusa. The southernmost speck of Italy, that former fisherman's stopover has become synonymous with "refugee"; the island's tent cities have hosted visits from two popes. By now, however, Lampedusa has proven too small. Authorities set the Campania camp in a flatlands, an anomaly. The driving was so easy I started to wonder about the Allied advance in '43. But then fences loomed ahead, tall, a cage blockaded by live-cargo trailers. Everything was gray or brown, topped by razor wire, and swiftly a couple of armed guards came visible. Their weapon was a hunting rifle, with a scope, rather than the semi-automatic we've all come, coldly, to expect. Still, their uniforms featured a belt across the chest, and they kept a German Shepherd on a tight leash. Auschwitz came to mind, yes.

I knew better, to be sure. By this time my reconstruction project was about complete, and I came prepared, with a small grant and a magazine assignment. At the gate all I had to do was unfold the letters from each place. Looking these over was another man in uniform (federal, *carabinieri*), and he also took my passport, but his colleagues with the guns ignored me until I asked to pet their dog. Inside I was assigned a young man with the *Protezione Civile*, affiliated with the Red Cross, and all the staff turned out the same; they wore the armband. One or two had on ties as well, though this was another day of Saharan air. The heat in fact proved useful, as I began my tour. At first, most of the camp-dwellers kept to the shade of their tents.

Perched on their cots, they eyed me from under flaps folded up and back, maximum ventilation. Four cots per tent, it looked like, and I didn't see any bad sagging or rips. The halogens overhead were clamped to sturdy poles, at regular intervals. Two marked the border of a commons, and against one squatted a boy with a soccer ball (rubber, not the real thing). Latrines and showers stood beyond, and my guide explained that the water set aside for washing never got what you'd call "cold," but they had a heater that kicked on once a day.

The infirmary was set up opposite the camp entrance. This tent ran double-wide, and a priest had dropped in for his daily rounds. As he took time with two or three bed cases, I spoke with the doctor on duty. He assured me he wasn't dealing with anything exotic.

"All we see here," he told me, "is the sort of trouble you'd expect. The sort of injuries that come with manual labor. Injuries to the joints, muscle tears ..."

Another tent-combo held the kitchen and serving area. I counted four plastic tables, each a four-seater, and in the cooks' cupboards I saw nothing but non-perishables in stenciled packaging. Still, they featured the Trinity: pasta, sauce, parmesan. Most days, one meal included meat, and insofar as possible the administrators found alternatives to pork. Then while I was asking about fire hazards, there arrived the bread-truck. Country loaves, baked that morning, their smell drew more campers, and I may have heard something about an early lunch shift. I never got that straight. I sidled out of the way of the folks coming in, but made it no farther than a step or two back into the sun.

By then, a good dozen men—all men, rawboned, none looking much past 30—had interpreted the semiotics: a white visitor in glasses, an unseasonable jacket, taking notes on a pad. They got it, and now when my guide made the introductions, he let slip those dangerous words *The New York Times*.

With that I was no longer taking notes. I had to spread my arms, clearing some room. At the edge of the gathering crowd there flitted at least one woman, and this settled me somehow, took me back to basics, asking names and trying out different languages. Like the doctor, I heard nothing I didn't expect. There was Omar and Abdullah, rough French and worse Italian. Omar, though, turned out to have decent English, and what's more he seemed like one of the camp's party boys. He had neck-length dreads and a swaggerer's grin that would, over where they sold the *New York Times*, make people think he was Jamaican. I threw a question back at him, perhaps a defensive mechanism.

"What's that on your feet? In America we call those 'flip-flops.' Flip-flop, understand? And just *look* at the design!"

A punk-rock design, with little black skulls running along bone-white straps. If any of these guys wore different footwear, I didn't see it, and I didn't need Omar to tell me the gear had been issued upon arrival. A donation, a manufacturer's overrun, they could've come from a mob sweatshop.

The kid in the dreads, however, put something extra in his answer. "We love Italy!" he exclaimed. "You smell that bread? Mm-mm. Italy people so *nice!*"

His smile switched to high-beam. "Give us the bread, the shoes and clothes …"

The men kept me surrounded, and I saw that only a few had on jeans or khakis, in either case badly threadbare. Most wore a limp pajama, with drawstring pants and short-sleeved three-button shirts. The color was wheat, or dun, or what the Sahara might look like at twilight. Omar was the exception, topping his loungewear with a silken bomber jacket. Across one side of his chest, a dragon spat fire, the style Chinese, and the *calde Africane* would have to get a lot worse before he'd take the thing off. He knew he had a miracle on his back.

"You want to stay in Italy?" I asked.

"No, I go the Netherlands. I have people Amsterdam."

"And where are you from, exactly?"

I thought I had a system, a set of questions. Reanimating the monster of my high-school French, I checked my sense of where they'd caught the boat over. Libya, to be sure, where rebels were at it tooth and claw with Khaddafi's last loyalists. Omar and these others, however, had no stake in either side. Most had come to Libya as wildcatters, working the oil fields. Omar considered himself Nigerian, he'd heard English all his life, though clearly he wasn't cut out for school.

Still, he had an advantage over the others, and with elbows and hips he kept his place at the front. He stood so near, I could tell that this morning he'd chosen tea, not coffee. I could've been back in some crammed Naples call center. I stuck with the program, asking country of origin and intended destination—taking as many as I could from Christmas to Easter.

After another round of question and scribble, I discovered a chair behind me. Nothing special, molded plastic, set at the base of a pole, but who'd put it there? And when had this crowd started backing me into a pole?

I didn't want a seat. The air felt heavy enough, sweat-soaked. How many were there now? Had I spotted three women towards the back? Each time I took down one guy's information, another handful would clamor for attention. Bracing my heels against the feet of the chair, wondering how much of my unease was about race—that's always in the mix, isn't it?—I found myself bringing up my father. Vincenzo Vicedomini, yes: his emigration and American Dream. I asked Omar for help even as it occurred to me that many of these guys might not understand whatever language my translator liked to use. Perhaps he was working in Arabic? Perhaps three-quarters of the crowd got it? In any case I stuck to simple English, telling a story. I threw in some exaggeration too, some melodrama. Pop would've had no patience for it, and the expression *nothing but the shirt on his back* (I went so far, yes) would've made him laugh. He'd have broken in with some tough-guy patter. Yet here amid the press of refugees, a throng with nothing but the shirts on their backs, Omar too got theatrical. Shaking his dreads, he yanked at his jacket lapel, the side with the dragon.

"And now," I went on, "look at me. I'm his son, and I was able to go to school." A mention of education out of a vestige of conscience. "And, and I'm a writer. I can come back to Italy and I can tell your story …"

Much as the recollection stings, I couldn't have rambled for long. I couldn't have kept up the drivel for more than a minute or so. Soon my friend from *Protezione Civile* was working through the crowd, with him one of the men in a tie. They waved Omar silent and announced that they would set up a tent for interviews. Campers would get the chance to tell me about themselves, one on one. For the moment, everyone—everyone—needed a break.

Early lunch? Late? I never got that straight. I was taxi'd to a hill town that remained decently populated, where we parked outside an arched gateway, flowering up top. An arch you might see in *Condé Nast Traveler*. At the restaurant, I wasn't allowed to leave without trying the *involtini*. These looked like meatballs, but turned out to be tightly wound and thoroughly cooked strips of horse or donkey. A local delicacy, I learned, going back to the era of the Moors. In those days beef was rare, and if a dignitary came visiting, some sheik with his retinue, you certainly couldn't set out pork.

* * *

The Q & A following lunch prompted a different sort of shame. I spared my interview subjects more hooey about my father the refugee, but I couldn't prevent them from grasping, not far into the conversation, how little I could help. Their faces would go hollow, after even the worst of what they had to tell me led to nothing more than another scribble and nod. The man with the Red Cross armband shared the tent with me, over in a corner by the fan, paging through a clipboard and keeping an eye on the time. Campers got 20 minutes each, and the half-dozen who ducked in under the flap seemed to have been selected for their command of English. Omar wasn't among them, but then he'd already had his interview. In any case I never had trouble getting the details. At one point we were interrupted by some ruckus in the camp, a squall of shouts that had my companion ducking briefly out.

Even while the man was gone, however, I got every single sorry detail. One young man spoke better Italian, but then again, who needs a translation for a gun-barrel finger at the side of the head? The runaway had been forced to cough up a second fare, halfway across the Mediterranean. Another man, a bit older, pulled up a pajama pants leg to reveal a foot-long scar, the slime-trail of a slug. There'd been a fire on his rig, he explained, and afterwards, while he lay healing, or half-healing, the boss took off with his wages. Every one of my visitors got agitated at some point, slamming back or rocking forward, their chair's plastic feet kicking up the ground's dust. A kid not yet twenty (I was taking down ages) brandished one heavy-knuckled fist, and at that the other white man in the room lowered his clipboard. *Eh, Abdullah …*

But the boy faltered soon enough, his aggravation draining away as I sat there spooling out words, words, words.

"I'll tell your story," I'd say. "I'll tell the truth, over in America."

Even a teenager could interpret the semiotics. Abdullah, once he relaxed his hands, could probably have predicted the email from my editor. Polite but brisk, the woman declared she'd had no use for over five thousand words about "people coming from nowhere and headed nowhere."

Of course, I could've been more flexible. I could've been more diligent. Setting aside the whole question of talent, I can't help but think I should've placed, at least, a thousand words about my interview with Jennifer.

The last of my subjects, she was the lone woman, 29, out of Ghana. She did without head-cover, and she had a certain prettiness, her cheeks full and flushed—aglow with the hormones of pregnancy at mid-term. What's more, unlike Omar, she'd completed her country's British-style curriculum. She never had to resort to gestures, though when she got upset she'd wring her hands. "I just wish I could find out what's happened," she'd say, and wring her hands. She worried about her husband, another wildcatter with a contract in Libya. Farther south, in Accra,

Jennifer and he had two other children. The family needed a bigger home, and she herself was taking classes in nursing. But the husband was another of those cheated out of his wages, and the suits who ran the outfit, like most of the rich, were Khadaffi men. So Jennifer's husband had thrown in his lot with the rebels. The last she'd heard he'd joined the fight for Misurata—that summer's Stalingrad. Finally she'd left the kids with her mother and made her way towards the war zone.

That she'd wound up here ranked as a greater miracle than Omar's jacket. Once or twice, Jennifer spoke with a swagger to match the man with dreads. She'd made it this far, hadn't she? And she could count on the Italians. The *Protezione Civile* had assured her of a safe birth, attended by both a doula and an obstetrician. Their Red Cross affiliation even allowed correspondence across the battle lines. Still and all, she went on, a well-run hospital and an uncrowded tent city weren't what she'd been looking for, when she'd left Ghana.

"I just wish I could find out something," she said. "I *myself*, you understand? I wish they'd let me go wherever I need to."

Jennifer had submitted a petition concerning her case. She was asking that, after the baby was born, the two of them be set free in order to make their way back across the Mediterranean. She and the baby both needed the father.

As for the risk, she knew all about it. "I know exactly what I'd be getting into," she said. "I know better than any judge in Italy." But she had resources too, she insisted. "We have family there. A big family, and others who'd help too. It's not as if we've got *nothing*. It's not as if we're *nobody*."

Towards the end of our conversation, I stopped taking notes. I realized that what she had to say, like so much else in this part of my Naples story, wasn't anything I'd soon forget. After Jennifer finished, her hands flat on her belly, I had my response ready: *I'll tell the truth* ... Yet I managed, at most, a croak.

A final astonishment, a smile, turning her girlish.

After she left, after I came back to myself, I could only stare at my new friend, him with the red cross up on one short sleeve.

"If you do something for her," he said quietly, "you have to do it for them all."

The camp's office-trailer, on the way out, had the paperwork for donations but no way to take a credit card. I emptied my wallet, and I mean, it never felt so flimsy. Then back outside, I learned about the shouting, earlier. That ruckus while I sat doing interviews—there'd been an escape, I learned.

I was shown the stacked plastic chairs, an improvised stepstool, in one corner of the fence. Above, over the razor wire, there still hung one of the camp blankets, a tough synthetic. Besides that, the staff didn't know much. They believed it was one of those who'd ganged up on me earlier, and I thought of Omar, he was wiry enough. But then, so was just about every man in the place, and meanwhile my guide explained that they couldn't pin down the escapee's name until dinner. At dinner they'd bring out the checklist. By then, the runaway might've reached the town where I'd tried the *involtini*. By tomorrow he could be in Naples, picking up a duffel bag of plastic-ware. The hardest part, really, was right here: scaling the fence and getting to the treeline, a couple minutes' run.

I turned to one of the guards, there at the escape site, working with others to get the blanket off the wire. Seeing my look, he smirked.

"The American thinks I should've used my gun," he said. "Shot the man."

But I didn't know what I was thinking. When I looked through the fence, what did I expect to see, out along the woodsy riot of the horizon?

* * *

My father's ghost, maybe. I wouldn't be surprised if there were something of him left in the Camaldoli scrub, imprinted there by terror and outrage. His gasp at seeing the Austrians overhead, his choked warning to Gigi, these might echo yet across the local evenings. In any case, like Omar once he went over the fence (if it was Omar), the two teenage boys fled for cover. They sought other protectors, others of their kind.

A world falling apart has lately become a staple of Big Entertainment. If it isn't a breakdown in the ecosystem, it's a zombie virus, and either way, staying alive is a job for the lone wolf. The One, the Road Warrior: you find him even in Cormac McCarthy, his end-of-days novel *The Road*. The text achieves poetry, perhaps—but it ignores society. Starving survivors too would forge allegiances. They'd create tribes and, given decent luck, in time they'd get back to *homo urbanus*. Doesn't Naples itself stand as a dusty and redolent proof of the deep human need for community? So too, when my father confronted the apocalypse, he and his brother sought strength in numbers. They joined the guerillas.

This part of his past my father kept hidden the longest, and even now I have only a pin or two holding the traces in place. One of those, what's more, first turned up thanks to someone else. My sister Amy stumbled across the detail, around the turn of the latest century, when Uncle Gigi took her and her boys on a walk through the *centro*. My sister recalls they were by "that nice convent garden, off Spaccanapoli." So, Santa Chiara, and there my uncle pointed out where he and Enzo had helped spring an ambush.

The brothers had joined the fight, fully armed. As Gigi put it to me: "We jumped out and shot as many Germans as we could."

The conversation took a couple of years to loop round to me. After I'd heard it from Amy, with my uncle I'd needed to find the right moment.

"You went for the officers first," he went on. "Or the SS, in black."

With another sunny smile, the old man worked up a bit of mime, a rifleman's aim-and-fire.

"We picked off a few of those, before the Germans left. The black uniforms, I remember. I remember—but not your father."

By this time, when I corroborated Amy's story about Gigi's story about Pop, it was too late for my father to have a say. Still, I'll take my uncle at his word. He and his older brother must've reminisced, during one of the emigrant's final visits, and so discovered that Enzo had long since banished the worst of the Four Days from his mind. Besides, I'm one American who doesn't require some local to point out the best place for getting the drop on the *Tedeschi*. Even I know the cross-street that hooks around the Santa Chiara bell tower. I'd seen the softening pockmarks left by the gunfire, too, thanks to the hipster Franciscan Henry. At the juncture with Spaccanapoli this street is wide, almost another piazza, and along its church side rises a high, blind wall, to protect the brides of Christ. From there, though, the way narrows sharply, in irregular increments, and it drops as well, descending with sudden steepness towards the water. Along the way, opposite the wall, a couple of narrow *vicoli* intersect. Even an SS man wouldn't know what hit him.

"With your father," Gigi told me, "I went back to stand at the very corner. The very corner! Still he didn't remember."

I nodded slowly, getting the larger picture. My father and uncle—schoolboys, church boys—had made themselves over as *scugnizzi*. To them the word was an insult, and not a little frightening, as it is for the women of Ferrante. *Scugnizzi* were mob material, kids with knives like Gennaro Caldore. In the States you might call them gangbangers. But when it came to turf war, they were veterans.

So Gigi and Enzo went from the nuns to the thugs. Neither man said a word about their gang initiation, but I doubt there was much to tell. Even in America, a boy has got to make it through middle school. Myself, as a pre-adolescent in Naples, I mixed it up with a local kid. This was up in the Vomero, the good neighborhood, and close by the war memorial. Neither history nor demographics, however, meant anything to a boy looking to make a rep. As soon as he detected my accent, he'd seen his chance: beat up an American, earn some street cred. In no time the two of us were squaring off between parked cars. What followed was inconclusive; the old woman on the block stepped in, screeching. Still, I imagine my opponent did better every time he told the story. For me, it's a story about the city, where you'll still find *scugnizzi* ready to rumble, the same in this century as the last. I've seen them erupt in a shoving match at the door of a commuter train; just as the car pulls away, they'll kick off a couple of *neri*.

In my father's case, no doubt push came to shove. It was up to the older brother, and he muscled their way in, and after that the crew kept him and Gigi safe for at least two of the Four Days. At times they may've been part of some coordinated military action. The ambush off Spaccanapoli sounds like something that had a chain of command. By and large, though, they were feral children with guns, lurking in the fog of war.

* * *

Yet when my father stood by the bell tower and couldn't recall, after the decades had lopped over and heaped up—wasn't he showing integrity? Sticking with his sense of what mattered? If you asked him, the shot-up remains along the convent wall were best hauled away and forgotten. He's far from the only one to prefer things that way; I think of the poet Wislawa Szymborska, her classic from about 1990, "The End and the Beginning":

> *After every war, someone has to clean up ...*
> *Someone has to push the rubble*
> *to the side of the road,*
> *so the corpse-filled wagons*
> *can pass.*

In the end, the old battlefield invites a loafer:

someone must be stretched out
blade of grass in his mouth
gazing at the clouds.

Szymborska might be thinking of Whitman, but for me that dreamer in the grass is my father, searching the clouds for his route from Christmas to Easter. The journey after all occupied his entire adult life, whereas the worst of his war, vicious though it was, lasted just a few months and ended before he turned 20. Better to put it behind him. Better to leave any deeper analysis to the people who made their living talking. That would be me, and naturally I think of a problem more recently diagnosed, post-traumatic stress disorder. But PTSD has all sorts of treatments, from support animals to anti-depressants, and I can't see anything wrong with the therapy Gigi chose. Pop's brother worked through his trauma the same way their father did. Like Nonno, the stay-at-home son had no choice but to revisit the worst. Well into the '50s, Gigi must've stumbled across bomb wreckage and bullet holes. Both sorts of damage showed on his former *palazzo* downtown; the piazza had been renamed, but the building stood empty, uninhabitable.

Later, my Nonno and uncle both saw the town take a different sort of hit, *Il Boom*. A lot of the money went to the Camorra, but among the better buildings were Nonno's in the Vomero and Gigi's in Soccavo. The urban renewal even included a couple of monuments to the Four Days. Neither sculpture, sad to say, rises to its occasion. The freestanding stone off the *Lungomare* suggests some Tijuana knockoff of Maya hieroglyphs, and there's even less to admire about the iron doohickey along Via Toledo. Still, veterans find healing in such *ogetti votivi*. The aging grunts of Vietnam still come to DC and stand at Maya Lin's wall, fingering its names.

My uncle, in fact, took part in the city's initial efforts at rebuilding. This was after the British and Americans arrived, the same time as my father started to work for the OSS. The older brother's job, I notice, required him to keep secrets, while the younger found more ordinary employment. Gigi worked with pick and shovel, hod and trowel. The new occupiers needed to repair what the old ones had trashed, and once again, most of the manpower was local. As for working conditions, those come in for a lot of invective from Curzio Malaparte and John Horne Burns; both their novels highlight the callousness of Allied command. Still, any sort of paycheck was better than none, plus the workers got lunch.

Or as the Cockney foreman put it: "Don't forget we feed you niggers!"

My uncle remembered the word distinctly, five and six decades later. Gigi even got the accent, his smile nasty for once. He could trot out a whole Tommy Atkins thing: *Get cracking, you lazy darkies.* Like all Neapolitans, he'd swiftly picked up some English. As for the older brother, no doubt he heard the same, and forever afterwards, Pop nursed a grudge against the British. Case in point, the story of the bread thief, the FS man looking to decorate his service record with a dead Neapolitan. And what was that Pop told me about his Dominican partners? *They want no part of these Anglo bastards.*

Mom shared his antipathy, actually. "These British," she'd snort, recalling an anal-retentive desk jockey in the supply chain for the children's camp. She and her Enzo had trouble getting milk for the kids. In Pop's case, though, the hard feelings must've gone back further. Back before the war, he couldn't have missed the clueless snobs who came in every August, filling the waterfront hotels. The yachts out of Southampton or Poole must've moored close by Farouk's, out of Alexandria, and when the King's piano player emerged on deck, no doubt he was dark as a walnut. It's not hard to imagine the looks from the summering Brits. The sneers.

Don't forget—my uncle remembered distinctly—*we feed you niggers!*

Now, the African in the Southern Italian's closet is hardly a secret. Two times it's peeked out recently would be Spike Lee's movie *Do the Right Thing* (a tragedy) and Italo Calvino's story "The Aquatic Uncle" (a comedy). The genetic connection's obvious, and yet it makes no difference to latter-day arrivals from the far side of the Mediterranean. Boat people and legal immigrants alike, upwards of 200,000 a year, they've got little use for the ironies of a filmmaker, a fabulist—or a memoirist. Someone like me doesn't trip the color line.

They're outsiders at first glance, even in Naples, the most mixed-race city in the country. Bologna may be a center for progressive thought, but it has nothing to match the scene across the twin piazzas *del Mercato* and *del Carmine*, both close by the old docks. The markets here have been taken over by buyers and sellers of color. One look, and a Bolognese would fall back on the old slur "everything south of Rome is Africa." Nevertheless, a genuine African knows better. The Italian South has slurs of its own; *Mercato* and *Carmine* are known as "Calcutta." No such insults are flung at the Vicedominis. We're the elite, the suits. A hustler in a T-shirt, we keep him running. Granted, for white folks we're not entirely clueless. Marcaurelio and Nando were quick to sympathize when I spoke of the refugee camp, especially when I got to Jennifer and her baby. Neither failed to understand.

"Let's say we give her want she wants," suggested Nando. "She has her baby and then, goodbye. Goodbye and good luck, on the streets of Palermo. What then?"

Marcaurelio went further, imagining the girl and her husband reunited. "She finds him, and he's still in one piece. What then?"

I thought of alternatives, in Ghana or Germany—none of them easy.

"A man with a new mouth to feed," continued my doctor cousin, "he wants work. Why did he leave home in the first place, if not to get somewhere *better*?"

At that he settled into a different tone, starting to sound *Napoli D.O.C.* This ancient city, claimed Marcaurelio, had always found a place for newcomers. Wave after wave, over nearly 3000 years, "this city took them all in. These Africans too, you'll see. They'll make a home."

Talk like that, sometimes salted with a proverb, amounts to a default setting for local whites. Even Bassolino, during our mid-'90s interview, availed himself of the comforts of history. Down the centuries, he assured me, Naples had always found a place for a wayfaring stranger.

The mayor spread his hands in welcome. Our metropolis has such a heart …

With Bassolino, I had better things to talk about. With my cousin, though, a couple of times I've tried to prod. The Africans, I've pointed out, certainly "made a home" in our family. Just look at us, our lips, our kinky hair. Then there's his son, darkening up over summer as if he were the one out of Cairo.

But Marcaurelio lets the bait dangle. He sees no point speculating about some Saracen who raped a great-grandmother. He gets it, the inferno of the melting pot, the ugliness that lurks within the promise of assimilation. He understands every bit as well as his professor cousin. But if you ask him, that only set me up for some teasing in return. I sound, he's told me, as I'm trying to claim not only that I'm Neapolitan—but also that I'm *African*.

"*Caro cugino*," he says, "I know better than you what my father put up with. The Nazis called him a monkey. 'Hey, little monkey!'"

Still, my cousin continues, in no way does that make me a soul brother.

"But, excuse me. These days, what difference does it make? The Nazis were run out of town 50 years ago. 60 years ago. But, excuse me—a *nero* in Naples these days, what does he care?"

* * *

Cousin, I doubt Padre Pio ever preached a truer word. Insofar as I feel like an alien, that's something for long paragraphs of reflection, buttressed with mighty planks of reading. With texts like *Are Italians White?*, not neglecting all 50 pages of Guglielmo's footnotes. But that's not my project. I'm laying my own wrangles over those of greater Naples, seeing how the city illuminates the self—and an honest portrayal must include the *neri* in town. On their journey from Christmas to Easter, the uprooted Africans have a rough go.

The problems extend well beyond any one metro. The entire European Union has signed off on the "Dublin II Protocols," for asylum seekers, which create suffocating tangles of regulation. In Italy, the Inferno of earning citizenship spirals down more than nine levels. Worse, things tend to change with each administration in Rome, so that what loosens under Matteo Renzi, in 2014, tightens a few years later under Matteo Salvini. In response, naturally, protests erupt. Naples usually suffers another garbage bonfire, reeking of toxins and accompanied by hollering knots of dark-skinned laborers. The disruptions get play in *Il Mattino* and, as the years go by, the letters to the editor grow uglier. One will call the *immigrati* "thieves," another "murderers." When editors respond (a feature in Italian papers), their soothing can seem almost worse. I read one that spoke of "Biblical changes," of "responsible controls": sweet nothings full of spit.

An educated Italian, such as that editor, ought instead to point out how little opportunity a person of color has for climbing any sort of career ladder, in this country. Anyone who's gone abroad, even within Europe, can attest to the better means for advancement elsewhere. Both my cousins have mentioned it.

"In Israel," says Nando, "I met Sudanese in uniform. Working in Defense."

"Up in a hospital in London," says Marcaurelio, "the woman in reception comes from Africa, and so do the orderlies. In London, in New York …"

I finished the thought for him: but not in Naples.

Then there's the murder of Ibrahim Diop, the right-wing raving about a "Nigerian Mafia," the full-figure black girls in outline against a bonfire—gloomy images abound, most of them worse than anything my father faced after he swapped homelands. What's more, Pop had help; he had a wife born and raised in New York. Around Naples too, for someone from Cameroon or Zambia, nothing so smoothes the way as marrying an Italian. A spouse whose name ends in a vowel won't, by him- or herself, undo the state's tangles. The right to vote, for instance, doesn't come with the marriage license. Still, more doors open, and when Neapolitans make reassuring noises about Africans "finding their way," often they mean "hooking up."

Which brings me to the case I know best, Leo the Moroccan.

His employment situation enjoys decent long-term prospects. In a good hotel, at your service, there's so much scutwork that a man can make himself indispensable. In time, he could step up to manager. The workers get lunch, too. They get enough to lay aside a few Euro, and with luck and the right connections, earlier arrivals who've learned the ropes, a guy might set up a stall under Castel Capuano. He might start to look like he's gotten somewhere. Back during the last century, over in New York, didn't a lot of transplants follow the same trajectory? My father drew his first US paychecks from a Manhattan YMCA; he worked as custodian and night watchman. Others went to the Garment District or the meatpackers. At the same time, if they hadn't been so lucky as Pop, coming over with a partner, they kept an eye out for the right person. In Leo's case, in Naples, he realized soon enough that the leather stall needed to pull in tourists. It's the white man's got the money. Leo needed to set his goods apart, to add some special decoration. He found a ceramic artist, a woman with a knack for piecework. A woman worldly and attractive, quick on the pickup.

Nunzia. She took Leo as a lover, and they were together three years.

The breakup with Elmo had been (why not throw in Joni Mitchell, Boomer Muse?) dirty for dirty. First the man's tomcatting had driven her out on the prowl herself, and then—in yo' face, baby—he didn't want her anyway. He'd found The One, he declared, and Nunzia spent an angry winter and more on her own, acting out. Still, it won't do to say she took up with the Moroccan on the rebound. That would describe the night with me. Her heartbreak seems in fact part of what kept us just this side of intercourse; the Oregon Cowboy, himself gutshot, couldn't ignore her wounds. But Leo came along later, and from the first he must've struck her as more serious than any cowboy. From the first, he was trying to build a life. Also I've come to believe that the arrangement appealed to her politics. She was making a statement, I believe: her mark amid the city's emerging stipple of dark and light.

I realize how this sounds. People don't select a lover as a social experiment, or not once they're out of college. But Nunzia, even pushing 40 and thwarted by economics, remained an artist. And how many times has an artist's yen to try something new carried over to his or her private life? Should I haul out an example that concerns Naples?

Sure: any excuse to bring up Ingrid Bergman. The actress risked her career to go work in Italy, about the same time as my father traveled the other way. A weepie like *Casablanca* was all well and good, but Bergman was intrigued by the challenge of postwar Neo-Realism, in particular the films of Roberto Rossellini. She stepped away from Hollywood in order to work with him, making two or three movies on a shoestring. The first had a title that couldn't have been more southern, *Stromboli*, and by the time shooting wrapped, the director and star were lovers. Ingrid from Stockholm, Roberto from Rome, neither of them kids, they seized this second chance at romance. Or third, or whatever—I'm putting a shine on the story of course, but I'm not making it up. They got together and gave us Isabella Rossellini (speaking of artists and freethinkers).

In Nunzia's case, I'm convinced she had in mind a private life that would, in its own small way, help the world assume a pleasing shape. She and Leo never set up housekeeping, and this probably wasn't just a matter of the cost, or of her hard feelings over Elmo. Besides that, the Moroccan had people in town, cousins or something. Everyone who knew him knew of his connections, unspoken but longstanding. So too, everyone got that these two were a couple.

* * *

On evenings when Nunzia held court in Piazza Bellini, the party never really got started till Leo came over after his shift at the hotel. He must've had a locker for his bellboy's jacket, but otherwise he'd cross town in work clothes, a starched white shirt with dress slacks and lace-up shoes. A good-looking guy, *certo*, and perhaps ten years younger than Nunzia. She began to use his photo in her compositions, switching from straight ceramics to mixed media, and even after the relationship collapsed, you'd still find a pastiche or two in her studio. The most eye-catching features Leo cradling a white mass across his shoulders, a lump with hair but no hooves and no face. The piece suggests a *presepe* figure, a black shepherd (Leo was dark for a Moroccan), except that his load might be a cocoon, a larva. He might be Abraham with Isaac, keeping the boy under wraps before cutting his throat. The conceptual layering feels right for Nunzia, feels smart, but the picture also puts her man in clingy knee breeches and a skimpy unbuttoned vest. The construct brings out his muscular thighs, the definition of his broad chest.

Not that the *fidanzato* didn't offer other pleasures. Nunzia brought him to art openings, and at these he gave us a new way of seeing. I remember he didn't like a bone-and-feather composition, with "Africa" in the title. He complained the thing wasn't African at all, its range of color skimpy and its imagination meager.

"It's just *primitive*," grumbled Leo. "It's like something a Neanderthal would make. A caveman!"

233

Also he returned the favor, taking his girlfriend places she'd never have gone on her own. In particular she caught a number of concerts, set up by *3 Febbraio* or the like, now featuring drums and horns out of Ethiopia, now juju guitar out of Mali. These were always well outside the *centro*, and once or twice I too dropped in. I knew the juju sound thanks to Marvin Gaye, and with Leo's help I learned more, an entire night's polyrhythmic saunter. I began to notice how such stuff muscled into Italian music, especially rootsy ensembles like Spaccanapoli. Back in the States, Spaccanapoli eventually turned up on the soundtrack to *The Sopranos*, so I heard again the wail and bump of those nights on the *periferia*. And the music hardly exhausted the gifts of these events. There were dancers out of a hieroglyph, goat dishes sopping and redolent, and potent hashish.

When Leo and I shared a spliff, lounging around those scraps of parkland, he wasn't so much the performer as when he showed up in the galleries and cafés. Nunzia's crowd was white, whereas the concerts were mostly others from the South, and if his American friend had questions, he could roll with that. He could take pleasure in tripping me up, tossing in the French, if not some variant of Arabic. Why not teach the ofay a thing or two? Why not clarify that, back in Rabat, a man had better get his French right? *C'est la capitale, mon ami*, and a man had better know the language of power. As for Arabic, his lessons always came with a chuckle. To begin with, a cowboy like his friend John—chuckle, smile—needed to understand there was a difference between the chitchat around a shisha, where they spoke a cultural mélange known as Darija, and the Arabic of lawyers and diplomats. The one phrase I remember from his midnight tutorials seems now to speak volumes: *shokk'ran bizz'aff*, thank you very much.

In and among all that, there leaked more personal information. When Leo declared he was "never going back," *jamais*, it came across without posturing. When he brought up his family, he wanted me to know that they still included "mountain people," villagers of the Atlas timberline. He claimed a solid Berber heritage, nothing so mixed-blood as the Moroccans down in the coastal cities. Just look at this chest and shoulders! Also Leo spoke of his new girlfriend, confessing that what he admired most about her wasn't much different from what I did, a quality he called "spirit." He didn't kid himself about the difficulties she'd taken on, with him, and acknowledged she was "better than most Italians." Indeed, as he talked I picked up the implication that Nunzia was more accepting than his own immigrant circle. Misgivings about friends and family, to be sure, emerged discreetly. I had to read between the lines, the dimples and crinkles around Leo's big, wordless smile. He never lost sight of the trouble I could cause, a clueless and clumsy American. He never loosened up enough to allow me a look at his work visa.

"I cannot," he'd tell me, suddenly formal. "*Je vous en prie.*"

Still, I happened on moments of revelation. When the boyfriend claimed that, in his circle as in Nunzia's, everyone was "friends," I could assess the friendship myself. I could watch the dried fruit being shared, the necklaces getting fingered—and notice as well an extra measure of silence, around the white girl. Nunzia and I both came in for some serious side-eye. Alternatively, we'd be waylaid by a sales pitch, anything from craftwork to berries. Either way, Leo would cruise on, perhaps nodding to the music. I thought of Marcaurelio evading talk of the Camorra, and also of lovers anywhere, convinced they can dance past whatever traps might be lurking. When the hookup is North-South, a couple might go so far as to wave off the legal difficulties.

I've seen such denial even when one of them was a *clandestino.* The men and women without papers, of course, prefer to keep it on the downlow. Outside a refugee camp, the less said the better. Yet I've met one who was glad to talk, largely because of the young Italian woman sitting alongside. He was the life of the party, really, breaking out the guitar, even swapping a few songs with me. The night was one of my blue-moon moments of Naples glamour, or its chimney-sweep stepsister, a party for people in theater and film. No doubt Paolo Sorrentino would recall a couple of the faces, all of them white except my strum-happy companion. I took him for a neighborhood rock star, in dreadlocks down past his shoulders and a suede jacket that seemed, in this heat, a sacrifice to fashion. When he finished "Redemption Song," when he soaked up the applause, you had no trouble imagining that smile in Hollywood. Then after another grinning toke, the man remarked that he was an illegal. What's more, back in Sierra Leone, he was an enemy of the state.

Back there, he'd gone for a Master's in filmmaking. He'd arrived in Naples on a study grant. But almost as soon as he came off the jet, his homeland had convulsed with regime change, and the new authorities had decreed his program a nest of traitors. As they rounded up his classmates and professors, he'd pocketed the money for his return. By now—another marquee smile—he doubted he'd ever go back. This was his home, the film community.

His girlfriend shuttled her chair forward, taking his hand with a grin almost as winning as his. She was one of those Italian redheads, a daughter of Barbarossa. She took over when I tried another question, asking how he got paid.

In the arts, she shrugged, they always found a way.

When I looked doubtful, she raised her chin. They always have it for him, some cash at the end of the week.

But her boyfriend, I pointed out, could be in danger. Up in Rome, some members of Parliament sounded downright racist ...

She looked past me, waving over a platter of sea-salad. As she arranged a plate, her chic fugitive handed me the guitar. He asked if I knew "Chimes of Freedom."

* * *

Following that night, I tried to keep track of the man. Show folk are good about that, and word was, my friend with the dreads had taken his act up to Rome, Cinecittà. Brother, I hope *everyt'ing i-rie*. I hope the same for Leo as well, though his situation was always more stable, his documents in order. He's still got his position at the hotel, I hear, and his stall by Porta Capuana. I know, too, that he owes some of his good fortune to Nunzia. She stood up with him at a hearing or two.

Back in 2008, was it? She hasn't shared the details. Still, *amica*—you stood up and made a difference. Here and there in the books of this city, a small bloom amid the lattices of names and dates, there's you and your Moroccan.

As for the specifics, just what she helped with, I could ask Leo. I've glimpsed him once or twice, over in the *mercato*, on-task as ever. The man straightened up to nod, but Nunzia had already asked me not to pursue the matter. "Whatever you're looking for in Naples," she said, "surely you can find it without him."

This was our first evening together after she and the Moroccan broke up. I'd been overseas, and she was glad to get a fresh perspective. She started at the end, when Leo had refused to take no for an answer. Nunzia used an American coinage, "stalking." She'd broken things off cleanly, frank as ever about her change of heart, and yet after a night of *intraliarsi,* as she left the piazza she'd find him emerging from the dark. Or come morning, he'd be waiting on her stoop, and he'd stick with her halfway to the studio. Again and again, she had to insist: *No.*

"I made it a point," she told me, "to stay on the busy streets."

She'd only begun the story, but I had to jump in. That night, did she want me to walk her home?

She trusted me, of course; she knew about my heart's fresh commitments, over in some odd locale with a name all vowels: *Ai-o-ua.* Still, when Nunzia patted my arm she set off a flutter within the ribs. "*Caro* John," she said, "you have no idea how hard it is to live in Naples."

In order to back Leo off, she'd needed more than an escort home. She'd needed another social experiment. "The shop," she said. "The leather goods, over by Capuano. That's where I had to go."

Yes: the setup went back to an earlier generation of immigrant.

"His people, there. I went to them and I asked, did they want such trouble?"

Leo had his angels, the men helping him through the relocation. To them, in Naples, it mattered to keep the peace. In other words, Nunzia had figured out her best play. She'd made it work—though as I got the picture you'd think I'd just taken a lungful of hash. I was choking up, ambushed by emotions.

Leo …? I tried to ask. What will he, where does he …?

My friend too was surprised, squaring her fine shoulders as I hunched over my Falanghina. Still, she had an answer. I was a sweetie-pie, "*dolce* John," but I needed to understand: Leo was doing very well.

"At the hotel, at the shop, very well. His visa too, every year the renewal comes through like *that*."

An abrupt gesture, not quite a snap of the fingers. This was one lucky African, said Nunzia, and the affair with her had been only the beginning. These days, he was even paying taxes. But Leo's immigrant success story, between the two of them, had played out less happily.

"John, he was no longer the same. He lost his lightness, you understand?"

As the boyfriend took on stature in his community, he developed expectations regarding the woman at his side.

"He even started to complain that I get out too much. That I meet too many people. *Per carità!*" She used the English, "network."

I pointed out that any client who came to the studio would see she had a *fidanzato*. He'd see the Moroccan's photo in five pieces, maybe six …

"Yes, and that too had to stop. A man in his position, he told me, he couldn't appear in such cartoons. Cartoons!"

She'd wondered about his background, and whether he had more religious feeling than he'd let on. "Perhaps he'd fallen in with, you know, the wrong sort of Muslim …" But she shook her head. Leo himself could've told me: back in Rabat, *mon ami*, a lot of us were brought up Catholic. Anyway, to him God's name made no difference; like my father, he hadn't left his homeland to go to church. He wasn't going to waste time with any *ogetti votivi*, unless it was one of Nunzia's ceramics. He did enjoy her Sacred Hearts, fire-engine red and trumpet gold. Yet even those had begun to seem like an offense, over their final months as a couple. Conversation after conversation sank into the sort of squabble Nunzia hated, about *piccole offese*, offenses in the least gesture or word. Indeed, after she'd announced that they were through, hadn't similar notions of What's Right carried over to the stalking?

To her, this wasn't even a question. To her the problem with Leo couldn't have been more obvious, and it couldn't have had less to do with Morocco.

"Once he got settled here," she declared, "he was just another man."

* * *

Towards the end of her explanations, as an African or two approached our table to hawk their wares, I thought I spied a decent journey's end for these latest Neapolitans. I thought I saw how they might "make their way." From where I sat, the love affair between Nunzia and Leo described a familiar trajectory, ordinary in fact. To her, his drive had soured to bluster, to giving orders; to him, she'd devolved from a creature of "spirit" to a crazy woman, making a spectacle of them both. Each one's dream of the other had fallen into decay, revealing monsters, and on either side of the Atlantic, how often had I seen the same? In my own marriage I'd seen the same, or damn near, and so once more I was the archeologist along Spaccanapoli. The latest artifacts brought to light indicated that the new immigrants were making the same old mistakes—and what could be more promising? What did "assimilation" mean, if not tumbling into the same old mistakes?

A joke, sure. To put it that way, I'm cracking a joke when I've no right, so far removed am I from those Frantz Fanon called *The Wretched of the Earth*. Consider, too, that the book appeared in 1964. Since then, how has history treated the flotsam and jetsam of the South? The powers of Europe have quit the territory but kept their businesses, and the consequences have often had the brute logic of that *Wehrmacht* squad leader, the night he returned to the Camaldoli nunnery. It's all about the "strong man," a commander in Boko Haram or Sudan's Rapid Support. Yet these men too soon enough find themselves up on a stool with a noose around their necks, and a half-century after Fanon, for many on his continent, the only route to some facsimile of civilization is via boat.

Of course, my sketch of the African nightmare is too simple. Of course the continent is anything but a monolith, bad news all over. A city like Dar es Salaam, to name just one, may offer a sweeter life than Naples. Besides, aren't we talking about a single case? About Leo, a long way from hand to mouth? Leo's success offers a counterbalance, you might say, to Omar in his dragon jacket and Jennifer with her swollen belly. Or you might say that the experience of migrants out of the South, in Southern Italy, presents so many variants and wild hairs that the real joke is seeing anything in common with what my father went through in coming to the States.

All of this was tumbling through my head, after Nunzia and I kissed good night. If her breakup left one of the *neri* looking ordinary, looking like he belonged, it also threw the hopelessness of so many others into relief. This larger tragedy reduced men and women to floating spores, only one in a thousand likely to take root, and that gloomy vision, back at the café, had choked me up. That'd been part of what caught in my throat, at least. Eventually other griefs came to mind, such as how the wreck of the affair had also drowned a part of me, my dream of the Artist Abroad. That ornamental figure sank deeper in the muck each time Nunzia moved on. On top of that, alone again downtown, I realized that this had been a hard visit. I'd seen the refugee camp and lost *Zia* Bianca. She'd passed before I arrived, the last of my father's generation, but now I recalled our talk and felt powerfully the good in its old lies: in the horrors kept from her.

A hard visit, this year, and I wished I could find a midnight mass.

The few churches that retain a congregation, these days, can't risk staying open after dark. They might make exception for a holy day, the Feast of St. Francis, but otherwise they shutter the entryways. The steps serve as a bed for the homeless or a stage for a street performer, if not an African girl in a micro-mini and boots. But if mass was out of the question that night, the next morning I found a service. By now I'd reached the end of my own Neapolitan affair, my 20 years courting the city, and I didn't need a relative (all out of the *centro* anyway) to take me to church. I even had a Naples publisher, something of a maverick, who didn't mind honoring my quirky request for some B'n'B down amid the *vicoli*. Lodgings like that hardly put a dent in his accounts, and I was never more than ten minutes from Santa Chiara. There, it was as if I had some sort of eardrum set amid the heart and lungs; it quivered even at the whisper of the tourists, between the bomb-denuded walls. I'd take a seat and offer my own whispers, bilingual. For a couple of years I asked help for my marriage, and despite how that worked out, I went on to pray for my father, and then for his brother, for his sister—and despite this lengthening stretch of tombstones I'd pray for my work as well, always some hurdle to get over, and every time, every visit, for my daughter.

My Protestant upbringing, Episcopal and Presbyterian mostly, hadn't kept me from knowing the rituals. In Naples I came to prefer the *vespro*, late in the day; as the city began to cool, I took the wafer.

Attendance tended to be sparse. A crowd such as gathered on that foggy Cilento mountaintop was the exception, and besides, I preferred the quiet of a weekday evening among a murmuring few. At services like those, not infrequently, I saw more non-Europeans than locals. I saw a color range from ebony to dun, and some hadn't just come from across the Mediterranean. Rather they were Filipino, Vietnamese, or perhaps Syrian, like the woman who'd shown me the worst of 9/11. Plainly this country had at least one career track open to refugees. Anyone was welcome to put on a robe or wimple, and take up work as God's helper. The vocation that'd given my family its name might've lost its appeal among them and their countrymen, but the faith was still winning converts elsewhere. After all, doesn't it derive from a dark-skinned visionary out of the Middle East? One who preached that the wandering soul is worth more than Empire? This message retains no small power, for a seed-spore looking to root, and as a missionary friend of mine put it, "Christianity no longer wears a white face."

The current Pope, *nota bene*, comes from Latin America and has embraced the new Catholic diversity. He seeks a return to the core mission of helping the impoverished and rootless. Then there's me, with my darker cousin and lighter aunt and so on. All of us hold the White Card, undeniably, yet all of us seem wired for the Church. The latest news is, my great-uncle with the plaque, down by the Black Blocks, won't be the last Vicedomini to make his home above a sanctuary. After Aunt Bianca died, her *mammone* son finally had to get a life. His relatives could only help so much, the welfare system even less, and his best resources turned out to be old friends who'd gone into the clergy. In the last photo this cousin sent, he's wearing a sparkling white robe, neck to shoetops, with flaring sleeves. Beside him stood the priest, his vestments red over white; Bianca's son must've kept them clean and pressed. My cousin's got a room in the church, and he's grown so reliable, he assists at exorcism. Totally wired for church.

Myself, in the consecrated spaces of Naples, it wasn't so cinematic. For starters, by the early '90s, I was all through getting down on my knees. Nonetheless, I couldn't deny the effect that prayer had on me, now and again. I tried to talk about it, first with the men's group in Portland. Still, I don't believe I got a grasp on what I felt until I sat finishing the first of my own Naples novels. In one of the final drafts, I awarded my protagonist a "spiritual muscle." Sometimes at Mass and sometimes over the rosary, the woman feels it flex. Naturally I can think of other ways to put it, a numinous brush-by, an impalpable quiver, but in any case the muscle's of no use when it comes to real work. "IRL" is a shorthand God doesn't bother to translate, just as when I'm at prayer I'm not In Real Life. Not in the way my American father would've defined it, the daily scuffle. Rather, the Mass helps me handle the scuffle. It helps me work with greater love. If that sounds like pap, a Hallmark card, then I guess I've failed again, and I'll just say that this lay Catholicism proved intrinsic to my Neapolitan engagement. No doubt, too, my spirituality's diluted, rather a mongrel. It's some part loneliness, I realize.

Still and all, by now I'm looking back over hundreds of hours in a pew, around the old city. Impressive totals, enough to raise a pointed question: how come I hadn't been raised in the Church?

For years and years, right through the first adult visits to my father's home, I never gave it much thought. Like my sister and brother, I'd heard from early on that church had nothing to do with why Pop had come to America. He'd come to make money, and even his new name helped to gird him for the hardscrabble. He'd shortened it to something every American ought to recognize.

"A word," he told me, "they'd know from the church down the street."

Ah, not every American, Pop. I can't tell you how many times I've had to spell out the name and then clarify, *it's Italian*. My father must've slogged though the M-I-N-I even more often. But that he should mention a church, when he explained his thinking—that seems significant. That's almost a red flag, since back in Naples, you'd see the word in plenty of places other than church.

I'd never deny that, in the States, what he intended to carve in stone was a dollar sign. He had other values as well, a larger vision of the good life, and as they say in Santa Chiara, *Deo gratias*. I was a lucky child, to take part in family dancing and soccer in the backyard. In time, however, soccer became too much for me, even my dancing lost its pep, and I got most of my exercise knocking around Naples. The more I did, the less the old man's economic imperative seemed to matter, as a reason for skipping Mass. Every parish had its wealthy congregants, underwriting the expense of a new *assistente* like my cousin. Every altar, every baptismal font, needed upkeep, and a few were detailed in goldleaf. In the Camorra's city, the money might even have bloodstains. A shrine to Padre Pio might be an attempt to cleanse a soul far dirtier than my father's. Still, I'd never seen him set foot in a Catholic place of worship. Rather, Mom handled our religious upbringing, starting with a suburban church the very definition of "white liberal." As for my father, the only time I heard him speak of God's place in his life was after he'd fallen into his final debility.

"I still know how to talk to God," he told me. "I still know all those *words*." An intensity seized him, surprising. "Long ago, I learned them well."

Did he have as much as a year left? Was his high feeling, his anger, due to the incessant pain?

"The nuns taught me," he growled. "The *nuns*."

About the anger and pain, I'd guessed wrong. Rather, I recalled how rarely my father visited any church, even the nice white congregation my mother found us. How would he have put it, in B-movie Americanese? *Once in a blue moon ...*

* * *

The American Enzo, the New & Improved Vicedomini, didn't care to speak with God. Where had God been back during the Four Days? Myself, I'm so troubled by the nuns' execution, it sets me imagining how the Mother Superior pleaded for her sisters. I see her up in *Kommandant's* face, arguing that she too holds rank, she gives the orders: *I am the one responsible, I alone ...* and if I can imagine it, my father must've gotten the picture even more vividly.

Then the next day or the one after, Pop saw worse, and by the end of the fighting his faith was gone. I'm convinced of it—just as I'm sure that, after he'd at last (perhaps) spoken with God, he spoke to me.

Twice, actually, in visitations about three months apart. Visitations, or whatever: every time I tell the story, the mysticism wears thinner and the mitigating factors loom larger. I was up in Chicago, the first weeks after he passed. The chill of spring by the lake bore down, and the workload, managing students and writing a dissertation. My child was out in one corner of the country and my mother down in the opposite, each grieving in their way, but I wouldn't get back to either of them soon, not with so many i's to dot and t's to cross. Mitigating factors, all these emotions resonating around me, along with the other voices in my building. Nevertheless I know what I heard. It was a Saturday in April, a moment free of demands, or nearly. I was out of the shower, following a workout at the Y, cold sober. As I started to towel off, I heard my father: "*Eh*, John."

Just that, a word and a half, in what sounds to me like a mix of Naples and New York. Plainly the emotions were mixed: first a heavy sigh, then a fond name. A name like a friendly sock in the shoulder, no less, for the message came through plainly enough: buck up. A sad business, *eh*—but, John, okay. Buck up.

This much I could take in, it registered deep down, even as I sank against the cold tile of the bathroom wall. There may also have been a stirring, another brush-by, a rustle across my chest hair, but then I was nothing but wet and slack. I was limp and jellied, sunk for untold minutes on the floor, beside a towel, an adult in the shape of an ampersand. Only, at some point I tuned in my own voice, repeating what I'd heard: *eh*, John … *eh*, John …

With that, out of the deep down, the encouragement emerged, the affirmation he'd intended. I rose to it, aware at last of the towel for my chills and the towel-rack to help me stand.

Over the weeks that followed, I kept my ears cocked. The only sounds were the traffic outside, the neighbors upstairs, and more than once I scolded myself: come on, a grown man hearing voices. Yet I did as he'd suggested. I got my head up, striking a balance between student papers and my own bibliography. I found where the extra effort was needed and put my back into it. Then once my dissertation was submitted, and my kid and I enjoyed a round of calling me "Doctor," I spent much of the summer in a serious attempt to relocate overseas. I could swear I'd heard that as well, in the two notes Pop had played for me: getting to Naples for good deserved my best effort. I had an inheritance in hand and friends who could set up an open-ended rental off Tribunali. I made my most extensive round of queries, arranging to meet professors at the *Orientale*, *Federico II*, smaller schools, and (switching to English) NATO's U of Maryland branch. Then shortly before my flight, I had my second spectral visit.

My father came in a dream, this time. A dream, and naturally it retains a certain mystery. I do get the encouragement intended, the same message as before, but in this case I have to feel around for his helping hand.

The opening offers nothing like comfort, a bowl of bloody ground meat. No sooner do I come upon the bowl than I realize it's hamburger, raw and heaped in its own run-off, and one other thing as well: it's my Ph.D. The coursework and committee and Post-Its in multiple colors—the whole multi-volume shebang sits here, straight out of the grinder and bleeding in a white ceramic bowl. Maybe it looks a little like a brain, my freshly certified brain, but it looks a lot more like hamburger. Small wonder that later, in

Naples, I wound up praying for insight. Right there in the dream, I'm casting around for help. I'm heartened by the approach, off to my right, of two figures. Or is it three? It's a blur, smoky, spattered, even as two of the entities drawing near resolve themselves into cousins. They're Marcaurelio and Serena, though neither comes in clearly, and the third remains indiscernible. A smudge, standing upright. Still, now I've got someone to ask.

Gesturing, trying for a comic bafflement: *Ma questo, cos'è?*

But this, what is it? How can it be? The answer too comes in Italian, in a choral voice, more than two voices. Besides my cousins, it's my father speaking.

In suffering, there are always three things that can help. The most important is the will of God, and the next is the will of the one suffering. The third, the least important, is the will of the doctor.

* * *

"Doctor," my latest title. The one featured in the latest byplay between my child and me. It pegs me as low man on the totem pole, in this Message From Beyond, but I can venture an interpretation. I'd say my father's again calling for balance. He's warning me about limits—indeed, my "terminal degree" hasn't got me far, neither around Naples nor Stateside—but at the same time he's affirming my other resources, more sustaining, like a family in two worlds. Indeed the Old World offers some of the few memories that match the power of this dream. In my mind it remains as vivid as the deathbed wave from Gigi, the cold and angry night with Nando, or my twenty airless minutes in the tent with Jennifer. The bowl of meat and speaking smudges may even reveal a connection between last century's lighter-skinned emigrants and this century's darker immigrants.

Those twinned odysseys, it bears repeating, come in a rainbow of nuance. Sorting out every hue would take a dozen dozen dissertations. Nevertheless, I'm confident that the unconscious of just about every new arrival stables a few funeral horses. What haunted my father must haunt others, and if it doesn't take the form of horses and a hearse, perhaps it's a farm family dead of drought. Such remnants linger like columns of smoke, of dust, in the soul of the transplant. No box in the closet can contain it, finally. Of course, smug Euro-America prefers to say *fuggedaboudit*. Of course, any culture largely about cost analysis and return on investment won't know what to do with the violated prayers of a teenage boy, his holy scrip collapsing to ash between his hands. My father's renunciation of the Church and Leo's embrace of machismo in fact appear two sides of the same coin, two forms of aggressive therapy to deal with the destruction of the landmarks they used to steer by. The immigrant success knows he's built a home on that ruin, as well as on the crushed seeds of so many others who floated off alongside him yet never found landfall. I too can feel the crunch underfoot, though I endured nothing like my father did, and still less anything like the refugees in their pajamas. Any of us with a hyphen in our makeup can suffer the defining nightmare of this latest turnover from century to century, a vision of a world without homelands, but rather only trailer parks and tent cities. Living catch-as-catch-can, these days, is hardly confined to folks who started out in Aleppo or Brazzaville. Hasn't the same taken hold here in the land of the U-Haul and the corporate re-lo?

For a sensibility like mine, this glimpse of endless diaspora, what Salman Rushdie termed "a century of wandering," prompts a terrible need to find out about the lost tribal homeground. The old mysteries begin to ululate irresistibly. "We beat on against the current, borne back ceaselessly into the past." That's *The Great Gatsby*, of course, another of the prayer-objects that decorate my interior chapel. Like a million other bookish boys and girls I first read it as a teen, and nowadays I see that my family had its own Gatz-become-Gatsby. "Larger than life," right? I loved hearing that about my father, and the friend who said it first got to know him about the same time as I first devoured Fitzgerald. But decades later, as I got into my own reinventions, our Gatsby had more and more trouble just getting out of a chair. Between infarctions, he found himself borne back ceaselessly.

So Pop shared his last bad memory: the last of the three talks that define my text. A horror out of old Naples, he shared it in a setting that couldn't have been more American. In Boston, we'd gathered for a family Thanksgiving. As ever he sat at the head of the table, though before the end of winter I'd be clearing away his last wine and biscotti, and over the November repast his face again suggested a crumpled brown bag. I wonder, too, if the menu called the past to mind; our soup was thick with mushrooms.

Towards the end of the meal Pop spoke of an autumn long previous, when he'd helped Gigi get some shoes. Earlier I used the term "meat-grinder," and now that expression takes me to my dream, but at this Thanksgiving with his grown children, my father went back to that blood and stink soberly, his voice level and his gaze clear. For the first time, he confessed outright that he and Gigi had joined forces with a band of guerillas. *Scugnizzi, sì.* The crew could see the use in him, at least, the older brother, quick and muscular. The younger remained barefoot, however, a serious disadvantage whether it's fight or flight. So the homies came up with a plan. Another harsh rite of initiation, it seems, another night-sea journey that might end in someone washing up dead. As the story unfolded I thought often of such voyagers, now getting somewhere, now falling back, never wholly at peace.

The toughnecks of the Four Days knew better than to try and scavenge. By then the city had been picked clean. Rather, the best source was the same as for the guns. The best boots, sturdy government issue, belonged to the occupiers. Also, any kid who'd survived this long knew where the troops liked to go for a drink, off-duty. Likewise they grasped the advantage in getting Gigi out of his shirt. He needed to look ragged and harmless, a "little monkey," circling among the uniforms with a hand out and surreptitiously checking shoe size. Out in the alley, meanwhile, the other kids got a deceit ready, perhaps a boy with a girl's voice, raising a love-call in the dark. Once they lured away Gigi's pick, it made no difference that the soldier too must've been a teenager.

At the table, my father never broke down. Was he seeking forgiveness? Redemption? Something like that, and in any case he had to get across. He wasn't just talking to himself. Even as he sat giving thanks for his New World and grown children, he was still striving to get somewhere.

"First thing," he said, "is you cut his throat so he can't call for help."

The victim must've flopped around, his carotid spurting blood, but the gang stayed on him. They knew the formula, should one of the *Tedeschi* turn up dead. Their boy had got his shoes, and he could go far, he could scamper off wherever he liked. But first, "You cut him up," my father said, "so you can get rid of him."

PART FIVE:

'a capa è 'na sfoglia 'e cipolle—
A brain peels like an onion.

ERRIBLE THING, A HORROR ABOUT which he held his tongue for half a century. He kept his peace even when, a couple of decades along, his adopted home began to provide daily reminders of war. The '60s, right? Television technology perplexed him, worlds apart from the gears and springs with which he loved to fiddle, and yet its arcana could deliver the bombing and gunfire right into the living room. You saw street fighting as well, as close by as Detroit or Chicago. At times Pop must've felt his own brush-by, hellish rather than divine. And how'd he handle it, another world threatening to collapse? In our family's circle, he was among the first to oppose the conflict in Vietnam.

"You Americans," he told some *Mad Men* extra, "you don't have any *idea*."

My sister and brother and I of course suffered our own '60s turmoil, fighting with him and Mom over hair and music, flirting with the wrong lover or worse drugs. I recall an acid trip on a hot night, far from home, during which I looked in the mirror and saw that the sweat running down my face had turned to my parents' blood. Some guilt there, hippie boy? Unnerving as the psychedelia was, though, I came down from those few hours, and the others, in the same place as when I'd lifted off: work-study as a college student, and trial-and-error as anything else. My siblings must've gone through something similar, some apogee of flight from the family, before they too settled into orbit. Whenever there was a falling-out, there followed a hauling-in. Even at our surliest, too, we were solid behind our parents' anti-war work. Often Pop was the sharpest-dressed man at the rally, going for *la bella figura* in a checked coat, creased brushed-denim bells, serious sideburns, and what were then called "Cuban heels." Superfly. Yet Enzo Domini could be counted on, whether the job was circulating petitions or getting out the vote. We loved him for it, and later all the more for his willingness to share a joint.

Once when Pop and I got a buzz on, he told me about his teenage smoking. Before his hometown went to pieces, he'd been part of a soccer squad, semi-pro, and the coach used to pack a bit of hash. They'd break it out before a game in the hills, he told me, up where the wind got raw. Up in a town like Camaldoli.

The place had its happy memories, yes, and after decades of other stories, this one still rings true. Coaches have always sought whatever advantage they can get (God knows the stuff is better for you than steroids), and even during the War, perhaps especially during the War, every ship out of North Africa must've concealed a few bricks of hashish. Yet while I see no reason to doubt my father's recollection, I suspect that once again there's another tale to tell. There's another leaf of the onion to peel, one that uncovers those bad nights at the end of September '43. The O.G. types who took in Pop and Gigi must've known all about the brown-black goo. The stuff was contraband. Besides, *scugnizzi* too suffered the cold, with never much to eat but always plenty to fear.

The logic behind an easy line of talk, *dietrologia*: I've gotten pretty good at that. Most people do, don't they, as the wrinkles deepen and the joints complain? Most people learn to tell when they're not getting the whole story, and whether it's worth digging out the rest. Certainly that's how I've notched a number of Neapolitan benchmarks. Certainly I've found an aphorism, on-point: *'a capa è 'na sfoglia 'e cipolle*, ah KAH-pah EH nah SVOY-lah eh CHEE-poh-leh, "the brain peels like an onion." The slang for "brain" or "head"—*'na capa*, savor the bite—I take to mean any tricky knot or conundrum, and what could be trickier than this city? The place loses it layers only slowly, streaming juices, fetching tears.

Even now, as I look back on my walkabouts, what I notice is all that they've failed to uncover. The songs, for instance, *"'O Sole Mio"* just for starters. I've never gone a day without hearing a couple *canzone Napoletane,* and when John Turturro came to town, he fell so hard for the music that he had to make a documentary, *Passione.* A celebration flecked with graffiti, itself all juice and tears. Myself, I roughed out chords for the sighing *"Reginella,"* but soon quit trying. The song demands a player who'll do it justice.

Then there's the lottery. In Italy this is run by the state, not the *malavita,* but playing the numbers nonetheless has a rich mythology. It provided the great Totò with a couple of signature bits, and for the Vicedominis it was a job. My father's mother, tugging another of her Carro family strings, found work in her precinct. Important work—she was the dream interpreter. She received a government check for suggesting the numbers on which to bet, judging from whatever had troubled the player's sleep. In this my Nonna relied on a text fat as a dictionary, the *Smorfia.* The book turned up in many households around town, but the average Neapolitan could never match the expertise of the state appointee, at her desk. She knew which questions to ask, narrowing down the selection amid the labyrinthine columns of dreams and numbers. "House of corpses," #33, "new world," #38. Only a skilled hand could pluck out the winners from the Collective Unconscious, and my grandmother kept the job right through my teenage visits.

The woman's battered *Smorfia* sits now on my shelves in Des Moines, but the world of those numbers, like that of the city's songs, is a spice left out of this *Ragù.* To use the other metaphor, the archeology, my trowel has scooped up a number of items that still resist interpretation. I've no idea what became of Jennifer, well-spoken and hormone-honeyed, up from Ghana and headed God only knows where. As for Flavio Gioia, distinguished musician, old family friend, I've turned up nothing after 1945. Nothing at the Conservatory or the Opera House. The Synagogue claims it had close to 600 living members following the War—a testimony to the old city—but if the name's on some list of temple-goers, I haven't found it.

Then too, I had the onion aphorism wrong. I had *sfoglia* wrong, a signifier as flexible as the thing signified: a leaf, a flake, a page, even a strip of dough rolled flat. You hear it in the English "exfoliate." Everybody tells me, however, that the saying's not about exfoliation, the peeling. Rather it's about the thing peeled: *'na capa*.

"The brain, the head," says a professor at Federico II, "this is the onion peel."

"*Mutabile*, changeable," says Marcaurelio, "that's the head. The mind."

Everybody acknowledges, too, that the city's proverbs are themselves flexible. Nunzia even claimed she liked my interpretation—"but," she went on, "*caro* John, you have no idea."

She swept an arm across the studio, then, taking in the changes in her work since we'd met. The earliest was a photograph blown up the size of a flag and doctored by hand, before anyone had dreamed of Photoshop. The piece had been exhibited as part of Bassolino's renewal. Ten years later had come the construction small enough to fit on a bedstand, a white throne in which sat a figure wearing a white pelt: her golden-brown Leo. Then there were the pieces featuring a sail or a seashell, inspired by her latest *fidanzato*, a man with a grown son in Marseilles and a small boat in the marina under Castel dell'Ovo. A good match, for a woman forever testing boundaries. Still, the standouts around her workplace, whether an early piece or a late one, remain the ceramics. These ranged from a crooked *corno* the length of my pinky to a bas-relief as large as my doctorate in its frame, presenting the Madonna of the Arches. An icon for troubled women, here she was faceless and ferocious, all hard color, even the gold.

"Like a peel of an onion," Nunzia said, "*mutabile*, we fold and bend. Don't you see it, just looking around? Eh, and what about looking in the mirror?"

At the moment, actually, I was thinking of my child.

* * *

By that time Vera had one of my old friend's Madonnas, an icon of hope for the lost. Over my double-decade of reconstruction, my only child went from 10 to 30, from Portland to L.A., and from impressing friends with her guitar licks to carving out a career as DJ, sideman, producer, and more. These changes alone suggest a coil of onion, bent this way and that, glistening in an array of colors. Recently my daughter even worked out a way back to Naples. A soul-satisfying visit, alongside a girlfriend, it left both young people swearing they wanted to move to Southern Italy. A happy ending, right? A sweet port of arrival ...

Eh. It's high time I exposed the rotten underside of my Neapolitan layers. Gallivanting off, I fell down as a father.

When I tumbled back into the Crater, I was full-grown. The wife who wanted no more of me had been at my side for twenty years. Yes, that figure again: you could say I'd been married since my last visit to Naples, and honestly, I needed no Siren to wind up on the rocks. I had a life and understood its basic makeup. My child however suffered tremors throughout the edifice of Self; she'd lost a load-bearing wall. A sibling might've helped, but she had none (in retrospect, my wife's and my reluctance to have another kid seems like another critical flaw). Worse, when the breakdown came, she was stuck in a young person's worst, most fragile stretch of "mutability." She was in middle school.

And that's when her father starts to take himself far away, for two weeks a year at least, if not three or a month or more.

Yes, I kept up the gifts and phone calls. A postcard every day, always, opening with "Ciao, V," palsy-walsy. I kept it up for years, at roughly a buck a card. Given the Italian mails, damn it, often the first didn't reach Portland till after I got back myself. At least she was spared the worst delay, one I heard about over the phone, during a snowbound Chicago February. The call came from Portland, an old friend, thanking me for his card—dated the previous July.

The recollection still makes me laugh. Then, however, there's the *dietrologia*: the two homes far apart.

A damaged teenage girl, contending with the trials of a musical calling, had lost her father not just temporarily to Naples, but permanently to Chicago.

The job, no question, was another *colpo d'oro*, a wallop anyone would want. I had a professor's salary, benefits that covered dependents, and the laurel crown of *Visiting Writer*. The security didn't extend to that infinity known as tenure, but I could count on a few years, longer than most such gigs. To have a stretch of my future set up also allowed me to look back, and to confirm I'd helped Vera bank a sizeable account of childhood happiness. My efforts weren't anything out of the ordinary: the bike helmet and *The Little Mermaid*, the Oregon trout farm and the basement construction projects. I'd managed a pair of Italian getaways, one a homestay program (a position as teacher liaison), and one an actual vacation (my final assignments in PR, stretching my conscience as far as it would go). Then too, my wife and I had worked through our "good divorce." All things considered, it looked as if everyone would benefit from my getting a real job. Granted, my office was across the Great Divide, and the girl hadn't yet turned 15. Still.

Our best connection, our most enjoyable, was via music. Years ago my child and I jammed a bit, on guitar and recorder, but by the time of the divorce she'd moved on to better partners. I favored another ancestor, the monk with a mountain of books, while she was the one whose playing might yet land her on a yacht in the Mediterranean. Back while I was briefly a Portland bachelor, back before I again could call myself a professor, she supplied the better soundtrack for my new digs. The two-bedroom space felt most like a home the evenings that she and I put together dinner while bopping to some cassette (the cheapest, most portable format) from one of her hard-hitting women. She'd kept old favorites like Salt'N'Pepa, while adding the rage-metal of L7 and, later, Sleater-Kinney. The ruckus they raised must've gone straight to her troubled heart.

L7 was my gift to her, the evening she turned 14. The group was playing a club in town, and I treated Vera and three of her BFFs. One of those nights. One of those moments amid the wreckage, when it felt like I might yet reassemble some form of the good life. I knew the sweetness of the Oregon city, its comfortable drizzle, its neighborhood venues and their all-ages arrangements. I reveled in the anti-glamour and total command of the four women onstage, the crowd-surfing frenzy they triggered with an anti-anthem like "Pretend That We're Dead." In my memory these images, my daughter and her girls dancing and laughing, come together in a montage with the best evenings around Naples.

V and I enjoyed quieter pleasures. We prowled the stacks of Powell's Books, then winnowed through our selections in the coffee shop. When Madeleine L'Engle came to town, my daughter not only accompanied me to the reading, but also stood up with a question. She wanted to know more about the heroine of *A Wrinkle in Time*. Then there were the movies, the post-*Mermaid* fare, which in the days before Netflix entailed a lengthy ritual of selection. By the time I left for Chicago, her viewing tastes could surprise me. Once as we settled in for a matinee, she announced that her new favorite was something called *The Karen Carpenter Story*, performed entirely by Barbie dolls. Quite the idiosyncratic choice, very *Portlandia*; the director, Todd Haynes, had family in town.

Our shared interests, in other words, could leave us miles apart. I do think we made a connection over L7, something like their twin guitars, shredding in synch. Grateful as Vera was, though, she made sure I knew that the band wasn't the first she'd seen tear it up. She and her friends had been sneaking into clubs for months. When I heard, well, I couldn't say "attagirl," but I could remind myself that she was no longer a girl. She was an adolescent, and "developing autonomy," as my doctoral reading put it.

Come to think, if my advanced studies in the postmodern had taught me anything, by '96 or '97, it was the same as I got from the aphorism—that identity's fluid and easily bent.

But this was my child, and my job was to get a sense of what lay beneath the surface. I worried when, for months following the divorce, she left her room in my apartment barren. I don't mean only that I found next to nothing in her bureau, when I gave the drawers a fatherly check. Her wardrobe had shrunk to a few boyish pieces anyway. I've already mentioned that, the last time I saw my daughter in a dress, she'd put it on as a joke, one night during her learning program in Italy. Nor was I especially concerned about the absence of postcards and artwork from Naples, here in Papa's Portland digs. Those would find their place in time, right? Or they would if she ever outgrew this white nakedness, wall to bedroom wall, a complete scrub of what I'd grown used to. Back in the house that was now Mom's, she'd strewn her space with a cornucopia. The liners out of cassettes and CDs of course, but also headlines and ads, wittily cropped, also artwork from friends, souvenirs … It was Nunzia's studio, West. In my apartment, however, she wouldn't even put up a poster. I bought her two to start with, a Madonna and a Marilyn, the latter in a butch pose, on a weight bench pumping iron. V left both rolled up in a corner.

When at last I asked her about it, my timing was impeccable. My first Thanksgiving without a family, and I'd hardly started to speak before I broke down, bawling out of control. We fell into role reversal, the daughter comforting the father, and by New Year's the walls of her second bedroom were brightly littered. She even got more color into her wardrobe, tying a bandanna around one wrist. Nevertheless, no decoration could express the grief and terror that weighed on her, and those storms must've surged up worse when, over uncaten turkey and potatoes, she saw me express the same. Thank God she never had to hear the howl I fell into the following year, the morning I moved out. With my books already shipped cross-country, with my bachelor's Jetta packed to the gills, I fell into half an hour and more of wailing helplessness in a corner of her room. The sheetrock above my sunken head, my sopping, burning head, had once again been stripped bare.

Then on one of her first visits to the Midwest—back before 9/11, the TSA, and the barnlike X-rays—her backpack reeked of pot. It cried out for a fatherly check, and in one pocket I found the pills.

* * *

Now, where's Naples, in all this? Naturally, as I inhaled the dank of Vera's backpack, I thought of those evenings with Pop. Naturally, too, I calculated the difference in age between my daughter's experience in the late '90s and mine in the early '70s. A vast difference in so young a life, as much as seven years. Then there were these pills in a baggie.

V's mother and I never found many pills, but they were always bad news. Her drug of choice was speed. Now and again this included street product, some methamphetamine knockoff, and on party nights she'd chase that down with alcohol. The combination set off hideous alarms, sleep-obliterating; speed and booze had killed one of my high-school friends. Her Mom and I struggled for information, gleaning what we could from therapy and AA, or taking pills to the hospital. Our child offered only partial admissions, and trying to read her, I thought again of Naples, trying to uncover its secrets. The city showed in her maturing looks, too: the hair's black-seaweed richness, the chin's Vicedomini sweep.

If I'd achieved any insight over on Spaccanapoli, it meant nothing if it couldn't help me now. A couple of connections, at least, came to mind. For starters, I understood that I was dealing with someone like young Enzo Domini, a teenager crawling out of the wreckage, worm-eaten by PTSD. With that in mind, my adult father provided the best tone for me to strike, when dealing with my child's change of life: the same as he'd used for mine.

Twenty years after his War, in our Vomero kitchen, he'd spoken to me adult to adult. Now, I'd best sit down with her the very day I searched her backpack, giving soft-spoken emphasis to the danger—on top of everything else, she may have carried illegal goods across state lines—and also to how swiftly and easily we could find help. That weekend I drove her to an AA meeting out in Skokie, and back in Portland, again I've got to give credit to my ex. She arranged more meetings, both for mother and daughter, and found a counselor who specialized in juvenile abusers. Like me, too, she went on the wagon a while.

As I learned the 12 Steps, it set off rugged spasms in my spiritual muscle. "A searching and fearless moral inventory," ow. After every visit back to the Northwest, what a hollow ring my Chicago apartment gave to the words "health benefits." Because didn't I work in a free market? Couldn't I have gone back to PR? But here I was, a Visitor, walking to class talking to myself. Usually I rehearsed my resignation speech: *no choice … my child.* Some mornings, I was only babbling, murmuring. I found a church, and for icons I had my desktop photos, both at home and in the office. I touched them each time I bowed my head.

Whispers of another kind, more hurtful, came out back in Portland. The therapists kept twisting the leaves of V's suffering this way and that, inspecting them for one particular strain of infection. They kept asking about abuse in the home. Naturally I'd braced myself for this, an inevitable question, whenever a girl starts to self-medicate. But how was I supposed to feel when I got the question a tenth time, a dozenth, over a few years? How were either of us, Vera or I, supposed to handle it? If some counselor wanted to explore a youngster's concepts of sex and love, still in development, surely there was a better way. Myself, I'd striven to be open and receptive, careful about introducing my daughter to my first lover, post-divorce, and more careful still as we talked afterwards. But two or three years later, in therapy, I never heard a word about V's likely sexual orientation. Rather, the whole question of intimacy, too complex even for the cliché "layers of the onion," was reduced to a single dirty secret. And I was that secret; I was the Camorra. Indeed, when Neapolitans opened up about the Camorra, they sounded less obsessed than the folks in recovery did about parental abuse.

Wrong from the get-go, the ugly suggestion kept on nagging. I'd see Vera wave it off at the beginning of an hour at the therapist's only to have it come back again by the end. But unlike me, she was in no position to insist. She couldn't put her foot down, not when the adult who was supposed to back her up wasn't even in the same time zone, nine meetings out of ten. That's where my guilt lay, my failure—nowhere else. Small wonder V learned to duck behind evasions, bobbing and weaving like my cousin in Secondigliano. Then too, when Marcaurelio refused to give a straight answer, like Vera he had good reason. My daughter's commitment to staying sober deepened despite these glitches in her support system; I felt her determination even when she put some tricky spin on the language of recovery. Besides, over in my own neck of the woods, wasn't I also putting a spin on a specialized language? Didn't I placate my doctoral committee with favorite terminology? Here the "heteroglossia" of Bakhtin, there the "mirroring" of Lacan? Yet I wasn't playing games with my profs, no more than in Al-Anon. Likewise, my daughter was smart enough to balance the few times the people trying to help were wrong against the many they were right.

Between us, meantime, the give and take grew uneasy. Throughout the end of the '90s, with me on Lake Michigan and her by the Pacific, the relationship suggests another piece of therapy-speak: avoidance behavior. Vast tracts of Vera's life went off-limits, and when she and I did enjoy something like free-flowing conversation, it nearly always had to do with my work. She didn't want to talk about assembling a band or cutting her first songs; she wanted to talk about Dante and his *Divine Comedy*. The poem, or Poem, had been a touchstone for me long before

I'd left Portland, in my own "bitter exile." Now Vera adopted it too. The Twelve Steps, after all, first took the downward spiral into *Inferno* and then reversed it, climbing through *Purgatorio*. At the top, once and for all the soul was cleansed. Besides that, my daughter's ear, long attuned to rap, enjoyed the interplay of *terza rima*. One of the best talks I recall from her later teens took place before the poetry shelves of Powell's, as we swapped a few translations back and forth. Together we enjoyed something like ten minutes of shared goodwill.

* * *

Her mother wasn't getting much further. Half-truths, if not quarter-truths, dominated their home life as well, and Vera suffered at least one relapse. According to what I heard, though, this was only a matter of sharing a joint or two. According to all I was getting, long-distance, we came through Y2K in decent shape. In Chicago, on First Night 2000, I made sure to leave a voicemail at Vera's Portland number: "This is the Third Millennium saying hello to the Second!" When she and I at last spoke, in January, she seemed to indicate she'd enjoyed the message. Seemed to, halfway or a quarter's worth, still saving her energy for the work within. She was sitting on self-discoveries that must've felt immense, and I struggled to hold my peace. Parent and child, I figured, each had to cook in their own water.

That spring, when my university awarded me a grant for my Naples work, my best funding to date, I followed through by arranging a long stay. I even lined up a magazine assignment. So too, when Vera's mother enrolled her in one of those sobriety hikes, out in one of Oregon's wilderness areas, I co-signed and paid my share. Such therapy was popular in the Twenty-Aughts; the idea seemed laudable, taking teens away from temptation and into a natural high. But on her trek, Vera was somehow found lacking. She didn't fall within the norms, on the rubrics the therapists preferred. By the time I returned, she was in a facility in the semi-arid outback, a "transition home."

At least I'd armored myself, by then, against the questions about abuse. This time I had a formula for shutting them down; I offered to take a polygraph, "under formal circumstances." With, ahem, a lawyer present. That would back off the guys on the other end—and they *were* all guys, I noticed, these "directors" laying down the rules for a young woman at risk. But there's no need to make things any worse than they were. I'll just point out that such wilderness treatments resulted in a number of lawsuits, a kid or two died on the trail, and nowadays it's strictly regulated. At the time, I stood firmly by my argument. Before V went on that hike, neither she nor I had known the stakes; she'd been shanghai'd.

In dealing with her, meanwhile, I went back to old technology, working by hand. I abandoned the smudged keyboard for yellow legal pads. In this, I should add, I was simply following house rules; parents were allowed no contact beyond a 20-minute phone call on Sundays. More than that, though, as I filled each long sheet and turned it over, I'd also turn over, and over, the scattered onionskins of her makeup and mine. I faced up to the worst we'd done, perhaps "fearless and searching" or perhaps the Southern Italian equivalent, and I offered more apologies. But then, there's no place like Naples to show you that "making amends" is just another step, and that there are many more than twelve. Every fix is just another patch of mortar, helping to bolster a fragile older structure. In my letters, mostly I spoke of the future; I scratched after core elements about me and my loved ones in the hope that, brought to light, they'd help in rebuilding. My child could yet be her best—that was the hope, as I worked into the night, the letter always the last to-do of the day, easily some of the most exhausting days of my life, and as I sat over my inky scrawl (ink, because if I stopped to erase one word, I'd erase a hundred), I got somewhere, I sensed the strata of trouble yielding up strengths of character, both hers and mine. I could spell out that she was gay.

My child was gay, sure. Gay, and it made no difference. However she defined love, she was herself loved.

These letters also had more neutral moments, newsy. Whatever dialogue Vera and I had enjoyed, I strove to keep it in play, and I usually sent along a book. This reading, wouldn't you know it, took up a lot of my Sunday calls. She wouldn't say a word about her sexuality, but she gave me a rave review of *The Scarlet Letter*. In particular she marveled over how Hester Prynne had ended up, "a moral example to young women." Exact words, those, and what father could forget them? Or fail to work with them, next letter?

By way of reply, I still didn't get much. But then the men in charge of Vera's program kept me busy, as I grew more explicit about legal action, and as the summer wound down she showed everyone she'd kept working, herself. She'd mastered her own new map, one that sketched a future outside the "home" and back in Portland. Soon she'd registered as a high-school senior, and over the year she became a leader with the school's AA program. To me all this couldn't have felt any sweeter, a gratifying obverse of my howling misery on the day I left for Chicago. Still, I understood that this wasn't the year for her to visit. Rather, between Vera and me, the next substantial exchange was a long time coming, and a long way from either Southern Italy or the Pacific Northwest. My sister had arranged a rental on the Massachusetts coast, *Scarlet Letter* territory, and she'd agreed that a stay would make a nice graduation present for my daughter. But there by the Atlantic, our conversation felt like a miracle:

Vera, I'm so sorry my work took me away from you at such a hard time.
Pop, the worst that happened, it would've happened anyway.
Maybe, but my not being there made it harder.
Maybe. But you were working, trying to make something of yourself, and maybe that made it easier. If you got somewhere so could I.

This time I can't be so sure about the actual words, because we talked quite a while. Still, I've got the gist. As for sex and love, for instance, we said next to nothing. V had come out a while back, and now she had a steady girl, another Sober Soldier. Together they'd made plans for a summer trip of their own. While I was back in Naples, that year, they'd be out at Burning Man. Out in the Nevada desert, of course, they'd be offered plenty of pills, plenty of fat spliffs, but then, they had to handle the same at home. That was the everyday, for my child, and there in my sister's rental we had only a single still moment to honor it. Around us whirled more uncertainties than I'd care to count—myself, I had another few years before I met my new wife, and more before we settled in Des Moines—but among these, teetering between what the voyage discovers and how the home consoles, we found a still point of sharing and caring, together by the Atlantic on an evening when the sun's glinting might've stretched to the Gates of Hercules.

* * *

On our latest Naples visit, the one that might provide a happy ending, my "girl" had taken to sporting a sketch of a beard and mustache. I rather liked the look, and during the trip, the same as on every trip, I called the U.S. This no longer required a Call Center or Internet Bar, we had good wi-fi and the latest Skype, and I loved what I heard when V took my place before the screen.

"Man!" exclaimed the person Stateside. "You look so *Italian!*"

Great as that was to hear, by then the most Italian part of my own story was over. Halfway through the second decade of the 21st Century, Naples could do no more for me. It'd unraveled my onion, *si sicuro*. Every peel had been put through a wringer; the city's key revelation, for one of the world's comfortable few, was my own vulnerability. It showed me how easily a cozy setup could go to pieces. Finally, though, this discovery became only another passage in the John-journey. Along the way, I've also got the little girl I encouraged to play, to tootle on recorder while I strummed guitar, and the heartbroken teen in grunge gear, a young person I both hurt and helped. In these too I can identify what's Neapolitan: the music, the caution, the resilience.

My child's all done, I should add, with the trials of ten and fifteen years ago. The years since have seen plenty of traffic, clamorous arrivals and muted departures, but there's been no drug abuse, no destructive therapy. Lately, the worst wrangles have been the same as most Americans, home and work and health care. Naturally I wonder how my father would've reacted, but he's long gone, and his ghost remains quiet. I'd like to think that, whatever exists yet of the expansive spirit I knew as "Pop," it's pleased to catch the occasional strains of another relative making music.

Also Vera speaks freely of the scary past. Our recent return to Naples was certainly a happy time, but once as we shared a seat on the funicolare, I learned some unhappy news. An old friend had died, I learned. A former Best Friend Forever, no less, a girl easy to recall and always a live wire. During the high school's *Midsummer Night's Dream,* a disco version, her dancing stood out even in the ensemble numbers. Before she turned 30, however, the poor kid was gone. She OD'd in some Portland crackhouse. Down in Los Angeles, where my grown child was building her career, the news had been slow to arrive. But then, someone so close as V had long known the real problem.

"A terrible family," I was told. "Christian creeps, you know, talk like a preacher and neglect the children. Total neglect."

As I say, I heard about this in Naples, and then that same night, the duo I'd brought to town stayed out late. Myself, I had work the next morning, a meeting with a publisher. The struggle never ends, does it? Of course there's a good side to that, a calling that doesn't tap out at 40 or 60, so long as you feel up to the effort. How's that core? Doing your planks? But while I went to bed, that night, the younger generation had a party. With cousin Rikki, they made the old center their playground. They stayed out till after the bars close and the *scippatori* get busy. I don't imagine the three of them went long before spotting a whore, a junkie, or an illegal African. Out on Spaccanapoli, bad trouble lurks everywhere.

The next evening we were down in Paestum, spellbound before the ruins. The floodlights come on after dark, turning the temples to glacier cliffs. There's Hera the mother, Athena the city, and then the one consecrated to some deity nobody can agree on. Immense, plainly the largest of the three, this mysterious sanctuary is lined with columns thick as redwoods, six across and 14 deep, while amid the shadows within you make out smaller divisions: shrines, passageways, an innermost Holy of Holies. As for the deity who claimed that sanctum, I like the idea that the place was a Pantheon, open to any god who might be handy. That's how I've used it, laying a hand on the base of one column or another and calling, wordlessly, on some ill-defined Spirit.

A Paestum temple is another risky construct, to be sure. Should the wrong stone give way, it'd be a cataclysm. Difficulties like that help make the Campanian crescent unique—no keyboard around the world presents quite such a "QWERTY problem"—and yet recently I've been seeing Naples everywhere. Whenever I get to a new place, now after so many returns to the old one, I start to spot landmarks I came to know over by the Tyrrhenian. In DC one January, following a sea-change in US politics, I found myself in the same swank hotel bar as a thousand blue- and black-suited lobbyists, all stinking of "dark money." Camorra money, sure: the natural analogy, once you've lived in Naples. The mob can always find a well-dressed front, even Ivy League. But if life in the States can reflect some deplorable element of the ancient seaport, its better sides also turn up. The good life, even in a Midwestern center like Des Moines, now includes a *centro* and a *Lungomare*. "The Riverwalk," they call it, but I know just where they're coming from. "Walkability" and "mixed-use," I know it well. In those same cities, too, they've caught the passion for Neapolitan pizza.

The menu always leads off with the Margherita. Another writer and I have a standing joke that if we've ever got books out at the same time, we'll go on a Pizza Tour.

Then there are my ever-more-frequent visits to LA. Impossible city, right? Every visit, I'm hearing it again: *you have no idea how difficult it is in LA.*

When it comes to facing the apocalypse, nowhere else in America offers such rich potential. The threat brought on by climate change is only the latest of the Doomsday scenarios. An earthquake could rip the freeways to pieces! So too, when it comes to sustaining a mature and genuine love, where have you got a harder row to hoe than in Hollywood? Where are face and body more of a commodity, an item on the ledger? Then there's the crime, shredding families and neighborhoods. If it's not the Crips and the Bloods, it's the Mexican Eme or the Korean Triads. Nevertheless, despite these dangers and more, newcomers keep streaming in. Some arrive with as little going for them as the Mediterranean boat people, but they believe in the city. They can't shake its song of promise, as every year the vast nexus of Angeleno cultures hatches a fresh cluster of successes. One of them, I daresay, is a musician and DJ named Domini.

Like Naples, in other words, the Southern Californian metropolis refuses to dry up and blow away. It's too big for that, too deeply connected to vital economies, and on top of anything else, it's too goddamn beautiful. Granted, LA has no single viewpoint like up in the Vomero, no sweeping panorama across land and sea, with its array of dangers all somehow confounded. Still, over by the Pacific, you'll find plenty of nooks and crannies to lift the heart. A surprising number of these—views out towards the sky, or in towards a shrine—can only be found on foot, but then I'm lucky enough to have a knowledgeable guide. I've even given some thought to LA as the place where I might grow old. I'm frightened about it, sure, growing old. I'm frightened about a lot of things, and yet I'm flexible, I'm open, and in getting to that, nothing's mattered so much as Naples. I could go so far as to say I'm nothing without Naples, but then if you ask me, neither are all the hymns raised, and all the husks left rotting, across our entire vertiginous world.

ACKNOWLEDGMENTS

THE LONG GESTATION PERIOD FOR *The Archeology of a Good Ragù* became itself part of the story, and over those twenty years I was lucky enough to publish many of my reflections on Naples, in *GQ*, *Ninth Letter*, *New York Times Travel*, *Southwest Review*, *Zone 3*, and elsewhere. Such publication has continued, too, in *Literary Hub*, *Hopkins Review*, and *Virginia Quarterly Review*, among other places. Naturally, these pieces all went through changes for the sake of the text. Nevertheless the magazines and journals, along with their editors, have my infinite thanks.

Grazie infinite as well to the entire busy crew at Guernica World Editions, and in particular Michael Mirolla.

As for early readers, naturally those include the writers kind enough to commit blurbs. Among the others, I've got to salute George Colt, Fred Gardaphé, Joseph Salvatore, Robin Hemley, and Lettie Prell.

Financing for the work always seemed a miracle worthy of San Gennaro, but here on the earthly plane, I'm grateful especially to the Iowa Department of Cultural Affairs, various Oregon and Portland city commissions for the arts and humanities, and the Center for the Writing Arts at Northwestern University.

Cover artwork: "Partenope," by Oni Wong, *Cortile Artestesa*, Naples.

Seems to me that *al fondo*, at bottom, a book like this is its own Acknowledgments. I would hope every page trembles with gratitude.

ABOUT THE AUTHOR

JOHN DOMINI'S FICTION AND NON-FICTION has earned praise from Salman Rushdie and Richard Ford, among others. He has ten previous books, including a trilogy of novels set in Naples, the latest *The Color Inside a Melon*. He has a Fellowship from the National Endowment for the Arts, as well as other awards, in all genres. He publishes regularly in *Lit Hub* and the *Washington Post* and elsewhere, and he's taught at Harvard and Northwestern. He's lived all over the US, as well as Italy.

ALSO BY JOHN DOMINI

SHORT STORIES

Bedlam
Highway Trade
MOVIEOLA!

NOVELS

Talking Heads: 77
Earthquake I.D.
A Tomb on the Periphery
The Color Inside a Melon

POETRY

The Grand McLuckless Road Atlas

ESSAYS & CRITICISM

The Sea-God's Herb

TRANSLATION

Books & Rough Business, a memoir by Tullio Pironti

Printed in June 2021
by Gauvin Press,
Gatineau, Québec

fingers behind his head and crosses his legs at the ankles. In her pink scuffs, Slomka shuffles into the kitchen and pours two American bourbons, neat.

He calls out into the kitchen, it's a question premised on the assumption that she was more erotically exciting in a former time.

Speaking from the kitchen, she tells him not to start again, then shuffles back into the bedroom and hands him his drink. His rib cage is convex, like that of a chicken. His shoulders and knees and hips are sharp thrusts of bone, his arms and legs are long and skinny. Slomka told a girlfriend that sex with Götz was like sleeping with a bag of wooden toys.

No, really, tell me, he says.

Silence.

Slomka says she does not remember, she thinks she was prettier before the war, that's all she meant. She meant nothing.

That's when you were coaching Faith and Beauty girls, right? he says. Rhythmic movement, which I like?

She says she does not remember, that men found her attractive before the war.

Silence.

He says he had a couple of Faith and Beauty girls before his unit went to Africa, that they were amazing.

They weren't whores, she says sharply. She says they were fine women, but it doesn't matter any more, so she wants to stop talking about it.

Perfect wives for German heroes, he says. Isn't that what they were supposed to become? What garbage. Nobody believed it, even then. Nobody.

They were lovely girls, Slomka says, lying down on the bed and stretching out beside Götz's naked body. They did believe it, everybody did. None of that matters any more, so stop talking about it.

Silence.

I never believed any of it, he says, and takes a long drag on his cigarette, flicks off the dangle of ash into a saucer on the floor beside the bed. I never believed anything, that was the best way to go. I knew some real fanatics in Africa, guys in my outfit, all up everybody's ass with it, all the time. There was this one, from somewhere in Bavaria I think, he couldn't stop talking about it, but I didn't listen — just kept my head low, did my job, and that was that, all I paid attention to, since the desert was full of unfriendlies trying to shoot our butts off. You didn't have time to think about it. But even after the unit surrendered, even in the POW camp in Texas, where the big shots among the prisoners bossed everybody around, making us keep on being soldiers when there wasn't any point, some guys were still going on about it, how great and noble it was, and all that. The GIs made us watch movies of what they said were prison camps run by the SS, and the movies were supposed to prove how bad it was, but I never believed that, either. I never believed anything, except that we couldn't lose, and I was wrong about that. I was right about everything else.

Slomka tells him he was so smart, smarter than everybody.

He re-crosses his legs at the ankles, takes another long drag on the cigarette. He slides his free hand under Slomka's backside.

Not smarter, he says. Maybe dumber. He said he survived, he is good in bed, he likes women and, in that sense, is dissimilar to the artist in the house next door, who has not been visited by a woman in months.

The rarity of this conversation should be noted, Alexander observes. Götz and Slomka almost never talk after sexual congress. They normally have little to talk about. His teasing her is unusual, at least as unusual as her snapping at the bait. You are writing about a singular occurrence, Alexander says, one hitherto unheard of, at least as pertains to Götz and Slomka. You should not let anything stop you.

Silence.

Slomka tells Götz he is obsessed by the artist who lives in the house next door.

Götz denies being obsessed, but says that one has to wonder about a man on the young side of 40 who, in the winter of 1956, never leaves his place or has female company, and almost never answers a rap on the door. But there was one time, Götz says, when I stopped by, this was last month, and this time, he wanted to talk. He told me — me, of all people, I didn't even know him — that he could not remember anything before June, 1945, when he was in the POW camp at Cuxhaven, and that was why he didn't have the money for the rent. He said he couldn't work, couldn't draw, or whatever it is that he does, because he had stopped remembering in Cuxhaven, and now he wanted to remember something from before 1945, but he couldn't.

I said he had to pay the rent, the rest of it was none of my business. He was saying crazy things like that, but I let him go on, since there was no shutting him up. I said that wasn't my problem, that he had to pay the rent, or move out, even though I didn't want him to move out, since the old house has been so hard to rent, now that there are so many new houses, I thought nobody would take it.

So he said his mother would send him money for the rent, it would come the next week, or the week after that, and he asked me if this would be all right. I said, yes, because I didn't want to try renting the place to somebody else. The money did come, or he got it from somewhere, and he paid the rent, Götz says.

～48

Alexander says I can stop writing now, because it appears that Götz is confused about his recent visit with Jupp, which had nothing to do with rent, and because I am going to describe nothing further of an erotic nature, which is what interests him.

Alexander is a curious child. At dusk, when we watch the edge of the asphalt parking lot, waiting for deer to come out of the forest, he wants me to shoot an animal so he can see it die. When not with me or Mr. Steinway, he spends hours reading the adventure books by Edgar Rice Burroughs that the owner, long ago, bought from a jobber in old volumes and shelved prominently in the lounge, apparently in a bid to make the Occidental seem like a literate place. There is row upon row of books published in the 1920s and 1930s. Among the used books that the owner bought as a job-lot, and the existence of which he had been unaware, are works by progressive sexologists of the 1920s, written for ignorant maidens about to be married, and Alexander has found and read them, and asks me what they mean. I have nothing to say to him about pessaries or urnings. I was a curious child, until I saw my naked father do something to a woman in a motel on the frayed edge of a city in the South, something he seemed to enjoy, but that had nothing to do with me. Since that time, I have not been naked. I have been curious about nothing other than modernity, the prospects of my race, Jupp's transfixing art, and certain words that pass across the silences between Götz and Slomka on an unseasonably warm German night in 1956.

Alexander does not permit me to record Götz's reply to Slomka's statement that she has heard two men and a woman talking on the sidewalk underneath her window. It is not like her to eavesdrop, but she listened when one of the men said he saw a movie he liked last year, then described it.

Slomka tells Götz she saw the same one. The film was set in an Alpine valley, on a farm in the valley, or, at least, that was what the film was about, a farm in an Alpine valley. A village girl, engaged to the farmer's son, is seduced by a smooth-talking stranger from the city and so lured away from the village to the city, where the stranger neglects her and abuses her trust. Ultimately abandoned by the stranger, she finds her way back to the village in the Alpine valley, where the farmer's son forgives her and resolves to marry her despite her disgrace. The film ended on the wedding day, all church bells and dancing, for that is the law of German *Heimat* movies created at the enormously successful Berolina studio during the Cold War. The man on the sidewalk, Slomka tells Götz, said he liked the film because it resembled movies made during the Third Reich. She says she liked the film because the wronged and redeemed girl resembled Sonja Henie in *One in a Million,* the Norwegian ice-skating star's first Hollywood movie, which Slomka saw four times after the film's release in 1936.

Dr. Goebbels superintended the distribution of *One in a Million* throughout Germany as a personal favour to Henie, his celebrity acquaintance, who bewitched him and Slomka in 1936. Unable to have Henie, Slomka followed her attraction to Nordic beauty into fleeting affairs with blonde, athletic girls of the northern Aryan sort before discovering Götz, beside whose naked body she lounges in her flat in Heerdt, a district of Düsseldorf, Germany. This is the kind of detail Alexander would like to hear more about, but I choose not to gratify him, since he refuses to allow me to write things I urgently want to.

In another film produced by Berolina, one that defied the *Heimat* formula by having an unhappy ending, and so became a box-office flop

— a movie that Slomka has watched — the girl who looks like Sonja Henie plays a simple, lovely maiden living with her elderly, widowed father on an ample dairy farm in a Bavarian valley. A mammoth national agricultural concern has plans to take over the farm, an outcome the girl thinks she does not want. But the girl is in love with another farmer's son, who explains to her that the results of conglomeration will include peace and prosperity and certainty. After they marry, he says, the pair of them will work for the company, and so continue to live their pastoral lives, but on a regular salary.

Persuaded, she persuades her father to sell his land and dairy herd to the corporation, which introduces high-performance machinery and migrant labour, making the young couple redundant. The old father is forced out of his house and sent to live in a public institution for the dying. In the final scene, the girl and her husband bid a sad farewell to the father in his white room at the institution and promise to write after they find work in the city.

Alexander says that Slomka did not weep during the film's concluding moments, that she was sensual and cruel, being merely interested in the flesh of the actress who looked like Sonja Henie looked in 1936, that Slomka was uninterested in the sad story. I would perhaps answer Alexander's assertion, were there not a disturbance in the street under Slomka's window at this hour past midnight in 1956. Götz hears it, shushes Slomka, rolls out of bed and goes, still naked, to the window, peers out into the warm darkness, in the direction the noise comes from.

∾49

No disturbance interrupted for long the calm of the Occidental Hotel during the Cold War. Disputes erupted occasionally between lovers, or between husbands and the lovers of their wives, but they never ended in bloodshed, and they were kept from becoming public scandals by Mr. Steinway's timely, discreet interventions with the parties involved. Since only white people were permitted to register at the hotel, and all of them were conventional and modest, ruckus of any sort was unknown. Faulty toilets and smells in hallways were attended to immediately by handymen armed with the latest weapons of their respective trades. In his autobiography, Henry Kissinger calls the hotel a haven of peace in a stormy world, and commends Mr. Steinway (while not mentioning his name) for the efficient management of all details pertaining to the comfort of white people.

Rudolph Sandman, the novelist, soaked for hours in the enormous tub in the spa, thinking of plots and characters for her forthcoming books, though she imagined only ones identical with those that had made her previous novels best-sellers. The hotel was new then. Her ideas, like the menus in the dining room, like the music played for guests in the evenings, like the pleasures guests drifted among, were old. They had once been fresh and electric. Then they became popular and banal, and, around the time of the missile crisis, they were stale and tawdry. But no guests noticed, least of all Rudolph Sandman, who believed everything she thought, while she soaked in the tub during the Cold War, was miraculously original.

This is information of the sort that Alexander appreciates. He is a sensuous child. Like Rudolph Sandman many years before, he took long baths in near-scalding water when the travelling folk he lived among gathered at the Occidental Hotel. Had he not done so, he would surely have been as dirty as they were. While I found much about them disagreeable — their manners were coarse, their music vain and raucous, their bodies noisome — their thoughts, in several instances, accorded with my own.

The travelling folk, for example, do not allow negroes to move with them. They settle disputes by main force, which ensures the sovereignty among them of strong, well-knit men. They do not tolerate traitors to their race, especially when imprisoned. In the jails of the United States, indeed, they maintain peace with manly violence, or so I am told, having never been in prison myself — but I believe the reports are true, since peace can no longer be assured by any other method. At times like this, thinking these thoughts and writing these words, I become hopeless, but Alexander encourages me to stand firm and not relent. The travelling folk, off-scouring of the earth, do not relent. I do not approve of the religion that seems to attract them, especially when they are imprisoned — unironic reverence for the old Nordic gods and heroes that merely mimics, but does not supplant, the worship of the Christian god I detest. (The missionaries of Odinism are prodigiously busy among prison populations, and the kindreds they have spawned can be found in jails across America.)

From his schoolbook translation of the Old Norse poem *Hávamál,* Jupp learned of (but did not worship) Odin, who hung, grievously wounded, nine nights on the windy tree "that no-one knows" in order to win the intoxicating mead of poetry, vision, wisdom. The biographer states that Jupp was an atheist — but only to suggest that his spirituality was therefore opportunistic, manipulative, basically unfelt. The contrary is true, as the artworks themselves prove: They embody deep spiritual feelings, albeit ones divorced from Christian dogmas, open to organic unities and pluralities, and to savage nature and natural power.

Indeed, the tyrannical humility of the Christian god is absent. But so are the obnoxious materialism of the modern "atheist," and the moral defeatism of the contemporary "intellectual." Present, in all Jupp's work, is the sweet drink of poetry, which he won by hanging on the windy tree early in 1956, undergoing all that in the darkness of the box.

Figure 7: A 1971 graphite drawing by Joseph Beuys, entitled *Young Blacksmith with his Work* and now in the collection of the National Galleries of Scotland.

In a point-form chronology, Joseph Beuys framed his life-story as a series of "exhibitions," Austellungen or settings-out, or manifestations, or actions, or theophanies that came to him or in which he was a participant. After listing the year 1929, in which he turned eight, he wrote this line: "Exhibition at the grave of Genghis Khan." An anonymous curatorial note that accompanies the drawing states that Beuys believed a translation of Genghis Khan would be John Smith, "meaning he would have been a blacksmith. In this role, working with fire to create tools and objects from metal, Beuys compared Khan to a shaman ..."

The creation or work of Genghis Khan, the shaman-blacksmith, is Eurasia. "From the beginning of the work ... Joseph Beuys has shown his interest in the ancient cultures of the Eurasian continent, and looking back at his oeuvre we can already discern some early connections with Tibet too." (Wijers, Writing as Sculpture.) There is a 1958 watercolour that presents Genghis Khan's daughter riding an elk. In Applied Grammatology, *page 234, the critic Gregory Ulmer remarks on Beuys' "childhood fantasies about Genghis Khan (he carried a cane with him everywhere and imagined himself to be a nomad herdsman)." Mircea Eliade (in* The Forge and the Crucible: The Origins and Structure of Alchemy, *page 85) recalls that, in Mongolian epic poetry, "the word for 'smith' (darkhan) signifies both 'hero' and 'free-horseman'." Beuys was aware that, according to some traditions cherished by the Eurasian nomads, the first occupation of the world-creating Genghis Khan was that of a smith. (Eliade, op. cit.)*

The smith, the consecrated one, the hero — but also the stranger: "As early as 1880 or thereabouts," Eliade writes (pages 88–89), "Richard Andrée ... had succeeded in showing that metal workers, almost everywhere, form groups apart; they are mysterious beings who must be isolated from the rest of the community." Late legends show the smith to be a superior man, a shaman and visionary, yet the servant of all, even an outcast — he who forges the weapons with which the warrior fights his battle of initiation.

But in the myths that come from the youth of the race, or in the historical figure of Genghis Khan, the smith and the warrior are one man, united are the smithy and the field of war (sites of transfiguration). Siegfried, in the third music-drama of Wagner's Ring der Nibelungen, *welds the sword Nothung from the fragments of his father's weapon, then executes his heroic feat of slaying the dragon Fafner with it. Eliade again (page 106): "There would appear to have existed therefore, at several different cultural levels (which is a mark of very great antiquity), a close connection between the art of the smith, the occult sciences (shamanism, magic, healing, etc.), and the art of song, dance and poetry." The hammer's rhythmic striking of the anvil is the origin of music, and the smith's powerful songs bring wholeness to the dying or infirm. In European folktales, "Jesus Christ (or St. Peter, St. Nicholas or St. Eloi) plays the role of a blacksmith who heals the sick and rejuvenates the old by putting them in a heated oven or forging them on an anvil." (Ibid., pages 106–107).*

The smithy is a kind of kitchen, in which the raw is cooked. In a footnote appended to his Felt: Fluxus, Joseph Beuys, and the Dalai

Lama, *Chris Thompson complains that the many accounts of the artist's near-fatal crash in Crimea and his alleged rescue and revival by Tatar nomads universally fail to deal with the "commingling of the signifiers of healing and food-preparation" in Beuys' oft-repeated narrative. His injured body, in the story, "is not so much treated as it is kneaded and worked, smeared with fat, rolled in felt, cured in both the medical and culinary senses of the word, baked back to health in a makeshift oven—producing, literally, a rising from death. And in Beuys' tale the healing scene has the same ending as would a certain kind of satisfying meal: it concludes with the enactment of communion in the sharing of food and the enmeshing of the guest in a palpable sense of kinship and belonging." (page 281)*

∾50

Within an old neighbourhood of the city—though no part of it is truly old, this Southern city now having become much like any place in America—my brother found a room for cheap rent in what had been the mansion of the Witherspoons, prominent cotton brokers until ruined by the collapse of commodity prices. The oldest Witherspoon boy, a contemporary of my father, was a man of the vague sort, who, in his will, bequeathed his dry, disintegrating collection of Civil War paper memorabilia to the city's principal chapter of the United Daughters of the Confederacy, who did not want it. The son had inherited the heap of yellowed war-time and post-war clippings, flyers, posters, political and pious pamphlets, quotidian diaries of the widows with whom she surrounded herself and so on from a maiden great-aunt who treasured every evidence of the Southern struggle while it was ongoing, and for years after the defeat, and passed on this obsession to her nephew. He lived alone with the scraps and tatters in a trailer beyond the city's edge, working on and off for decades at a descriptive catalogue of his hoard, which he did not complete before his death.

I consider this devotion to papery ruins reactionary. The battle for Southern culture will be won by red-blooded partisans, true men, not archivists. That is what I told my brother when he first approached me for money to flee American depravity. That is what I told him after his return from inner Asia, where his taste for the archaic had been inflamed by an acquaintance of the boy Jules. My brother took the advice I gave him on the latter occasion, and decided to seek activity.

～51

For a while, his desire, or the desire I had invented for him, was gratified by the standard-bearers of the neo-Confederate cause, the partisans of which seek to rid the South of American cultural hegemony and restore the inner South's Cavalier values of manliness, cleanliness and unyielding resistance to voluptuousness.

He went to meetings, and dutifully attended lectures by judges on the primordial right of secession and the righteousness of armed defense of one's home and property, lectures by historians on the origins of Southern folk music, lectures by scholars of grits and blood-feuding and Presbyterianism. He turned out for rallies organized by leaders of the movement to celebrate the free flying of the Southern flag on public property. At these events, nationalist preachers harangued the crowds, which could be large, about the coming day of Southern independence, about staying armed, and vigilant with respect to the dark races and the enflamers of their crude passions in high places. My brother listened to the lectures and speeches, and was pleased by what he heard until he began to tire of the endless talk, which did not satisfy my orders to him to seek action.

I hate the prattle of racist intellectuals. It does not prevent one instance of pollution, or the uttering of one lewd remark by a mulatto to a white woman in the mountains. My brother has seen them in the mountains, conversing as a praeludium to intercourse. None of this could happen at the Occidental Hotel during the Cold War, or that part of it before the missile crisis, when men with negro blood were not allowed to register or dine there.

At the time my brother had begun to weary of racist talk, the first robbery of a two-man armoured currency transport took place, on a desolate road in the Southern mountains. The robbers were five in number, according to a guard who was not hurt, who was allowed to live and talk. On national television, the unharmed guard said he courageously foiled the robbers for a bit with reminders that they really did not want to get into trouble with God by stealing his shipment of cash, until their leader, a quiet, unruffled man in no great hurry, instructed the two guards to kneel, which they did, whereupon he shot one of them dead. At that moment, the living guard decided he had no choice but to cooperate in the transfer of 3.6-million dollars from the armoured vehicle to the robbers' truck and listen to what they said, what they wanted told to the world.

The police forbade the ineffectual young man's divulging on television what the robbers had to say, but he could not keep his secret to himself. He told it to his wife, who told another woman on the firing range, who told it to her alcoholic boyfriend, who kept it quiet until he blurted out a version of it during a drink-soaked call to a phone-in radio show broadcast from the city. The notorious, lethal robbery, he said he heard, had been, according to the gang's leader, the handiwork of a hidden group without a name or charter, motivated to commit their crime by neither greed for money nor lust for revenge. No, they were gathering funds to fuel mere war for the salvation of Southern whites from the social and cultural depredations of the United States, for the preservation of the race, and its primal values, for the integrity of the West. Having thus reeled off what he had heard was the robbers' agenda, the boyfriend of the woman on the firing range then indulged in some fantastic embroidery of his gossip. The radio host and his audience were given to understand (quite misleadingly) that the robbers were heroically fit, violent young white males at war with the United States over sexual access to white women, which the Second World War was essentially about.

Just a hunch, prevaricated the caller agreeably. I listen to this show all the time, he said — I know what you think about the right-wing gun nuts, my wife is one, which I'm not saying I like, but she has the right to choose. Anyway, I love it when you take out after the right-wingers, though I am not a liberal, and I didn't vote for the half-negro president. Thanks for taking my call.

The host disconnected him, then pressed the next flashing button on his telephone switching mechanism, which had suddenly begun to sparkle.

I listened to the broadcast for its remaining 87 minutes. Many men and women who phoned in were offended by the male caller's conjecture about the ideological flavour of the gang. They accused him, and the host, of smearing and slandering Southern patriots, who would never stoop to robbing a cash truck on an open highway. As my brother discovered, the callers were right. The patriots never would.

$\sim$**52**

Near the old Witherspoon house, where my brother lodges, is a little street named after an ancestor of the son who was an archivist. There is nothing architecturally remarkable about this wide alley that cuts through what was once a fashionable residential district. It is lined by magnolia trees and by decayed two-storey buildings with glass-fronted shops at the level of the sidewalk, flats above. The shops were occupied, in the age of white people, by stylish milliners, couturiers, confectioners, stationers and other merchants, from whom the respectable and would-be respectable families of the city and the countryside beyond obtained the material costumery and equipage of their class. The arrival of department stores uptown doomed the commercial enterprises that once attracted the traffic of the wives of bankers, lawyers, doctors, the wealthiest cotton planters, and marked the start of the street's decline to what it is today: a shabby row of second-hand outlets, cheap appliance emporia, and the like, most of them catering to the impoverished negroes who now live round about.

One shop, however, stands out from the downmarket commercial clutter. It is a bookstore, and a sort of reading room, operated by a Mr. Smith, who has fortified it against marauders by placing tight steel grids over the windows and doors. I do not go there when I visit the city. But I know about it from my brother, who does, or, I should say, did.

The publications stocked by Mr. Smith and neatly shelved, floor to ceiling, in old-fashioned oak bookcases, include perennial favourites of men who, like my brother, are curious and spiritual. One can slake his adolescent thirst for futuristic fantasy with *Turner Diaries,* in which white militants based in liberated California rain down nuclear destruction on the eastern cities, then eradicate the dark races, and with other novels in this tradition. He can learn, if he chooses, the northern, white-power mysteries and rune-lore of Odinism, as retailed by the American visionary and murderer David Lane, whose penitentiary guards charitably allowed him to write and publish numerous occult testaments that continue to win converts (especially among prisoners) to the cult of Thor, Balder, Tyr and white man's blood. Young customers are encouraged to browse and not leaned upon to buy. For their entertainment, Mr. Smith keeps two cupboards stacked high with ephemera quick-printed and prolifically disgorged by death-metal bands and fans, boys' clubs, racial associations, Satanist churches, Eurasianist youth leagues. My brother, who is not young, has no taste for this juvenile matter, about which I know nothing.

For more mature and discerning clients, the proprietor keeps works by the Chilean diplomat Miguel Serrano, author of *The Golden Thread: Esoteric Hitlerism* (1978), by the extraordinary Frenchwoman Savitri Devi (*née* Maximiani Portas) and other seminal evangelists of National Socialism at its most spiritual. The faith of these intellectuals had not been extinguished by the downfall of 1945. "And the atrocious end? The agony of the proud Third German Reich?" Devi asks in her most famous post-war book. "It was but the beginning of the Via dolorosa leading to the great New Beginning. All the horror of the present and of the immediate future would pass. The hell in which the German people were to live, for years, would pass. National Socialism would rise again because it is true to cosmic Reality, and because that which is true does not pass. Germany's Via dolorosa was, indeed, the Way to coming glory. It had to be taken, if the privileged Nation was to fulfill her mission absolutely, i.e. if she was to be the Nation that died for the sake of the highest human race, which she embodied, and that would rise again to take the lead of those surviving Aryans who are — at last! — to understand her message of life and to carry it with them into the splendour of the dawning Golden Age."

Her footsteps dogged by the West German political police and spies from the occupation armies, constantly exposed to danger by her penchant for befriending and succouring survivors, Savitri Devi made her way through Germany's post-apocalyptic wreckage, distributing leaflets that encouraged bravery and promised swift vindication, writing in the waiting rooms of train stations and borrowed rooms and jail cells, always writing. In the most difficult circumstances, Devi composed the manuscript of *The Lightning and the Sun,* dedicating the work "to the god-like individual of our times; the Man against Time; the greatest European of all times; both Sun and Lightning: Adolf Hitler, as a tribute of unfailing love and loyalty, for ever and ever." Mr. Smith's copy (first edition, Calcutta, 1958), which he occasionally shows to his most devout clients, is autographed and inscribed by the author, to whom the future bookstore's owner took the rarity when he visited her in Delhi. He was as slim and eager as he had been during his last military tour in Vietnam, just before the fall of Saigon to the nationalist revolutionaries, whose valour he appreciated. My brother tells me that he has become stout.

Devi was very old then, living alone, but not lonely. She enjoyed the company of numerous, much-beloved cats and birds. A guiding principle of her life was the defense of the right of animals to protection and human loyalty; she had not eaten flesh since girlhood. And she accepted with grace and gratitude the attentions of the many, mostly youthful admirers who came from Europe and America to render homage. Wonderfully energetic, acute and animated, despite her great age, Devi enchanted the young devotees with stories of adventures in postwar Germany, of the persecuted former soldiers and activists and camp guards she met in the course of her missionary labours — each man and woman a living witness to the Third Reich, as she was not, having lived and worked for the Axis cause throughout the war years in India. They knew, as she did not, that briefly triumphant incarnation of the vision she followed and adored.

The Lightning and the Sun, written when its author was on the move in post-war Europe, testifies to the moral electricity that galvanized three world-historical men. There is Akhenaton, the Egyptian king and sun-worshipping idealist (the Man *above* Time, in Devi's reckoning); Genghis Khan, brutal creator in Eurasia of history's largest land empire (the Man *in* Time); and Hitler, the Man *Against* Time, in whose astonishing personality were combined the world-transcending solar esoterism of Akhenaton and the utter ruthlessness, the "lightning," of Genghis Khan. Who will grasp the meaning of Hitler? Very few. "Nobody can understand him," Devi writes, "save a true artist who is, at the same time a true revolutionary: a person of one dream and one aim, like himself." Those who do understand him recognize the roots of his power in the worship of Life and Nature, and the depth of his resistance to all man-centered systems of thought, including Marxism and the "diluted (and. moreover, obsolete) forms of Jewish poison for Aryan consumption known as Christianity and Western Democracy."

Hitler's was and remains a hard way, according to Devi. "His Gospel of Germanic pride and glorious healthy earthly life—'freedom and bread'—coupled with the hard blows of the early Storm Troopers' fists, that kept order in his public meetings and, when necessary, fought his battle in the streets, broke down whatever opposition stood in his way to power. There was, in that blending of mystical insight, elemental logic and well-organized brutality—of truth and youth—that characterizes National Socialism, a grandeur that appealed to the masses and to the very best of the best people: to those exceptionally intelligent and reliable men who have retained the raw vitality of the masses within their psychological make-up."

Upon finishing *The Lightning and the Sun,* my brother decided he was one of these exceptionally intelligent and reliable men, and told Mr. Smith so.

The bookseller responded to this confession with a long-practiced shrug. Occasional visitations by the police, hysterical outbursts by mothers who had traced the source of their sons' reading material to the shop, the raving of certain patrons, the prying of journalists in need of a sensational story — all of it had reinforced the natural reserve and indifference to respectability in his disposition.

He considers himself a responsible businessman in what the city's elite perhaps thinks is a disreputable trade, but which tolerates him, as it tolerates the salesmen of pornography and love. Unlike those salesmen, he believes in something. Clean-shaven, his hair cropped close to the skull, he minds his shop dressed in neatly pressed khaki slacks and a khaki shirt. He does not have a telephone.

During business hours, he sits at the cash register and reads books about the wars. After hours, he goes to his apartment, which is above the store, and watches television. Sometimes after work he drives out to a catfish house by the lake and eats dinner and drinks beer with friends met at the store. Or the friends come to the apartment and drink beer and watch television. Had the friends not been quiet, they would have talked with him about politics. They do not do so. They are quiet now in the long evening of the West.

Berlin, April 1945, the quiet, the world-historical quiet in the bunker after it shoots itself. "Oh, now — now under the ceaseless fire and thunder of the Russian artillery; now, on the brink of disaster — how the Man 'against Time' clearly understood this!" writes Savitri Devi. "Above him and above the smoke of the Russian cannons and of the burning city, above the noise of explosions, millions and millions of miles away, the stars — those same stars that had shed their light over the adolescent's first prophetic ecstasy, forty years before — sparkled in all their glory, in limitless void. And the Man 'against Time,' who could not see them, knew that his National Socialist wisdom, founded upon the very laws of Life; his Wisdom that this doomed world had cursed and rejected, was, and would remain, in spite of all, as unassailable and everlasting as their everlasting Dance."

$\sim$54

Despite his initial rejection by Mr. Smith, my brother persisted — I would not have imagined, before then, that he had perseverance in him — and eventually engaged the proprietor in a conversation of sorts. He described his unsatisfying odyssey through the societies of the aggrieved and resentful. He avowed his impatience with racist intelligentsia and Southern nationalists, whose words, endless words, he had read in books and magazines and pamphlets, and heard at rallies and congresses. They talked, but the rot continued. He said the words pestered his eyes and ears, like gnats on sweaty afternoons. He said he wanted the silence.

Mr. Smith, who eventually found the silence, had wanted and found and learned many words after his honourable discharge from the army of the United States. Unwilling to hold a customary job, charmless, but already entrepreneurial, he squatted in a condemned building at the forward edge of the expressway's advance through the city, and earned almost enough to eat by changing light bulbs on communications masts atop skyscrapers. He loved to read, and he tolerated no interference with his daily reading regime of race lore, white-power literature, extreme racist erotica. Most men who congregated around him were desperate, so he entertained them during the long summer evenings with stories about the wars, and with audiotapes illicitly made at the black-metal concerts he attended. A clutch of benevolent neo-pagans rehabilitated him following his near-death from starvation, and sent him on his way to Delhi and his interview with the elderly Savitri Devi. Returned to the city, and after saving up money from his mast-scaling jobs, Mr. Smith founded the bookstore in the old shopping street near the Witherspoon mansion. He believed in something, several things, for a while; he could be exasperated, even appalled. Then, like my brother some time afterward, he wanted the silence.

It came to him gradually, the way sleep comes to a crowded mind. At first, it registered as weariness with his clientele's fear and predictable outrage. These men, he was finding, were ravished by one demagogue after another, flashing up out of obscurity, enjoying his transit across the zenith of the racist cosmos, then vanishing. Mr. Smith's clients wanted to be angry and offended, so they attended to the angry political voices who could rouse them to new, excruciating pitches of anxiety. It was then that Mr. Smith began to welcome the presence of the quiet men who, from time to time during the stiflingly hot days of late summer, came into the shop near closing time, wanting to be friends. They became Mr. Smith's friends after a while, and drank beer and watched television with him in the apartment over the store, or met him at the catfish place out on the lake. They talked a little, then they talked hardly at all.

Mr. Smith introduced my brother to the quiet men in that late summer, one evening after the sun had sunk behind the towers of the financial district and fireflies had begun to pulse bright and off among the wide, waxy green leaves of the magnolias on the street outside the shop. The city was at peace in that hour. The indolent negro youths had not yet sidled from their rooms in the dilapidated mansions of the district into the stale, humid cool of night, and gathered under streetlamps, where they would smoke and gossip and make lewd remarks to the negro prostitutes until dispersed by police. Inside the bookstore, the air was warm and close, but calm embraced them all — Mr. Smith, my brother, the quiet men — as the owner locked down the steel grids on windows and doors, then led the party upstairs to the flat where the beer and television set and the fixings of their dinner waited.

As men should, the quiet men ate and drank heartily in the hot, bare kitchen, but not greedily. I have no patience with greedy eaters, or with fastidious ones. Eaters of both sorts are products of bad breeding, the great moral affliction of the age, as Alexander knows. One can learn proper manners from a book, as the nouveaux-riches in the city do, with varying degrees of success. But breeding is a matter of blood, the work of centuries. My grandmother had it. She infallibly adopted the correct tone when speaking to inferiors, she ate plainly and gracefully, neither pondering her food nor treating it as something ignominious. Though raised in poverty, my brother inherited a measure of good breeding through the seed of our father, and so ate heartily, like the quiet men, but not like Mr. Smith, who picked at his meal of ham, black-eyed peas and cornbread in a way I would have disliked, had I been there.

Another sign of decent breeding among the quiet men was the pacific charity in their manner and in their patient (if telegraphic) replies to the occasionally long-winded questions of my brother. The men had once hated, but they did so no longer. They were no longer political in any partisan sense. The insurrection for which they longed would be fought not by themselves, but by other white people, ones with principles, and with visions of a world free from the dominion of the dark races, a world in which white men couple cleanly with white women in clean beds free of taint. Those idealists, armed and encouraged by the quiet men, will struggle and die, while the quiet men yearn only for the silence in the bunker after it shoots itself, the silence of the ruin after bombardment ceases, of the sea wreck, all sailors lost, the silence of the central fire and absence.

After dinner in the kitchen on an evening that summer, Mr. Smith told my brother and the quiet men jokes I will not repeat about the liberal host of the call-in show. They all laughed, and my brother laughed and said the world would be a better place were he off the air. One of the quiet men who was also laughing, I do not know which, said he had the same thought, and he knew what needed to be done. Mr. Smith told another joke about the host, and they all laughed again, then Mr. Smith told my brother that the time had come for him, my brother, to become one of the quiet men, so he would do it, and then he would belong. My brother laughed and said he did not know what Mr. Smith meant, when, of course, he knew exactly. So Mr. Smith told another joke, which he had learned in the army, a coarse joke that featured the host of the radio show doing things to a negro man, once, twice, three times, things meriting the death penalty for both of them, and everyone laughed and each knew from this moment that, soon thereafter, the host of the radio show would never have the chance to do to the negro man what was described in the joke, or to anyone else, ever. A quiet man said he thought Mr. Smith's joke was the funniest one he had ever heard, so Mr. Smith told it again, and they all laughed and laughed until they stopped.

$\sim$**55**

I could not abide my brother's whimpering, though my heart had always been kind. He stood in the library of my grandfather's house, his shabby raincoat dripping water into the ruddy pile of the Tabriz carpet, and complained that he could not do what the quiet men demanded of him.

From the day he had made himself known to me, when I shook his flaccid hand and rebuffed his attempt to threaten money out of me, I knew he would become a traitor to the race. His mother's blood, after all, ran through his veins — she, a wanton from the womb, who seduced our father when he was a youth, innocent and unstained, tall, strong and steady as a young oak, in my grandmother's words. He fell into the woman's embrace, he was naked and he begot my brother on her. I know how this happens to young men, because I have seen it. My brother was stained by my father's seed when he was begotten immorally, but none of this was my father's fault. How could he, an unbent oak, have known? There was the consequence, however, my brother, it dripped rainwater on the library carpet as it told me what it could not do.

Though it was weak, I loved my brother then, so I said I would take its place, and I was kind, very kind. I told it that it could garner all the honour from the quiet men for stilling the voice of the radio show's host, who sat before a microphone in the city every Saturday evening, taking the calls of those who entertained him, curtly dismissing and disconnecting others, uttering venomous words against callers whom he identified as race warriors or patriots, and defaming the silence. I told it that I wanted neither reward nor recognition, that I would accomplish this deed for love of it, and this was the truest thing I knew, so this was what I would write. It, my brother, knew that I had never seen an adult negro's phallus, or a Jew's circumcised one, or, except once, the phallus of our father, and that was in a motel on the edge of a city in the South.

Another true thing I knew, which Alexander reluctantly allows me to write, is that Jupp and Michael Fröhlingsdorf walked deep into the countryside of the Lower Rhineland in the late spring of 1937, the fourth year of the revolution, Jupp's sixteenth year of life. the teacher's thirty-second. The ostensible reasons for these excursions were that Herr Fröhlingsdorf needed to gather plant specimens, and Jupp wanted to practice drawing from nature. Perhaps Alexander resists this writing because he senses it will turn out badly, especially for the teacher, whom, I suspect, Alexander loves more than Jupp does.

Be that as it may, the two of them walked, one Sunday afternoon, through the fields to a damp copse in which Jupp had found a deformed oak he thought worth a sketch. A large gall, a sort of infection, had ballooned on one side of the trunk when the tree was young, forcing its growth to twist and tangle outward rather than branch upward normally, gracefully, gradually.

Alexander lets me record Herr Fröhlingsdorf's puzzlement at Jupp's choice of a subject, a tree that exemplified, in the teacher's politicized view, the perversion of nature's essential energies, hence unworthy of representation. I am not permitted to write details of the exchange between the man and the youth concerning this matter. But there is a moment when the force of life is thwarted, when the wildness is undone and powers in the loins degenerate. That is the death of a man or a race, Jupp's companion said, the weary failing that comes just before the end, at which time the folk-soul penetrates and fecundates matter again after so long a celestial exile. Karma, not the will of the flesh, ordains the hour of this death, Dr. Steiner said, according to the teacher, citing an esoteric authority much resorted to by leaders in the Party even after the dissolution of Germany's Anthroposophical Society in 1935. This death of the folk-soul must take place in the body of every male true to his race, Herr Fröhlingsdorf said, as Jupp sketched the malformed oak, and listened.

The ensouling gives to each male his true racial self, its parts and principles, Dr. Steiner said — to the Chinaman, his submissiveness and impassivity and cruelty; to the negro, his docility and brutish sensualism; to the Aryan, especially the German, his princely bearing, aggression and keen intelligence, but also his loneliness. From German males thus ensouled, from the old warriors of the Party, emerged the supreme idea that rejects both materialism and the otherworldly spirituality of the East, and especially the Catholic Church — that embraces Nature and Life, and endures the Death of Spirit in world-transfiguring passion, pain and flame. While drawing the twisted tree, Jupp listened with his body to the music of Herr Fröhlingsdorf's words, of Dr. Steiner's words and thoughts, and he assented to the melody, and the idea.

↷56

An hour before the disturbance in the street, which will cause Götz to rouse himself from Slomka's bed, go to the window of her flat, and peer out into the mild darkness, Jupp sits in the box, in Heerdt, in Düsseldorf. Remember for him, because he cannot now remember, the heavy sweetness of the air in the low copse in which he first heard of Dr. Steiner's knowledge and lore, of the rapture of matter and flesh by soul, of the prophet's teachings about the body politic ensouled by the idea of the healthy and best.

Though the Party forbade traffic in Steinerism among its faithful, Jupp's teacher enunciated no doctrine the youth had not heard before a thousand times, at rallies and during ideological indoctrinations. But Herr Fröhlingsdorf's language was elevated, mythic, free from the didactic coarseness of the usual Party propaganda and pregnant with pious, petty-bourgeois meaningfulness of the kind that appeals to young men disposed, like Jupp, to think in images. I forgive Jupp's seduction by the music of Steinerism that spring afternoon in 1937, when all Germans were spiritual; he could hardly have resisted, given his age and his desire to embrace whatever Herr Fröhlingsdorf proposed as truth.

As he sits inside the box, remembering nothing, remember for him the storm that bustled suddenly, unexpectedly out of the south-western sky that afternoon, surprising the two companions. No sooner had they hurried away from the trees and reached the road, lightning flashed and the downpour began, Within a minute, their outerwear was wet through. After another minute, they were soaked to the hide. Because they often walked abroad, Jupp and his teacher were no strangers to dampening by seasonal showers. But on this day of revelation and seduction, the wind-driven rain did not lessen, so very soon the cold drench of it penetrated the skin and seeped into their muscles and skeletons, and thence into their minds, like discipline.

Yet they were joyful. Outwardly bedraggled, but inwardly still glowing from their soul-talk in the copse, they were trudging in the direction of Kleve against punishing wind and rainfall — uncommon in fierceness in this part of Germany — when they heard a man's hail from the doorway of a sturdy farmer's house beside the road. The call was a summons to come inside, out of the storm. Grateful for the invitation, the man and the youth answered by quitting the road, and coming through the low doorway into the front room, where the wife of the bee-keeper (for this is what he was) kept watch over a fire that smouldered petulantly.

She said they could not very well join her at the fire in their sopping, muddy clothes, which she then offered to dry for them, if they were not in a hurry. She looked at them for a long moment, gauging their size, and said there were workingmen's rough trousers and shirts, too big for Jupp, but about right for Herr Fröhlingsdorf, in a cupboard within the upstairs room of her son, who now lived and worked on pictures as a set-builder in California, USA, and would not be coming home, having emigrated years ago, before talkies.

He wrote letters to his parents after his arrival in Hollywood, regularly and dutifully at first, less punctiliously later on. In one, from early 1923, he told of his young body's aches after the hours-long journey with other carpenters in the back of a Ford truck — one truck among dozens rattling over poor roads, ferrying workmen to an oceanside place, far north of Los Angeles, of high, gradually drifting sand dunes. He told of his labours on the tent city that was to house the thousands of Egyptians and Israelites, horse-wranglers and technicians, the orchestra, the stars (Charles de Roche as sleek, rich, arrogant pharaoh, Ramses the Magnificent, Theodore Roberts as the valiant little Jew, Moses) needed by C.B. De Mille for the most epical scenes in *The Ten Commandments*. And the son and his hundreds of fellows did more than construct a sizeable town for crew, extras, cast and themselves: they also erected and plastered the colossal walls and gates and the ceremonial avenue, guarded by sphinxes, of Ramses' many-godded treasure-city from which the monotheists would be led away into oblivion.

I appreciate De Mille's silent masterpiece, or at least the Old Testament dramatizations that celebrate national liberation, the leadership of the strong and forceful and vengeful, and that graphically depict the betrayals of the weak. The film's more prominent story, set in the present day, is less satisfactory. Danny (Rod La Roque) strives heroically for renown and great fortune, accidentally killing his mother in the process, and being damned by the pusillanimous Christian god for seeking to rise above the herd and attain mastery. The raw drive to overcome, which is *Nature,* is frustrated continually in the pious world in which Danny is punished for being strong. Iron, blind destiny does not exist there, as it exists here, at the Occidental Hotel, where Alexander knows that the lonely, worn voice of the radio host, broadcast each Saturday night to the South, must be stilled.

Though he did not say this in his letters, the bee-keeper's son succumbed to biological destiny at the production site, where he met and fancied an extra from Santa Monica named Clara. After the filming and a short, chaste courtship, he married Clara, who subsequently bore him three daughters. His most recent position was chief carpenter on the extravagant sets for Warner Brothers' *Gold Diggers of 1937.* Released in Germany early that year, the movie had attracted the son's parents to a theatre in Düsseldorf, where they marvelled at the architectural spectacle and fantasy of it, for which, they knew, their son was partly responsible. But, being convinced Party members, they also opposed its Americanism and materialism. The boy, they had known for some time, was lost to them. He had taught himself to speak English after the manner of white California natives, and did so with only a slight lilt of foreign accent. He did not conduct sexual affairs outside his marriage, he belonged to the union. He became an American, and voted for Roosevelt. He became a Christian Scientist.

The mother had altered nothing in the dim, shuttered bedroom since the son's departure for America. His work clothes were folded neatly in the cupboard. When the youth and the man were changing from wet clothes into the son's dry ones there, they were simultaneously naked for a brief interval. Alexander, a curious child, wants to know what happened next, because he is impatient with his immature body, its tiny, hairless scrotum and unevolved penis, and is thus eager to hear more about naked men than he learned from the sexology manuals for maidens that have been inadvertently shelved among the Edgar Rice Burroughs books in the lobby of the Occidental Hotel.

I respond to Alexander's curiosity by writing that there is nothing to be said. Had either Jupp or Michael been so inclined, which neither was, a touch, a caress, a gesture could have physically expressed the love that coursed between the man and the youth that afternoon of soul-talk and wind-driven rain. Each could have fumbled with the other's body — and they would have merely fumbled, since neither knew the mechanics or etiquette of love-making between men, except by rumour. They could have done these things in an effort to impose a certain resolution on the disturbed drift of time they moved within. They might not have done these things. But I will not write about matters of which, in any case, I possess no certain knowledge, having never been naked, and the day was darkened by storms, a circumstance, as Dr. Steiner said, that makes mating impossible.

In the second of his Nine Lectures on Bees, *Dr. Steiner said: "The fecundation of the bee is indeed a very special affair; there is nothing like a marriage-bed to which one retires, it all takes an entirely different course. It takes place openly, in the full sun-light and, though this may seem very strange at first, as high as possible in the air. The Queen-bee flies as far as possible towards the Sun to which she belongs ... and the drone alone which can overcome the earthly forces — for the drones have united themselves with the earthly forces — only that drone which can fly the highest is able to fecundate the Queen up there in the air.*

"The Queen returns and lays her eggs. So you see, the bees have no marriage bed, they have a marriage flight; they must strive as far as they are able, towards the Sun. One must have, is it not so, fine weather for this marriage flight which really needs the Sun? In bad weather it cannot take place."

Bundled into the box, its door shut and latch engaged, an hour before the commotion in the street that distracts Götz, Jupp cannot have heard the final arguments and contentions outside his window before conversations lapsed and the talkers drained away from the sidewalk. He is unaware that Götz, seeking information, almost approached the green door of the studio, and that Götz was lured away by Slomka before he could knock on it. Jupp is aware that the atmosphere inside the box has become warm, stiflingly close. Because he was not there, he does not remember the warmth, the heavy closeness of the air inside the circle of men and boys who sang songs of defiance and manly honour around the solstitial bonfire that burned in a pasture near Kleve on the longest evening of 1937.

The firelight cast long shadows on the field behind the boys and men and threw flickering blush on the slow, east-trending procession of low midsummer clouds. Swarms of sparks scattered upward into the night sky, glowed for an instant, vanished into the still, smoky air. All this is right, he might have thought while singing with them, each uniform and voice proclaiming solidarity of mind and sinew and bone with the idea and movement. All this was right and righteous, Jupp would have thought — the fragrance of the blaze and hay and sweat of hard bodies, the bright heat in cool night, the singing — had he been present with other Hitler Youth at the celebration of the solstice.

Instead, on that midsummer evening, Jupp sat in the fat chair in the teacher's study and listened to Herr Fröhlingsdorf tell him that the research for the project that had prompted their ventures around Kleve, Herr Fröhlingsdorf's commission to co-author a handbook on the flora of the Lower Rhineland, was complete, so further walks abroad would be redundant. From now on, the two of them would exchange greetings when passing on the street or in a corridor at the school; but private meetings were to cease.

Alexander knows that nothing untoward had happened between the youth and his teacher, though he wants to believe that something did so that I will write about it, rejoicing Alexander's lascivious heart. The child knows a little of the Uranian transactions between men and youths from the sexology manuals for maidens he has found shelved among the Edgar Rice Burroughs novels, but he knows nothing about the jealousy and fear that Ingvild Fröhlingsdorf nursed within her bosom. She hated Jupp more pointedly, but no less sincerely, than she hated and feared Michael's other students, who were his reasons for not seeking preferment in some grander town, where she could rise in society and in the Party. She knew she would not rise there or anywhere were Michael talked about by Kleve's women, whose talk was always about love. They would say, or she thought they would say, that she had no babies because Michael's love had weakened, his seed become decadent due to infrequency of discharge. They would say that the writing of Party tracts and botanical papers distracted him from marital love. Or that something did, they would speculate.

Or someone not his wife did, or someone who was not a woman at all. The wives of Kleve had been mindful about the love of men and youths since the summer of 1936, when the younger son of Frau Schneider, a locally celebrated needlewoman, had been sent away to an educational camp by the police for allegedly engaging in an act of love with a male acrobat employed by Zeller's Astounding Circus, in town at the time. (The acrobat, who was being blackmailed by the Gestapo, was, for that reason, not punished.) During Kleve's harvest festival, 1936, Frau Schneider received, by regular post, an invoice for the cost of her son's incarceration, a statement that he had died of a heart attack, and a packet containing his ashes.

Until that summer and fall, the women had regarded sodomy as a metropolitan vice, quite foreign to pious little Kleve. Now, however, inattentive husbands in the town were suspect, and shy sons. Deviation in the practices of love became a fashionable topic of discreet conversation among the women, who imagined their vigilance to be patriotic. In front of Ingvild, they speculated about the preferences in love of certain men and youths in the town — never Jupp or any other student of Michael's, of course, at least not within Ingvild's hearing. But what were they saying when she was absent? She worried.

In a moment of pique and fear, Ingvild Fröhlingsdorf briefly considered pre-empting the gossips by reporting her husband and Jupp to the police. But she immediately decided against doing so, since their disgrace would surely precipitate her own. Besides, she could provide no evidence of impropriety other than her empty womb, her suspicious thoughts, and her lonesomeness on the lengthening spring evenings when Jupp and her husband withdrew into the study, and talked or drew. Those evenings must be given back to her, she thought. The walks into the countryside around Kleve must stop, she decided, before they raised questions in the inquiring minds of the women, before they threatened to loosen her grip on the ladder leading upward into the higher circles of the movement, in which she imagined she could belong.

The air in the box Jupp sits in is hot.

∽58

Remember the summer of 1937, when Jupp loved the man who thought well of his botanical drawings, and introduced him to the thought of Dr. Steiner about bees, and with whom he hiked across the fields and marshes around Kleve. Remember the stormy afternoon on which Jupp and his teacher were naked in the same room. Remember these things, and you will remember the July day when he travelled by train from the Lower Rhineland to Munich with other lads from his Hitler Youth unit, and discovered certain matters there.

Horst had received orders to see that he and the boys under his command went on the outing for the sake, as they said, of solidarity with the racial community and of moral improvement: For there was to be in Munich a parade of costumed marchers and spectacular floats to see and cheer for, all of it in celebration of the German culture then being reawakened. So they went, and joined the spectators who lined the broad alleys bordered by elevated torches, and joined the surge that followed the procession as it wound past the reviewing stand installed before the gleaming, becolumned, stripped-classical façade of the new House of German Art, where Hitler climaxed the day by opening the first Great German Art Exhibition.

Jupp's waters were not deep, and his shallows were still disturbed by the events of the midsummer evening with Herr Fröhlingsdorf, after whose rejection Jupp had considered burning his notebooks and sketches and copies in misdirected revenge against the man who encouraged him to make them. He did not do so, but he resolved to be hard from then on. He would be a scientist of the sort his teacher was not — exact, cruel, dispassionate, positivistic. He would be an uninspired experimentalist like the biologist of amoebas who had disillusioned Herr Fröhlingsdorf during his first year of studies at Marburg.

After the lavish parade of marchers, bands and floats, called *Two Thousand Years of German Culture,* after the push and thrust of the crowds had ceased and the people had stopped cheering and disappeared back into their flats and houses, Horst directed the boys and youths under his supervision to see the museum show of painting and sculpture that the regime officially honoured. Jupp and the other Hitler Youth obeyed, going up the steps of the House of German Art, past the square columns, and into the first hall adorned with sculptures and paintings by artists who enjoyed the patronage of the National Socialist state.

Enormous bronze and stone statues of naked males with powerfully knotted shoulders and muscular hands and with narrow hips and dainty genitals — hands ready for capture, bodies about to penetrate and dominate — loomed in the corridors and galleries. Jupp did not know the names of the artists, but he recognized the style, since it spoke to the imagery of the masculine that he and all other German males carried around in their heads. At first, pausing in front of the statuary, he feigned indifference to its gravity and monumentality. Then he was impressed, and his thoughts gradually turned from the new but familiar images in front of him, which did not arouse him, and settled on the artists who had made them.

What must it be like, he thought, to be the creator of such sculpture? The answer came up to him from memories of articles he had read, and from the masculine art itself he saw in the museum. A man to whom other people, important people, pay respectful attention. A rich man presiding over a palatial atelier peopled by assistants and minions, a man kept busy by official commissions for war memorials, dramatically rhetorical decorations destined for public buildings, foursquare portrait busts of the Führer and other leaders in Party and society. This is what sculptors do, he imagined, this is what they are — and the imagining appealed to him, touched some hitherto unawakened department of his sensuous mind. He had drawn, and enjoyed drawing and copying, though never seriously considered becoming an artist of any sort, let alone a sculptor. He had lately decided to become a stringently materialistic scientist, unromantic and acute. But in a letter dated 18 May 1943, he will announce to his parents that he has decided to become a professional sculptor after Germany wins the war. Now, however, on this day in the summer of 1937, he was first imbued with the fantasy of becoming a sculptor — a stern master surrounded by disciples, resiliently anti-bourgeois — should his plans for a career in science not unfold as he wished.

Jupp then thought what it must be like to be a painter of the naked women he saw, who were unlike either the Greek nudes seen in books or the stout, flayed females he had seen portrayed in anatomical charts. But speculations about the lives of artists soon gave way to more primitive sensations provoked by content.

Here, after all, were women golden and gleaming, their limbs and hips sleek and barely muscled, their breasts alert, with taut little nipples, their bodies as relaxed as those of the sculpted men were tense. To Jupp's imagination, these women seemed available, unlike stone goddesses — willing to be caressed, wanting to be overpowered, possessed by men of the sort illustrated in the male statues.

Jupp's manhood stirred, then stiffened. He wanted these almost transparently fine women, he wanted to maul their idealized breasts and thighs, thrust his hard body into the compliant, perfectly complicit flesh.

He had stooped a little to accommodate the erection bulging at his trouser fly, when he heard a snort and laugh from one of his comrades.

There's nothing here, the comrade said in a loud whisper to the others close by, that you can't get from some girl in the League of German Maidens. I know because I've had them, he continued, and they want it as bad as we want to give it to them.

You've never had any of it, a second boy said to the braggart, who, still whispering, to the annoyance of respectable people touring the show, insisted that he had had it lots of time, usually on sports trips, especially at Party rallies where Hitler Youth and League girls were expected to turn up.

Jupp had of course heard about the loose morality of League girls from the other youths in Kleve, who often joked about getting the young ladies into bed, and sometimes may have done so. He looked back at the paintings around him. He looked at the smartly uniformed SS men strolling with their stylish wives through the gallery. He looked back at the flesh in the paintings, thinking about what the men in the gallery did with their women after they took off their uniforms at night and went to bed naked. The thought of it had been unsettling him lately, before the trip to Munich, and he had wondered, in fact, if this trip would be the right occasion to end his virginity. He thought about it, and about the women in the German paintings cherished by the regime, and decided the time had come to satisfy the mixed curiosity and craving and wish for extinction, which he did, in Munich, with a dark-haired League girl on an afternoon in July, 1937.

Figure 8: A photograph, possibly from 1982, that depicts Joseph Beuys planting a tree beside a basalt pillar before the façade of the Museum Fridericianum, Kassel, Germany. This tree is one of thousands that Joseph Beuys proposed be planted, each alongside a rough-hewn basalt pillar, throughout the Hessian town, an effort that he called *7,000 Oaks — Urban Forestation instead of Administration.*

The center of Kassel was almost completely destroyed by Allied bombs in 1943. It was rebuilt in the 1950s according to deplorably banal, bleak plans supplied by the conquerors. With the inauguration of Beuys' project, however, Kassel began to regain its character as a clearing in the German forest. It would be again bowered by oaks, the great Teutonic trees, symbols of virility, magnificence and celestial mystery since time out of mind. It would be a settlement of strongly rooted men in the midst of a holy grove.

The Christians found the German affection for oaks intolerable. Early in the eighth century. the militant Anglo-Saxon missionary Boniface, egged on by local converts to his creed, felled a prodigious oak sacred to the lightning-god Donar (or Thor), and built a church on the Hessian site from the timber. The event is narrated in the Latin

Life of Saint Boniface *by the monk Willibald, who lived and wrote in the century that saw this vandalism. It has been conjectured that the heathens who watched Boniface hewing Donar's oak became Christians because of disappointment with the god, who had failed to avenge this desecration by striking the missionary dead. If Christians similarly interpreted the famously familiar non-intervention of their god, there would be no Christians. They have a way around apostatizing because of the silence, Sister says, a way I do not understand.*

The Lonesome Tree, an 1822 canvas by Caspar David Friedrich now at the Alte Nationalgalerie in Berlin, presents a storm-battered oak standing tall and alone in an Arcadian plain. A village nestles in the middle distance beyond the tree; blue mountains rise in the background. A shepherd takes his ease under the lower boughs of the tree, while his flock grazes around a placid pond shadowed by gathering clouds at dusk. I have found several exegeses of this picture, none wholly satisfactory. But viewing it through the lens of 7,000 Oaks, I see in Friedrich's oak a wounded German rising from the ancient ground of blood and language, and it is Beuys, steady as an oak in his confrontation with contrary weathers. Or it is Germany; or it is the South, the inner South, indomitable.

An oak is a man, or something like a man. Writing in the seventeenth century, John Aubrey (as quoted in Geoffrey Grigson, The Englishman's Flora, *London, 1960) states that "When an oake is falling, before it falls it gives a kind of shriekes or groanes that may be heard a mile off, as it were the genus of the oake lamenting. E. Wyld, Esq. hath heard it severall times." A modern druid tells us that "a famous mistletoe-bearing oak in Derbyshire had the reputation of being semi-human as late as the nineteenth century. If its branches were severed, it screamed and bled, and spoke with the voice of prophetic doom. Aubrey also tells of an oak whose mistletoe was cut and sold to some London apothecaries, all of whom met with horrible misfortunes thereafter.*

The assignment I had assumed on behalf of my brother was easy to carry out. My brother had observed the movements of the radio host on several Saturday evenings—how, after the show, he invariably walked from the studio to a Chinese restaurant he apparently admired, how he ate with chopsticks for an hour, then sauntered the long way home, through the financial district and alongside the park, which, my grandmother once told me, has long been a trysting place for male inverts, and on to his rooms in the old Crockett Hotel, on Milam Street, which was formerly a stylish downtown address.

I knew what he looked like from newspaper photographs my brother gave me. In one, he is shown turning the sod for a new children's hospital the city does not need, but that is backed by influential Baptists and negroes. Attired in the only suit he owns, a dark one with worn sleeves and greasy lapels, his greying hair long and frowsy about the ears, he presses the shovel into the ground with weak arms and a too-smart shoe. His belly is large and round, his face is fleshy and very bright, with a widely smiling mouth of nicotine-darkened teeth. He is obviously sedentary and given to eating sweet pastries.

Another picture shows him accepting an award from a Southern lawyers' organization that is famous (as he was) for defamations of Southern patriots, nationalists, racial warriors. The image reveals him to be somewhat swaybacked and off-balance, as if suffering from a spinal disorder or vertigo. The negro attorney who hands him the plaque is young, nimbly slender, faintly awkward in the way negroes usually are (or were) in the presence of white people. Unlike the quiet men, who do not hate, I disliked the radio host in the photographs, I found disagreeable his suit, his globular, sagging face, his expensive shoes, all of which told me that he was white trash that had come up in the world, become an on-air bully of decent callers, commanding a huge audience of mostly hostile but fascinated white people in the South.

~60

He did not die immediately. His dying heart pumped blood to his head for a while, and blood spurted with ever-lessening pulses into the broadening puddle on the sidewalk beside the park where inverts rendezvous. I had not watched anything expire since Essie shot the coyote in the head, and that was when I was a little boy, long ago, in the summer my father died, just as the Cold War was beginning. And this memory of the bleeding coyote brought to mind certain matters I did not remember from my own history, because they did not touch me, but that I thought about after reading of them in the books and articles I kept in my grandfather's library, including ones that treat of Jupp's life and career, such as the ponderous, defamatory German biography. The radio host did not die quickly from his head injury. Jupp did not die, soon or late, when his Luftwaffe aircraft failed and crashed in Crimea, Eurasia, 16 March 1944, but he endured a grievous head wound from which blood spurted into the Eurasian steppe and that quite probably would have killed a man older, less fit than Jupp was at this time. The pilot, Hans Laurinck, had died instantly. Jupp, the radio operator, would have bled to death on the cold steppe had he not been quickly evacuated, unconscious, from the wreckage by a German military team, had his wound not been treated promptly at the base infirmary, where he regained consciousness and convalesced until the Red Army came, forcing the Germans, Jupp among them, to retreat westward.

Years later, Jupp would claim he was saved by nomadic Crimean Tatars, who wrapped his injured body in fat and felt, and fed him, and recognized in him a true soul-Tatar, though one unfortunately born in German flesh. None of this happened, but the story served as an aetiological myth of Jupp's subsequent deployment of fat and felt as symbolic materials in many of his assemblages and mystery-dramas, or *Aktionen*. In fact, according to the biography, he knew only one Tatar in Crimea, one of the base veterinarians and obviously an anti-Soviet collaborator whose speciality — unsurprising in a non-urban son of the steppes — was the care of horses, and whose given name was Ahmed, but who called himself Çobanzade.

Ahmed had studied animal medicine at Aqmescit in the 1920s (or at Simferopol, as the city was known after Crimea's annexation by the Russian Empire), when the cultural fluorescence of the new Autonomous Republic of Crimea was under way, deeply affecting him with charitable feelings. Tatar literature was encouraged, taught, written, performed during this period. The Tatars' Turkic tongue and history were studied and celebrated with zeal hitherto unsurpassed, not least famously by the Tatar poet of landscape and folklore, distinguished linguist and cultural activist Bekir Sidki Çobanzade, whose surname Ahmed would adopt after the successful (if short-lived) German liberation of Crimea from Soviet tyranny. (Bekir, one of Crimea's outstanding offspring, was murdered in 1937 by Stalin's police after torture and trial on charges of bourgeois nationalism, subversion. terrorism and spying.)

It was when he was still in veterinary training that Ahmed, a secularized Muslim quite assimilated to Russian custom, was moved by Bekir's patriotic preaching and example to begin an exploration of traditional Tatar ways of healing. This venture started with an eager review of the most accessible sources — family recollections of traditional remedies (they knew none), the poetry and prose of his nationalistic contemporaries — an effort that produced little useful information. Frustrated but still curious, he was soon scouring the archives and libraries of Simferopol for whatever documentation existed on Tatar shamanism, and in the university's library he found what he was looking for: the trove of Tatar oral poetry collected in the nineteenth century by the orientalist Vasily Vasilievich Radlov (born Friedrich Wilhelm Radloff, in Berlin), and numerous narratives of the shamanic work and ecstatic trance and sacred costume by eighteenth-century Russian and German travellers, most of whom, following Enlightenment intellectual taste, found the shaman outlandish.

Ahmed studied, and, enchanted by those traces of vanished racial heritage, he learned; and at last decided to apprentice himself to a shaman, who, he thought, could teach him the art he had read about. He had heard the call, faint at first but steadily louder, of the Swan Woman, who dwells in the underworld and may be one or seven or nine — whose eyes are dull as lead, whose fingernails are long and yellow, who feeds on the souls of the dead. He heard her cry and answered with a secret cry of his own. He wanted to fly over the steppe to the entrance, in barren hills, of the underworld, and struggle there with darkness until he strangled her, then call for the Moon to let down her radiant hair to the earth, where men and animals with head wounds suffer for want of moonlight. He found this Tatar poem in a compendium of such song:

> *I am a child created of nothing,*
> *I am formed of a ray of light.*
> *On the ray I hung my bow,*
> *I am quite alone.*
> *White Nothing is my father,*
> *Lofty Ray is my mother.*
> *I could not remain in heaven,*
> *And have been cast down here.*
> *The six corners in the moon*
> *Have I six times visited.*
> *The seven corners of the earth*
> *I seven times visited.*
> *He awoke the seven dead,*
> *The hero Baweddin came hither,*
> *Took me to his house ...*
> *Named me Kara Tschasch, the fair.*
> *This was my only father,*
> *Who held me below the earth.*

As the radio host lay bleeding on the sidewalk, the moon, ripe and bright, rose above the trees of the sodomites' park, and the beams of her late summer light grazed the injury. I saw the moon's damaged face, on which ordinary carnal men, who believed nothing, had dared to step and dig, reflected in the spreading black pool of blood.

Ahmed discovered no-one to teach him. Tatar shamans, it appeared, had died out or given up or gone into hiding long before the Tatar renaissance of the 1920s quickened the fascination of romantics with Crimean antiquities, monuments, curiosities, distinguishing attributes, and he eventually stopped looking for an esoteric teacher. Also, the cultural reawakening was quickly extinguished by Stalin, and Ahmed became silent, not being a man prone to make trouble.

After setting aside his studies of unapproved topics, he won employment at an impoverished collective farm outside a village called Argin, near Karasubazar (Belogorsk). There, he devoted himself to assistance with difficult calvings, curing the common distempers of mules and oxen by the currently official methods, gelding stallions, and to other duties of a rural veterinarian. But Ahmed was not lacking in other talents. He added lustre to his already solid reputation among the collectivized peasants, for example, by performing magic tricks to entertain them, the same tricks, in fact, with which he would later amuse Jupp in the infirmary, until the Red Army's approach to the German base voided all thought of amusing or being amused.

Like most men forever, at least until they are jolted from complacent resignation by catastrophe or a twist of compunction, Ahmed dwelt chiefly on what beset or distracted or fleetingly pleased him in the eternal present. He got along at the farm for years, appreciating in himself his status as an admired healer of animals and a performer of magic tricks for children and peasants, but essentially as nobody. This nobody looked around him and saw nothing that menaced him. Like the hungry tramp in the story by Maxim Gorki, Ahmed could say: "The silent and deserted steppes, all inundated with the bright glow of the morning sun, stretched out around us, uniting at the horizon with the sky, suffused with such a clear caressing and soft light that everything black and evil seemed impossible amidst this immense space of free open land shut in with the blue dome of heaven."

Alexander resents my citation of the Gorki tale, claims that I am indulging in literary digression to delay the re-introduction into this text of the Tatar philologist and poet Bekir Sidki Çobanzade. Alexander is an imperious child. His demands on me are unceasing. He wants salacious material, the kind of thing I do not like to write. He wants action, not reflection of the sort I think I do well. He wants scenes of Bekir Sidki Çobanzade's appalling torture by the Stalinist police, of the broken man's short, monstrously unjust trial before a fanatical judge determined to condemn the poet for crimes against the state, he wants to see the change wrought on Çobanzade's head by the executioner's bullet — all of which I refuse to give him. Alexander does not want to read about Ahmed's despair and shame upon learning of Bekir Sidki Çobanzade's disgrace and death — or about Ahmed's new sense of himself as a traitor to the light created in him long before by the poet's words, and as a man betrayed by the ruthless Soviet system to which he had sought to accommodate himself.

From battered trunks and suitcases buried under hay and sacks of fodder in the store-room by his cottage, Ahmed unearthed the many notebooks into which he had transcribed long passages of shamanic lyrics and the accounts by travellers of the rites and beliefs of the Tatar shamans. There also were the notes taken from books and records of thoughts that had seethed within him during his part-nationalist, part-pagan passion for the shamanism of his ancestors, who had practiced the mysteries of ecstasy until modernity erased all but fugitive literary traces of them. Ahmed read those jottings and transcriptions, and thought of the cruelty meted out to Çobanzade, conceiving a secret loathing for Communism more intense than any loathing he had known before. Forced to dissemble until the Germans freed his village from the reign of Red commissars, he thereafter offered veterinary services to the liberators, and renewed his covenant with the shaman's way, the religion of his books and of his Tatar blood.

He made a tambourine from withes and the hide of a rabbit he had killed and skinned, and taught himself to whistle and hum. Having sung the shaman's songs many times, he began to stink like a steppe-wolf, and became rough and scrawny like one. He would not often eat the food of normal men, preferring to make his meals of small, unclean mammals trapped on the steppe, and from wild plants he found there. In the first trance he sang himself into, he saw Jel Maja, Old Snap-Mouth, who slurps up humans and swallows them whole; and he was not afraid. In the second trance, Ahmed stole the horse of Kara Tygan Kan, who retaliated by stealing Ahmed's tongue. In the magical combat that followed, Ahmed stole Kara Tygan Kan's eyes, besting him, then, in exultation, he sniffed the bottom of a she-wolf in heat and mated with her. When she whelped, the pups she bore Ahmed were dreamers who dreamed of a white gelding, the property of the Germans and one of the horses cared for by Ahmed.

A day came in the late winter of 1944, after Jupp received the head wound in the plane crash, when the strong white horse, one of a team hauling a wagon loaded with munitions, stumbled in the frozen muck of a road. He heaved himself out of the mire and pulled the wagon across the steppe to the base, where Ahmed, the healer of animals on duty that afternoon, noticed the horse was badly lame. In his trance, dreaming the dream of the wolf-pups, Ahmed saw that he must shoot the white horse in the head, since the creature could not be healed. He did so, and Jupp watched the killing from a window of the infirmary.

Since the start of his military service, and even before, Jupp had not witnessed an act of compassion more morally unambiguous or one administered with more modesty and simplicity. I took seriously this superior example of killing, because it excited in Jupp solicitude toward the Tatar veterinarian whom he saw from the window. The men, Tatar and German, communicated after the killing; then they met, Ahmed and Jupp, on nights thereafter in the white sick-bay in which Jupp recovered from his painful wound. Ahmed distracted Jupp from worry and suffering with simple magic tricks, including the ventriloquism he had perfected, and with talk of the horses he tended and treated for the Germans.

But the Russians and the days of German evacuation westward approached, and Ahmed knew he would be left behind to the mercy of the commissars, who had no mercy. So he began to tell Jupp certain things—that, for example, he stank like a steppe-wolf because he had sung shaman-songs and spoken to animals, because he had carnally known a spirit-female and conducted the soul of the strong white horse to a place of blessing beyond the moon.

Then, on some evenings, after Jupp had become well enough to venture out of the infirmary for walks on the grounds of the base—he was still not fit to return to active duty, where Alexander definitely believes he should be—he visited Ahmed in his little shack on the outskirts of the encampment, and Ahmed shamanized. Ahmed crouched in a downcast pose on a mare's hide by the fireplace, facing south (as stipulated by the tourists' descriptions in the ethnographical volumes he had read) and holding the tambourine out in front of him. This material does not interest Alexander, but it makes me curious.

So I note that, at first, Ahmed made no sound, made no move, and Jupp dared not breathe; then Ahmed mumbled something, hiccupped, and became silent again. The quiet was broken when he suddenly yawned wide, emitting a harsh, metallic sound from his throat, and started thrumming on the tambourine. Jupp heard other sounds—a falcon's shriek high in a corner of the hovel, a dove's moan from somewhere else, the whine of a mosquito near his ear. Ahmed began to chant his shaman song, at first ruminatively and held close in his throat, eventually loud, and the chant was interrupted frequently by shouts, calls, chortles of animals and birds that seemed to come from every angle of the house.

In a 1936 article entitled "The Spiritual Ideas and Experiences of the Tatars of Central Asia," published in the *Journal of the Royal Anthropological Institute of Great Britain and Ireland,* Volume 66, which

I have copied out word for word into my notebooks about Jupp's art, Nora K. Chadwick writes: *The music becomes louder, the strokes on the tambourine become confused in one continuous rumble; the bells, rattles and small tabors sound ceaselessly. It is a deluge of sounds capable of driving away the wits of the audience. Suddenly everything stops; one or two powerful blows on the tambourine, and then it falls on the shaman's lap. Silence at once reigns. This process is repeated, with slight variations several times. When the shaman has worked up his audience to a sufficient pitch, the rhythm of the music is changed, and it is accompanied by broken phrases of song, gloomy in tone.*

Ahmed then threw himself at Jupp's injured head and began to suck the crown of Jupp's skull furiously, pulling the pain out (so he believed) with his mouth. *The fire has been made up again, and its bright gleam illumines the hut, which is now full of noise and movement. The wizard ceaselessly dances, sings, and beats his tambourine; first turning to the south, then to the west and east, he madly jumps and contorts himself …*

It should be observed that neither fat nor felt was featured in Ahmed's performance. Jupp's many critics are correct to denounce him for ascribing his deployment of fat and felt to the Tatars whom, he erroneously claimed, saved him from certain death after his aircraft had gone down in bad weather, in March, 1944. Alexander must not be taken in by this deception, of which Jupp was guilty on numerous occasions, not least grievously when he induced the Solomon R. Guggenheim Museum, in New York, to include the fat-and-felt legend in its catalogue of Jupp's 1979 retrospective at this otherwise prestigious institution. I was sceptical about the verity of the relentlessly repeated legend from the first moment I heard it, and, so that Alexander can remain innocent, I add my voice to the voices of the critics who have shown, in closely argued articles based on facts disputed by none other than certain clients, that the artist's use of fat and felt and other substances thought by the academies to be non-artistic was inspired simply by the force of his restless, autochthonic imagination.

Jupp, in short, was influenced by no-one and nothing that preceded him, including Tatars whom, in any case, he never encountered while stationed in Crimea, except for Ahmed. Jupp attended with acute sensitivity to Ahmed's shamanizing on several evenings, listened to the music Ahmed made with voice and tambourine, and ingested into his soul what the shaman song was in fact. This was true, though in the late winter and early spring of 1944, when the might of the Soviet army thrust the Germans from Crimea, he was not yet ready to commit himself to his great work. His education was not complete, so he could not be initiated by Ahmed into the mysteries of deep Eurasia — though he had for many years done service to the mysteries of inner Germany, which are shamanic in scope and shape, radically transfigurative, opposed to the soul-thwarting regime of instrumental reason. But he watched and heard and comprehended Ahmed's musical mystagogy, was moved by the choreography of the incantation. Recuperating from the injury to his head, Jupp smelled Ahmed's ancient stench, was appalled and fascinated by Ahmed's savage sucking of his wound, remembering everything until the imprisonment at Cuxhaven, when he forgot everything that had pleased him before June, 1945.

$\sim$62

I arrived at the Occidental Hotel in the late summer, when the travelling folk gathered here. I did not know what was on their minds, but Alexander later told me it was excessive rutting and drinking, neither of which I understood. I was put by Mr. Steinway into a room furnished with aqua plastic wall-covering, a narrow metal bed, a little desk and an ordinary chair with a hard green vinyl seat — a plain, armless metal chair of the sort once mass-produced in millions for schools and offices, but now out of favour with the decorators of such places. Alexander stayed in a room elsewhere in the hotel with the woman and man who had raised him until I met him, then he continued to live in that room alone after the travelling folk moved on and I started to feed him.

I came to the Occidental Hotel because I believed Sister would not find me here. I came here and began this writing after the ripe, bright moon shone on the black pool of blood, and my brother stood in the park, and told me, this time, of telling the authorities about the quiet men and Mr. Smith, how simple telling about them had been, how very simple.

Clean-shaven, dressed in starched uniforms that betokened civic rectitude and probity, attentively jotting down words in their notebooks, the hearers wanted very much to listen, so my brother concealed nothing. He said to me that he had related, through tears, all he knew about the robberies, and about the radio host, though he loved me, but he could not help himself. The hearers did not torture him for this information.

He had given it up freely, of his own accord, he told me in the park, adding that I should go away now, at least as far as the mountains.

I always knew my brother would turn out to be a traitor to his race. He died in the park, in a corner of it where sodomites meet, and I came to the Occidental Hotel when the travelling folk were here, the child Alexander among them.

When Mr. Steinway knew that neither Alexander nor I were leaving after he dismissed the staff and the hotel was shuttered, the manager dropped the officious manner that had endeared him to generations of guests, and became a less grand, less public institution. He corporally disciplined us seldom, preferring instead to use gentle methods to help us behave as guests should in this once-famous hotel. He gave us uncomplicated tasks to perform, such as making sure the fieldstone fireplace in the lobby was well-supplied with limbs and kindling from the forest beyond the parking lot. He set us to keep watch, rifle at the ready, for a buck that we could feed on in the winter should the owner fail to reappear, bearing supplies. Alexander was deputed as keeper of the paste and scissors for the scrapbooks in which Mr. Steinway mounted old, unharvested newspaper clippings about the hotel and the doings of notable people who had lodged or worked or entertained here. I cook our meals in wide skillets and pans designed for preparing the food of dozens.

After we eat our supper—always in the Tamarack Dining Room, Mr. Steinway having insisted we take meals nowhere less glamorous —we retire to the overstuffed sofas before the fireplace in the lobby, where the manager tells stories to edify Alexander, but also to distract me from worry. For I find troubling the thought of being discovered here by Sister or other Christians—or the idea is troubling perhaps only a little, since I seriously doubt that they would search for me in the mountains. Besides, I have merely done what any full-blood white Southern male would do were his woman or race threatened by defilement. Though terrible things have been done to my body, I have always remained clean. My brother knew this to be true, yet he told tales of impurity about me to the uniformed listeners of the United States. The upshot is that I came here and must dwell here, listen to Mr. Steinway talking after dinner, telling stories about the Occidental Hotel, and I must carefully attend to Alexander, who needs me.

~**63**

An hour before Götz hears the commotion on the sidewalk below Slomka's window, and bolts, naked, to the window to see what is disturbing his post-coital peace, Jupp crouched inside the hot, dark atmosphere of the box, thinking about nothing. Viewed objectively by a disinterested observer, looked at positivistically, as one might dispassionately regard any other object that possessed weight and extent, and that one intended to manipulate without respect to its nature, Jupp was in no way physically defective or inferior in early 1956. He had been injured in head and leg during the war, but his injuries, if still occasionally troublesome, had healed, and now physically prevented him from doing nothing he was able to do, such as draw and couple, though he had no desire to do either. As far as his body was concerned, he was in a far better condition than were many male contemporaries who, like him, had fought in the European theatre. His bowels voided properly, he was not old.

Nor would a wholly objective judgement find that he was creatively barren in the years leading up to his acquisition of the box, though one should be sparing in praise for his artistic production before the crisis that caused him to sit in the box. In art school during the first ten years after the war, he had won the respect and admiration of the figurative sculptor Ewald Mataré, his master in monumental sculpture at the academy, with whose daughter Jupp may have pursued a dalliance. He

had generated the proposal for a monument to the German dead of both
wars in which Germany fought in the twentieth century, a work in wood
and iron — a gate of oak wood into which Jupp would carve the names of
the war dead — that was later realized in a Romanesque church tower
in Büderich, a suburb of Meerbusch. He had drawn effusively and ad-
mirably, though his work in graphic media was little known beyond the
circle of the van der Grinten brothers, who collected it and farmed at
Kranenburg, very near Kleve, and who gave Jupp solace and refuge before he became famous, and long afterward. In the post-war years, also,
he had mastered the key ideas of Dr. Steiner's post-Christian metaphys-
ics and piety, and had begun to enunciate the words "creativity" and
"Christ-mind" with the decidedly heterodox inflections Steinerites gave
to such terms. He had displayed talent, if not brilliance.

Bent double in the box, Jupp drew breath laboriously. His legs
cramped, he thirsted. At first, Jupp felt only a slight constriction in his
head, in the crown of it, like the too-tightness of a hat. Then the invisible hat turned into something metallic, a clamp screwing down gradually, increasing the pressure on his temples, on the dome and rear
bowl of his skull. The tightening became insistent, persisting. His brain
could have been swelling like bread dough rising, its grey pulp inflamed, squeezing blood into its bone container — that's what I or you
would have suspected, had my head or your head suffered like this — but
Jupp did not imagine the possibility.

He did not unlatch the door of the box, unbend his body from the
darkness into the light cast by a single bulb at midnight.

He did not think continuous or discontinuous thoughts about the
pain, or about anything else, such as what it might be like to be without
the pain in his body, such as the other pains he has undergone, at other
times, when his war wounds hurt, such as what had caused the pain to
start this time. He made no connections, inferred nothing, drew no
conclusions.

His body felt the pain as, presumably, the body of a wordless animal
does, without the shrouding of it in meanings, explanations, mythologies, the usual excuses.

Then he did not thirst. Then he wanted nothing. I supply from my notebook words he cannot supply in the darkness of the box — "nigredo, tenebrositas, *chaos, melancholia," Jung's words for "a standstill that hampers moral decisions and makes convictions ineffective or even impossible"* (Mysterium Coniunctionis. *London, 1963, page 497).*

Nigredo: the blackening, putrefaction, the end of matters of time and history and identity, all elements cooked down in the alchemical furnace to inchoate darkness; a state in which males find themselves, their corpses stinking and busy with maggots. I remember the stillness in the room, in the mind, the great stilling of all chaos, after the decision has been made to disappear into the Blue Hole, drowning there, falling forever with the body of my father into the darkness, which has no bottom, because anything dropped into the Blue Hole never comes back, Essie said. Then a coyote bitch trotted by, and I could have gone off with her and become impure, but I wanted the white, non-fecund purity of the Occidental Hotel, which is my destiny.

Tenebrositas: the darkness in the streets after the last light in the windows has winked off, the darkness in which cats crouched motionless, watching for vermin's scurrying, at least in those nights before gas or electric street-lamps bathed laneways in eternal day. The darkness in which white children, long before abandoned by their fathers, sought the bodies of each other, but I will not write about that. In the winter of early 1956, in a place in Germany, the man I am calling Jupp — too familiarly, by his nickname, too familiarly, since I did not know him — went into the hot, dark box because he wanted to be nothing. Tenebrositas: the darkness of wanting to be nothing, of drowning in the Blue Hole and being nothing.

The day: the large, but finite, boredom of it before the box came, when Jupp sat at his drawing table in the studio, smoking, not drawing. The day was short, as it always is in winter at that latitude. Incidents happened in Heerdt, as they did every day. Outside the studio, the sky was blue, and the air was not cold. People standing on the sidewalk outside Jupp's studio talked about nothing until they wearied of doing so, or the day began to end, or both. The day began to end when the Rhine embankments did their ordinary job of holding the river in its course during nightfall. Barges pushed upstream and drifted downstream. as they always did. The warmth of the air at evening was the only unusual aspect of this day, but Jupp did not notice it, or anything else about the day after the box arrived.

The box: Late in the day, Jupp became naked and crawled into it, then engaged the latch on the inside of the door. As the evening came on, the air in the box became hot and humid. As evening persisted, Jupp's body began to cook, and his elements and excrements, bile, urine, blood, glandular fluids, spit began to blacken and fuse at the bottom of his maleness. I have known the vanishing of male desire, the languishing of the desire to persist in being like the evening that persisted without ceasing when Jupp crouched within the box. The Blue Hole is thought to be bottomless, endless, and so was that night.

∽64

In a brewery across the river from Jupp's street, Nylons sipped bitter beer with a recent addition to his circle of the injured and naive, for whom he cared unstintingly. This one, perhaps named Kurt, was attired that night much like any other young, working male Düsseldorfer, in dull grey and tan weeds and white underwear, but would have dressed in frocks and patterned panties continually had not law, circumstances and a measure of shyness limited his travesty to evenings of cabaret, when he sang, in a clear and unroughened tenor, the lovely songs made famous during the war by Zarah Leander.

I tell Alexander that I do not want to write about Kurt, but the child insists that I do so. He has become curious about the lives and doings of inverts, it appears, since learning of their existence from the sexology manuals shelved among the Edgar Rice Burroughs novels. Not that Kurt's inversion, of which I do not approve, was anything more intriguing than a case of ordinary adolescent gender-confusion that had been prolonged, for reasons unknown to me, into young manhood. But whatever cause can be adduced for Kurt's predilection, I consider the behaviour degenerate, and I cannot imagine any reason why a man true to his race would want to wear apparel appropriate to women, who work their will by wiles, not by the frankness and honesty native to manhood. Yet the age itself is corrupt, and perhaps long has been, even in the Germany of Jupp's boyhood — for are not Zarah Leander's shoulders too broad and waist too slender, did she not sing of her beloved with forwardness and zeal more proper to man than woman? I assume that Kurt, being perverse, loved Zarah Leander for her mannishness, which was of a forceful sort he did not often find in the German men with whom he socialized.

Kurt bore a peculiarly close resemblance to the star he worshipped. He, too, was tall and trim. He had the same dark eyes, like those of an Italian of the *mezzogiorno*; the same basket of ruly, coal-dark hair; something about the mouth, which looked (because made up in films to look) like Dietrich's. And his versions of her songs were credible, deeply felt if slightly stagey, mellow as certain young cheeses. He almost certainly would have known nothing about her tunes, or the canonical way to perform them, had he not made the unsanitary acquaintance of a young projectionist, the same one who lived with his sister in the block of flats next to Jupp's studio.

Getting to know him, Kurt discovered that the projectionist possessed and treasured a sizeable heap of movies produced in Germany during the 1930s and 1940s, films proscribed by the victors after the war. Usually portrayals of Germans as racially alert, but romantically inclined, these works were acquired from a network of Germans on the wrong side of the law, but loyal to the idea despite the country's military defeat, who trafficked in all manner of material detritus of the Third Reich and who kept the projectionist informed about the movies and movie memorabilia rescued from the general ruin and for sale. He secretly screened his holdings for Kurt at the theatre he worked in, after the last paying viewers of the latest Hollywood film, which he always detested, had departed.

Kurt was just old enough to remember the cheering, banners, high-stepping parades, and he remembered more vividly thundery nights passed in air-raid shelters with his parents, and the various stenches of fire and bodies in the streets of Düsseldorf after the bombers had passed by. But he loved the antique, heroic Germany of the projectionist's films, with the beautiful men who flew the regime's aircraft and the beautiful women who sang its songs. Sitting alone in the darkened theatre while his friend operated the projector behind him, Kurt adored

Zarah Leander's radiant face and voice in *The Great Love*, which had appeared in 1942.

The love of the title was that of Leander's character, a Danish singer named Hanna, for a boldly handsome Luftwaffe officer, Paul; but also the love of Paul for his menaced German homeland. Again and again, Paul must choose between his passions for the singer and for the Reich. He and Hanna argue before she releases Paul to follow his destiny, piloting fighter planes on the Eastern Front, a sacrifice necessary for German's ultimate overcoming and undergoing. In the final scene, frustrated in their pursuit of personal gratification, but strong in their resolution to defend Germany's freedom from foreign aggression, Hanna and Paul face the future together with light and courage in their countenances, as a flight of Luftwaffe bombers flashes across a bright sky.

Kurt watched *The Great Love* again and again, paying meticulous attention to every gesture of Zarah Leander — the toss of her head at the end of the performance for wounded soldiers, the flair and frankness with which she embraced Paul as both lover and racial comrade, the resignation in her dark eyes as she parts from Paul for what could be — almost certainly is — the last time. Kurt learned the manners of the star who filled the screen when people lived and died for something — not like 1956, he said to Nylons, when people believe nothing. Kurt fed on the projectionist's Zarah Leander movies hungrily, not fastidiously, nourishing himself on the silver-gilt lights and shadows on the screen, practicing the star's motions in front of a mirror, learning to be the singer he yearned to become. Here, he believed, was total love, of which the present day knew nothing; here was total art, devoid of American coarseness; here was total style — free of bourgeois flummery for the women, clean-cut for the men, like the uniforms of the lean Confederate cadets, my ancestors, whose daguerreotypes I looked at in the attic of my grandfather's house in the country. I lived for the first time in those images I found when I was a youth, I was alive in ways the sordid, shabby present could not make me, as Kurt was alive in the films of Zarah Leander, the goddess to whose fame Kurt had dedicated his art and artifice.

Nylons took his beer in the brewery, quizzing Kurt gently, mining him for the makings of a poem or story, and Kurt obliged, so in love was he with Nylons, until the time came for the younger man to go across the river to Heerdt and meet the young projectionist at the latter's flat, which he shared with his sister. Kurt mentioned the street, which Nylons knew as the address of his suffering friend, the artist Jupp, who was probably still awake. So, despite being slightly drunk and hence in no shape to drive, Nylons offered to give Kurt a lift in his Alvis Saloon to Kurt's destination beyond the river that night.

They arrived, and Nylons noted that the light burned in Jupp's studio. He insisted that Kurt meet Jupp. Kurt resisted, saying he was already late for his appointment with the projectionist. Nylons insisted more fervently. He said his friend had been too long sequestered away from the sight of men, that the singer's tales of Zarah Leander would distract Jupp from his melancholy. Kurt acceded out of love for Nylons, and the two men approached the green door that Götz had approached earlier, but not rapped on.

~65

Nylons rapped; no-one answered within. He then opened the door with the key Jupp had given him, and the visitors walked in, Kurt after Nylons.

A naked light bulb, depending by an electric wire from a plaster wreath in the ceiling, lit the studio, the work table, the box. The huge matrimonial bed was empty and unmade. The stench of stale cigarette smoke, the unflushed toilet, Jupp's unwashed, sweaty body in the box tainted the air the two men breathed. Kurt said he had to go; Nylons said not yet; Kurt stayed.

Crouched inside the box, Jupp heard Nylons command him once and then again to come out of the box and eat. Jupp told Nylons and his companion to go away and leave him alone. Then he heard Nylons say that he, Jupp, could die in his sweat and filth for all Nylons cared, but that Nylons and the man he was with were not leaving until Jupp died or came out of the box. These last-named remarks angered Jupp, who demanded again to be left alone. Nylons again refused to leave, which further angered Jupp. Arguments ensued, and there were long, tense silences between bursts of angry words before Jupp unlatched the door of the box, slid out into the light, stood up, naked and furious, to confront Nylons face to face.

Or such is the version of events that pleases Alexander, who relishes tales of altercations and conflicts between grown men, the more vexed the better, having been educated in narrative by the novels of Edgar Rice Burroughs. It would never suit him to see Jupp gradually coaxed from the box by Nylons, who quietly offers to ferry Jupp away from Heerdt and gently deposit him on the farm of the brothers, his long-standing patrons, far from any large city, and far from the box's suffocating heat and darkness.

There, in the house and rural holdings of the farmers, brothers after the flesh, his admirers — there, Nylons says, Jupp can mend and remember all that pleased him before he forgot it, all that you have been remembering for him since you began reading this text. There, doing slow, simple jobs in the farmhouse of the brothers and in the barns and among the coops where hens roost and lay, he can think of old poems and hymns and fragments he enjoyed during the early years of his life, when he walked abroad through the fields and forests. In the house he can rest, he can draw again — the brothers will encourage him — and he can sing shaman songs until he begins to stink like a young coyote, neither wild nor tame, despised by respectable animals that understand their place. It is a well-known fact, presented in every biography, even in the large German one I despise, that he recovered his strength on the brothers' farm near Kleve after his calamitous breakdown in Heerdt, having forgotten what pleased and shaped him before June, 1945, and having tried to be a German creature of 1955 or 1956, which he could not be without losing his mind and he would not willingly lose his mind, so he went inside the box instead.

But to please Alexander, who never leaves my side except to sleep or explore the length and breadth of the Occidental Hotel, I invent a contest of muscle and will. In this scenario, Jupp rages out of the box and stands naked and furious before Nylons and Kurt, then is forcefully argued into covering himself decently, dressing himself in the clothes he cast off at the outset of this narrative that I write for Alexander, argued into abandoning the box and accompanying Nylons and Kurt to the Alvis Saloon, which will take the three of them from Düsseldorf to the farm, Kurt having come too far in this adventure to exit now. It is a fact that Jupp recuperated from his severe breakdown at the brothers' farm near Kleve, but, for Alexander's enjoyment, I have invented the detail that Jupp abruptly changes his mind in the street and decides against going anywhere with Nylons and Kurt, resists abduction with the shouts and blows that startles Götz from post-coital leisure.

By the light of the streetlamp, Götz recognizes Jupp, who is manfully trying to prevent the two men from pushing him into the backseat of an Alvis Saloon parked improperly. Götz, who, like the woman who works in the post office, is not cruel, thinks for a moment of dressing quickly and intervening on Jupp's behalf. He thinks that, if the two men successfully kidnap Jupp, and he does not return, then Götz will have to find a new tenant for the property, something he does not want to do. But if he intervenes, and the men are serious about killing Jupp, then he, too, might be killed. Were he not killed, and Jupp were, he could be troubled by the police to give evidence, even implicated somehow (he did not know how) in the alleged homicide. Lights wink on in apartments overlooking the street, people come to their windows to see what transpires on the street. The presence of their faces in windows calms Götz somewhat. He thinks that, if the scuffle continues, one of the other neighbours will be alarmed and intervene, thus sparing him the bother. In the version I am giving Alexander, the neighbours do not intervene soon enough. They could so, but they do not. The two men, Nylons and Kurt, wrestle Jupp into the car, then jump into the front seat, and the car speeds away from the curb before Götz decides to do or not do anything. He returns to Slomka's bed. Slomka asks him what he has seen. He says it was nothing. Götz and Slomka do not talk about it, or about anything else. They love each other carnally, without affection, and they rarely speak after committing intercourse. They love each other as the white man with the remarkable knife, who climbed telecommunications masts, loved me at the time I decided to go to the Occidental Hotel, though Alexander should know I was never naked.

I look around the room in which I write and sleep, and I would tell him, but Alexander, the interesting child, is no longer present. He is surely exploring a corridor that has been, until now, unknown to him, since exploring is what he does when he leaves me. Though I do not approve of his wandering the empty hallways, I know he will not be lost, because he has a remarkable sense of direction.

Or he is visiting the office of Mr. Steinway, who clips articles about the hotel from old newspapers and otherwise prepares himself to be interviewed by the historian of dead resorts.

Or he is reading earlier drafts of this text, or the notebook about Jupp's art that I have assiduously written in the house of my grandfather, brought here, saved for Alexander's sanctification. I am not afraid for him. I am not afraid of anything, because I know Sister or some other Christian will never find me here, writing in a room with aqua wall-covering at the Occidental Hotel.

~

"WORDS AND SILENCE"

Anne Collins

I loved his words. The ones he chose to deploy and the way he deployed them. I loved them from the moment the phone rang, one early afternoon sometime in 1978, and I picked it up and this voice, carrying more than a trace of his Louisiana birthplace, asked me if he was speaking to the arts editor of *Maclean's* magazine. (I was twenty-six, and rarely answered the phone with my name, let alone my title, because I couldn't quite believe I was actually doing the job.) John Bentley Mays was eleven years older than me, already established as someone with intelligent things to say about visual art in the critical magazines and art publications of the day, and he told me that he'd decided he didn't want to write about art only for artists and critics anymore. We talked for the rest of the afternoon. Easily, relentlessly. I can't remember if we talked about art at all—we must have, because I hired him as our art critic—but I do remember the dazzle of that conversation and the exhilaration I felt all through it.

There were many more conversations over the thirty-eight years I knew John. At first our talks circled roughly around the pieces he wanted to write, but he would always digress, bringing me reports from the frontlines of his newest obsession. It seemed to me that he lived to understand and explain things, all sorts of things, including everything he noticed about his chosen city, his "emerald city," Toronto. He was desperate for what I could teach him about writing for the people who read *Maclean's*. But what did I know? I was making it up along with everyone else in the office who was trying to create a Canadian news-magazine with the same kind of reach and authority as *Time* or *News-week* with maybe a tenth of the staff and budget. That leanness, though, meant a kind of freedom. It meant room for a person with interests like John's—opposed (as he later wrote in *Maclean's*) to "the bankrupt, middle-brow notion that a country's artistic accomplishment consists of its masterpieces" and determined to champion artists who wanted "to cut art loose from the hot-air balloon of abstract 'high culture' and bring it down to earth again." As far as I was concerned, all John had to do was write like he talked, vividly and directly—shedding the art speak.

From the first article, once John was rolling, he was unstoppable. But getting a piece started, crafting the opening sentences to hook this new crowd, was a real struggle and sometimes he would disappear for a couple of weeks on deadline. I thought for the longest time it was be-cause he was wrestling with the lead, but of course I learned later that the words he launched out into the world were something John loved, something he lived for. The words that ran around inside his head, which were only let out in the pages of his diary, were something else again. But more of that a little later.

We learned together, really: that's the truth. Our opus, an incredibly long cover story in *Maclean's,* published in November 1979 under the corny header, "But Is It Art," was also John's announcement that a change had come, and that it was important for everyone with any interest in how we were living to recognize it: "this art—or at least this stuff—that the new Canadian artists of the '70s are making may look gooey or crumbly, may whisper gossip or talk dirty, or remind you of furniture or garbage. Sometimes it will be so ephemeral it can't be bought, and sometimes so suspect no one would want to buy it. As 1979 edges toward 1980, all the old certainties about art are about as contemporary as Hula-Hoops and bobby socks." It was no surprise to me that soon after this issue appeared the *Globe and Mail* came calling. John was such an intensely loyal soul, he was awkward breaking the news that he was taking the newspaper's offer of a full-time job as its art critic. I really didn't want to work with anyone else but John, but I was happy for him:

being paid to look at and think about art, here and everywhere, was heaven on earth for the man. It was a job he did with discipline, creativity and courage (never afraid to jab a sacred cow) for the next 18 years.

And there was no risk that we would lose touch: by the time he left *Maclean's* we were friends. By then I had come to understand that his intellectual obsessions, his need to write, his incredible manners, his affection for and interest in his friends (not that hot arguments didn't occasionally break out), his respect and love for Margaret Cannon, the wonderful woman he married — lovely qualities, each and every one of them — were also planks he laid as carefully as he could across the pit he risked sliding into every single day of his life. The pit he'd known since he was eight, when he first considered suicide. The pit dug by childhood trauma and betrayal, which he went on to so achingly describe in his books *In the Jaws of the Black Dogs* and *Power in the Blood*. The times when he disappeared were times when the black dogs of depression had him.

When I first knew him he self-medicated with alcohol, which was hard to pick up sometimes as he just seemed to become more eloquent. (I have vague memories of him teaching me to tango one night when we were both under the influence, and then there was the surprise fortieth birthday party he threw for Margaret. They always say there is no such thing as too much champagne. I beg to differ.) He self-medicated, too, with research jags and especially with writing: I think he never missed a deadline in all the years he was at the *Globe* no matter what terrible thoughts were whirling inside his brain. Through it all, John was the person you wanted to say grace at any family dinner, to give the toast at any celebration. He and Margaret stood up for my husband and me when we "eloped" to City Hall to get married after eight years of living together; they brought a sense of ritual to the utilitarian act of joining two people who had to run out the morning of the wedding to get the groom a pair of trousers suitable to be married in. From that day onward, I think they both felt a proprietary interest in the state of our marriage, or maybe the desire to make sure their witness had counted for something.

That abyss at the heart of John. It was inchoate at its centre, but reinforced with such cutting, annihilating self-loathing: swamps and sloughs of awful words generated by him in order to obliterate him. Sometimes we stared at each other across such a huge distance. I am one of those lucky people who wakes up cheerful in the morning, almost no matter what, like some reset button gets hit in the night. I also had a ridiculously loving and happy childhood, and parents I honoured; I was always hauling people home to meet them. Realizing that he and Margaret had no extended family in Canada, I soon began to include them and their daughter, Erin, in Christmas, Easter and Thanksgiving dinners at the family farm near Toronto.

My parents, Bill and Olive, took them all in, as if it was the most natural thing in the world to do. My dad was a farmer, a man of few words but great generosity of spirit: he couldn't have been more different from John, who must have seemed like an alien life form when they first met. But John really admired people who could make or build or grow things, and when he was near Dad it was as though he could relax. He loved both my parents, which made me love John all the more. He appreciated that wellspring of contentment he found at the farm, but he would also test me for fault lines. Given his experience, how could he trust such contentment?

For instance. In the early nineties, when I was working at *Saturday Night*—a now defunct general interest magazine that used to set the bar for long-form journalism in Canada, John started taking Prozac (he had stopped drinking, and had finally sought steady treatment for his depression, both through talk therapy and drugs). Treatment had given him enough stability and distance he thought he might be able to write about his black dogs, and he agreed to do so for the magazine. But he issued a challenge: if he was going to write about depression and the impact of Prozac I had to agree to take a couple days' worth of the drug and report back to him on my mood. John was sure that I'd take the pills, experience a lifting, calming or leavening, and then have to admit that I was not the more or less sunny individual I pretended to be. I took the pills. (That amazes me when I think back on it, but is a sign of John's powers of persuasion.) The only thing that happened was that Prozac seemed to upset my proprioception: I'd see my hand moving in front of my hand as if I was ghosting myself. I mention this only to say that my nature was as inscrutable to him as his was to me — until I agreed to edit the book that came out of that magazine article, *In the Jaws of the Black Dogs*, an account of living with depression that stands out in the company of books such as *Darkness Visible* and *Noonday Demons*.

He was brave to take it on, and at first Prozac kept him insulated. But it didn't insulate me. John felt that to truly describe depression, he had to demonstrate it with extracts from the diaries he'd been keeping all his life. The blast furnace of self-disgust and the horrifying despair he'd set down in those pages almost did me in, yet both of us had to weather them in order to find just enough to quote to give readers a sense of the real thing without causing them to abandon the book. My entertaining, loquacious, oh so considerate friend carried such a burden through his days that my throat still closes with hurt for him.

Other things in that book hurt too, such as realizing that John, who had given me so much joy, rarely experienced anything as simple as pleasure. Prozac, for maybe a couple of years, allowed him to wake in the morning to the sound of rain on the skylight and feel delight at both the syncopation and the sense that he was safe and dry inside. The beauty of the natural world, the beauty of music, the beauty of paint on canvas, the joy of cinema: all doors were open for a while. And then the drug stopped working and the doors slammed shut again. And John was left to do what he had always done, which was to put one foot in front of the other in the belief that there was no cure and that he would always carry that weight.

I won't go on for much longer; I don't want to write a list of what happened next. Between hospitalizations and through various drug regimens, John did so much, influenced so many, loved his family so thoroughly. I have never seen him happier than when he held his granddaughter on his lap. But as the years passed, my conversations with John grew fewer. Partly it was that my life as a book publisher and editor was so deadline-heavy it made finding simple chances to hang out almost impossible. But I also wonder whether words, those wonderful witty flows of exuberant analysis and story-telling, became less important to him. At family dinners he would watch and listen, rather than hold forth, though he still loved to engage my sons in long conversations about what was on their minds. I could be completely wrong, but it felt to me that he was most deeply interested in a place I couldn't go, which was the Catholic faith as practiced by a man who knew there was only consolation and never relief. I feel John's eyes on me as I write this, and I hope I'm not misrepresenting him. I am so happy that this book you hold in your hands partly refutes what I'm saying; I can't tell you how glad I am that among the last things John did before he died was to finish a novel. Deploying those incredible words of his.

I think often of his funeral, which he scripted. Trust John — who felt that if he wasn't able to withstand a particular moment of despair, suicide might take him at any point — to leave complete instructions for how we were to say goodbye to him. It was a mass and liturgy so classic and austere it became a universal ritual of human solidarity in the face of death and grief and unknowing. There was no moment as easy as someone standing to offer a story, to elicit a laugh, to bring us all together in shared remembrance of John Bentley Mays, to paper over briefly the hole he left in us. No, we stared, during the service, at what he knew in his bones: the void. The only defence against it being that you could see it, you could recognize it, you could articulate some parts of its nature and live on anyway, until you climbed a hill in High Park on a beautiful September day and left us all at the top of that hill.

Anne Collins is publisher of the Knopf Random House Canada Publishing Group and a vice president of Penguin Random House Canada.

JOHN JOSEPH JUPP

Richard Rhodes

In the end, he wrote the novel. It had been a long time coming. Other writing projects came first. I had taken photographs for three of John's books, all of them documentary subjects: experiential architectures of Toronto, his personal fight with depression, his family roots in Louisiana and Texas. One day, however, he said he had a new book underway. It would need a map, not photographs. The book was to be a novel set during the American Civil War and the story revolved around a Confederate submarine that successfully sank a Union warship in Charleston Harbour then sank with her entire crew.

Never finished, the book was to include scenes set in 19th-century Liverpool where the English helped hide and maintain the Confederate navy. All of this was news to me. I had never heard of the Confederate navy, let alone a Confederate submarine. But it was very John. He had an ironic take on himself as a Southerner transplanted to cold Canadian Ontario and he showed off an identity still attached to those roots. The themes of the novel — exotic early modernism, the pursuit of glory, self-destroying martyrdom — were Southern themes and very much part of a Southern sense of fate and drama. They were the fundamentals of its history; a tragic, often wrong-footed history, but for John this was the only kind that mattered, the only one worth imagining. His book would look to a past poised on the future. It would involve a voyage to sail unseen underwater. In the dark, he would find a battle to win, though not the war.

This finished novel, *The Occidental Hotel*, has a ghostly continuity with the earlier one. It too is a book about isolation, darkness and a lost war but with characters and events that have been recast in a 20th-century history. The story links melancholy remnants of the South and its Lost Cause nostalgia to the wrecked and repressed terrain of the Thousand Year Reich. Recounted by a narrator writing from an aging mountain hotel on the warmer side of the Mason Dixon line, the story shuttles between the hotel, the narrator's troubled childhood and a catatonic young artist in postwar Düsseldorf, Germany.

It is 1956 and the hero is an artist named Jupp who confounds his landlord and friends by retreating to a box in his studio. The invisible young artist is the focal point around which the narrator assembles episodes and witnesses to his prior life. We learn of his war service and his earlier tutelage under an instructor for the Hitler Youth. Jupp, shut inside his box, shapes the story as both a perpetrator and a victim. The narrator makes him a moral innocent subject to terrible times but also a sly manipulator who knowingly mines the darkness around him as a source for his creativity.

For anyone aware of postwar contemporary art, there is no mystery as to the model for the character. Jupp is the German sculptor and performance artist Joseph Beuys. John's book progresses as a complicated meditation on Jupp/Beuys. Through them it tallies the costs and consequences of the Nazi era and interweaves a parallel story set in a violent, race-conscious American South. The youthful Jupp/Beuys is impressed and overpowered by Nazi fantasies of a conquering Nordic and Eurasian heritage. The Southern narrator is captured by nostalgic memories of white cotton and summer crinoline. Like John himself, he also suffers the mystery of a father's sudden and unsolved murder. Together, the narrative threads create a transatlantic story where divergent histories meld in worldviews shaped by shame and loss and an abiding sense of disorientation.

The book, however, also constitutes a discerning appreciation of Joseph Beuys' art and legacy. Beuys' professional career is broached in a second text that is interspersed with the fictional sections of the novel. This "other" text paces the book with documentary photographs and critical commentaries. It makes a relief space from the fiction, a reminder of an objective reality represented by Beuys' achievements as an artist. The images, excerpts and annotations take the reader through key works and concepts in his art. They also serve as guides to some of the ideas driving contemporary art — ideas that drove John himself as an art critic.

John Bentley Mays was a by-line known to many on the Canadian art scene. His critical voice hovers like an alternate narrator to the book. The teller of the Jupp story and the teller of the Beuys' story are partnered. One builds a fictional setting, the other hovers around an actual art historical figure whose themes and works lend their aesthetic and philosophical weight to the proceedings.

As a critic, John's work was knowledgeable, incisive and, for some, dangerous. He came to prominence as a writer during the 1980s, first as an art critic for *Maclean's* magazine and then as art critic for *The Globe and Mail* newspaper. The latter role was one he held for a decade and half during the heyday of Toronto's downtown Queen Street art scene. As the grand sounding John Bentley Mays, he brought a new sense of engagement to what was then an insular and relatively poorly covered cultural beat, its secrets and accomplishments perhaps best known by grant officers at the Canada Council in Ottawa.

John changed that. Appearing with his wide brimmed hat and sunglasses, reporter's notebook in hand, he became a noticeable presence on the scene. He brought a fierce, articulate voice to a city where literary and performing arts traditionally held sway over contemporary art. His reports and Saturday essays were much anticipated. New reputations and ideas rose to push outmoded ones aside as the number of his filed stories grew. He welcomed, even personified, the postmodernism of the day and with his confident, irrepressible voice, he elevated contemporary art to a new relevancy for Canadians.

Contemporary art's 1980s moment was John's moment. He embraced the energies of the day to create fresh opportunities for artists and gallerists. He built appreciative new audiences for contemporary art with the wide-ranging intellectual interests that he brought to the page as a writer. More than a few itineraries were planned with his Saturday column in hand. By fostering a growing excitement for the visual arts, he created a special moment in the Toronto art scene.

It was moment when working artists began to feel a balanced reciprocation with the city that housed them and, with it, a gain in confidence and ambition. Local art institutions might dwell on the past with Group of Seven exhibitions, or heed the siren calls of New York and international art scenes, but John set his own course. For him, meaning had no colonial past, no nervous dependence on an agenda set elsewhere. He grasped significance where he found it and gave sophisticated voice to its presence in the art around him. John's strength as a critic was to presume the scope and interconnectedness of art. He underscored its inherent global nature, taking *The Globe and Mail* to places it had never been. His editors trusted his instincts that it and its readers belonged there.

I doubt that *The Occidental Hotel* was percolating as an idea for a book in 1987 but that June John planned a trip to Germany that headed toward what would be its eventual orbit. He had decided that he would take a week and report on the opening of the new Documenta 8 exhibition. Documenta was the largest of the curated international shows then beginning to dominate the art scene. It was much anticipated by more than a few art people in Toronto. After the previous Documenta 7, Ydessa Hendeles, then a leading gallerist in the city, hosted an evening for her artists and invited critics to share her excitement at what she had seen and photographed there.

Hundreds of slide images sat in carousel boxes on the long counter of her gallery. As the evening stretched to dawn, John, absorbed in conversation and debate throughout, made a promise not to miss the next one. By 1987 he had already started to prepare. He had first made a long car trip to Detroit to interview Docmenta 7's Rudi Fuchs who was involved in a new curatorial project. Then, as Documenta 8 neared, he sat down in Toronto with Artistic Director Manfred Schneckenberger who had come to town to research artists who might participate. Several Canadians were on his list. Two of them, Liz Magor and Ian

Carr Harris, were well-known local figures. They had each created a hybrid form of art that fused photography and sculpture into a timely understanding of how the pervasiveness of media images was increasingly shaping our culture and consciousness.

Documenta 8 was to be the "postmodern" Documenta. As a curatorial effort, it would show how contemporary art was setting aside more traditional aesthetic concerns for a deeper engagement with society and politics. Art was beginning to assume a state of wokeness and the event to mark its shift into a new relevance was happening over several months in sleepy, small town Kassel, a rebuilt former armaments centre north of Frankfurt.

John had rented a white GM Opal to make the two-hour drive from the airport. The town had become a favourite weekend spot for US servicemen stationed nearby and was only minutes away from the border with East Germany. The border cut a wide swath through the quiet farming countryside and John had arranged the car so that he could take a closer look after he filed his stories on the six-hour time difference with Toronto. Accompanying him in the car, we heard loud, low-flying American jets pass overhead, casting swift shadows on an otherwise verdant summer landscape. At one point, we pulled into a picture postcard farm courtyard stacked with fresh cut hay. As the sun shone down, John wryly noted that we had arrived at what would likely be the first farm in Hesse to face Soviet tanks.

He had actually done some homework on NATO ground war defence plans. His passing joke, however, was not a light observation. Forty years of post war tensions had charged the visible landscape. Medieval stone towers frequently visible in the area managed to feel more contemporary than they should have. They now seemed Cold War relics too, part of an endless history of war. This militarized frisson had marked the siting of Documenta from the beginning. The exhibition was initiated as a demonstration of the West's freedom in the face of Eastern Block threat. It was a call of action and change and now in 1987, two years before the Wall fell, four years before the collapse of the Soviet Union, its postmodern art seemed more than ever to signal that change was literally on the horizon.

An era was passing. Documenta expressed this in many ways and one of them was its inclusion of Joseph Beuys. Beuys had died the year before. Documenta 8 would be, in part, a homage to him. One of the exhibition spaces was devoted to his last major installation work. Beuys had played, after all, an important role to re-establish Europe's reputation in the contemporary art world after decades of American dominance (first by Jackson Pollock and the Abstract Expressionists, then the Pop Art of Warhol and Lichtenstein, then the Minimalists with Donald Judd and Robert Morris).

Beuys' esoteric performance-oriented works restored a missing sense of moral theatre to late modern art, returning a missing thread of European existential energy that delivered art not as a formal investigation but as a process of magic making and psychic exploration. Beuys' simple fabricated objects and symbolic performances offered a rawness that carried visceral memories of the Second World War and the time that had so darkly defined Germany and 20th-century Europe. Dressed in a Homburg hat and fishing vest, Beuys fashioned an iconic identity as an artist healer attuned to lost mythic energies. His work filtered a panorama of references to the cultural and human damage from the war. With felt and fat and clay, and a reductive palette of greys, browns and soured whites, he built things that felt like they belonged to a museum of ruin and diminished expectation. Each of his "Aktions" and built objects sounded a deep, resonant seriousness. In Beuys' artefacts of thoughtful remembrance, art had become an instrument to displace the oppressive history of the war.

The installation exhibited at Documenta 8, *Lightning with Stag in its Glare*, was completed the year before his death. It included earlier sculptures alongside more recent objects made of clay produced at workshop in Berlin in a space once used as a museum of prehistory. Beuys combined the elements into a massive monumental work. The tallest component, a flared shape of textured clay cast in bronze, hung from a steel beam mounted near roof. The heavy, earth-surfaced shape fell six metres to a scatter of rough-hewn objects on the floor. In notes for the installation, Beuys referred to the pendant as "Lightning." In front of it, another element with crossed ironing boards made from aluminum, was called "Stag." To one side, a wheeled cart with various clay forms, each embedded with a workmen's tool, seemingly had unloaded them onto the floor between. Then, standing apart like an observer, a sculptor's tripod topped with a planter's box and weighted with an excremental dump of clay completed the scene.

The concert of purposed horizontals and the dominating vertical took on the aspect of a mysterious frozen ceremony. Everything about the work fit the contours of Beuys' usual sculptural vocabulary. The imagined flash of "Lightning" and the tripod form, however, added fresh photographic references that newly extended the range of Beuys' work. They paid service to a recognition of photography, to the fact that at the time all things photographic were acquiring an era-defining materiality in contemporary art. But where other artists used photography as a sign of mass media's hold on contemporary culture, Beuys turned to it as a vessel of memory, a medium to be honoured for its evidential gifts. In the subdued colours and aspect of frozen circumstance, his installation expressed a kinship with our remembrance of 20th-century war images that offer such a terrible, unforgettable testimony to German war guilt.

The Beuys who haunted Documenta 8 is the Beuys of John's novel. Jupp's retreat into his box is a variation on an early Beuys performance work reproduced as the first image of the book. The grainy black and white photo shows Beuys' Happening event, *The Chief-Fluxus Chant*, from 1964. It turns us into observers in a smallish room in the René Block art gallery in Berlin, located not far from the Wall that was then expanding its grip across the divided city. In the picture, Beuys lies wrapped in a felt carpet on the concrete floor. Two dead hares seal either end of the carpet. Wedges of lard have been placed along the walls and in the corners of the room. A pole, wound like an electrical transformer, lies near the carpet; another leans against the wall. A snaking electrical wire runs to a speaker opposite that, through the caption to the image, we learn broadcasts the amplified sound of the hidden Beuys breathing, coughing and mumbling the alphabet. A quote from Beuys explains, "... my presence inside the felt ... was a parallel to the old initiation rite of the coffin, a form of simulated death ... acting out being dead, empty, emotionless ..."

The "dead" Beuys is a casualty of history, of course. So is Jupp. In the novel, his self-imposed captivity in his studio is a rehearsal of the "empty, emotionless" condition of the carpet-wrapped man in *The Chief*. The differing texts in the book keep the two separate however. They reside in different realms; one in fiction, the other in history. As the book progresses, the sections of critical text and reproduced images work to move our understanding of Beuys forward through a series of successive works and symbolic imageries from *How to Explain Pictures to a Dead Hare* (1965), to *Manresa* (1966), to *Eurasia Staff* (1968), to *Iphigenia/Titus Andronicus* (1969), to *I Like America and America Likes Me* (1974) and beyond.

Through them we take a place in a postwar professional world where Beuys moves on to become a famous teacher, influencing a generation of younger German artists, and an artist who eventually finds himself lauded in the art world. As an artist engaged with German legends, he becomes one. In contrast, the fictional sections with Jupp turn backward. We enter the jaded atmosphere of reconstruction after the war; learn of Jupp's experiences in the war then arrive at the most fully rendered scenes in the novel, the ones of Jupp during his time in the Hitler Youth. It is in this period that Jupp experiences his first aesthetic feelings and his first stirrings as an artist as he learns to draw and study the homeopathic properties of local plants. That he owes these experiences to a Nazi teacher is a disturbing paradox and this poisoned learning curve becomes the essential theme of John's book. He marvels at Beuys and the depth of his art but he anchors his fictional counterpart, Jupp, in a forbidden past that Beuys himself presumably shared.

The Beuys wrapped in the carpet is truly not dead. He has a relevant prehistory that animates the figure on the floor in the gallery as much as Jupp's personal history animates his playing dead in the studio. Both artist and fictional artist have chosen to hide themselves. The hiding is the vital condition of their actions. The same holds true for the narrator writing the book from his fading hotel. *The Occidental Hotel* is full of hiding from ugly pasts. It is also full of understanding how a disappearance, or a death, or the past, are not final subjective ends but rather ambiguous, unresolved states. Beuys' carpet death is a birth moment for meditations on time, history and ancient mythologies. Jupp's disappearance into his studio box is a healing manoeuvre, the prelude to a different beginning.

In the book, with Beuys playing dead and young Jupp in his box in mid-winter Düsseldorf, John makes an unlikely shift to a story by Mark Twain from the 1880s. Twain writes of a hostel in Munich where the dead are taken before burial so that they can be "monitored for signs of revival." Inside the hostel wires run from rings on dead fingers to bells as nearby attendants listen for them to sound. We are 80 years away from Beuys' *Chief* but clearly not very far. I stopped when I read the passage and thought that only John would look to Mark Twain as a guide to German funeral rites and a source for thinking about early performance art. I knew that somewhere close, the Mississippi flowed. I knew too that a Southern writer is a Southern writer no matter how many Ontario winters he spends listening to Wagner and remembering art exhibitions in a German town graced by a monument to the Brothers Grimm.

Richard Rhodes is a former editor of Canadian Art.

ACKNOWLEDGEMENTS

We acknowledge the use of the following images from the "Actions" of Joseph Beuys:

© **Estate of Joseph Beuys / SOCAN (2019)**

Figure 1: Photograph from the Action *The Chief-Fluxus Chant*, René Block Gallery, Berlin, 1 December 1964.

Figure 2: Photograph of Joseph Beuys from the Action *How to Explain Pictures to a Dead Hare*, Galerie Schmela, Düsseldorf, 26 November 1965.

Figure 3: Photograph of Joseph Beuys taken by Ute Klophaus from the Action *Manresa*, Galerie Schmela, Düsseldorf 15 December 1966.

Figure 4: Photograph from the Action *I Like America and America Likes Me*, René Block Gallery, New York, May, 1974.

Figure 5: Photograph from the Action *Iphigenia/Titus Andronicus*, staged for experimenta 3, an avant-garde theatre festival in Frankfurt-am-Main, 29 and 30 May 1969.

Figure 6: Frame from 16-millimetre film of the Action *Eurasienstab (Eurasia Staff)*, Wide White Space Gallery, Antwerp, 1968.

Figure 7: A 1971 graphite drawing by Joseph Beuys, entitled *Young Blacksmith with his Work* and now in the collection of the National Galleries of Scotland.

Figure 8: Photograph, possibly from 1982, of Joseph Beuys planting a tree beside a basalt pillar before the Museum Fridericianum, Kassel, Germany. This tree is one of thousands that Beuys proposed be planted, each alongside a rough-hewn basalt pillar, throughout the town, under the title *7,000 Oaks — Urban Forestation instead of Administration.*

Front cover image: *Portrait of John Bentley Mays*, **used with the permission of Margaret Cannon.**

ABOUT THE AUTHOR

The late John Bentley Mays (1941–2016) has been called *courtly, erudite, passionate and fierce* (by Sarah Milroy). The Louisiana-born Bentley Mays was a Toronto writer on architecture, visual art and design. He was a brilliant stylist and electric speaker as well as the winner of multiple magazine and newspaper awards. Many will remember him as the *Globe and Mail*'s dazzling art critic in the eighties and nineties. Dogged by a tragic childhood and plagued with lifelong depression, he wrestled with these afflictions while writing a first one book of fiction and four of nonfiction, and latterly this audacious and searing novel which he completed two weeks before his untimely death.

This book is made of paper from well-managed FSC® - certified
forests, recycled materials, and other controlled sources.